MEMORIES
OF MEMORIES

*****

Essays on the Bicultural Education of a
Second-Generation Member of America's
Italian Hebrew Diaspora

*****

GEORGE S. SACERDOTE

ISBN: 978-1-7333541-0-3
Library of Congress Control Number: 2019910469

Book design by JD&J Design

Dedicated to the loving memory of my late parents and brothers who made me what I am, and to my wife, sons and grandchildren who have inherited this legacy.

Special thanks are due to Lisa Colleen Moore of Sibley House Publishing Services for her editorial guidance and support without which this book would never have seen the light of day.

TABLE OF CONTENTS

Introduction

Some branches of my family claim descent from the Hebrew families that were already settled in Rome at the time of the Caesars, while others arrived in what we now call Italy in the 1400s, primarily from Spain. We had been comfortably off as far back as I have been able to trace, working as bankers during the Renaissance, and later moving into manufacturing in the 1600s and wholesale trade in the 1700s. Beginning in 1848, when Italian universities were reopened to Hebrews, my ancestors jumped into the learned professions. Both of my grandfathers were lawyers as had been their fathers before them. While neither of my grandmothers had gone to university, both were very cultured women whose brothers, children, nieces and nephews all did. Both of my parents earned doctorates: my father in electrical engineering and my mother in chemistry.

In the late 1930's, as Italy's Fascist dictator, Mussolini, invaded Ethiopia and subsequently drew ever closer to Hitler, Mussolini adopted much of the latter's racial programs after having previously denounced them as "idiocy." This reversal of course culminated in Mussolini's promulgation of the Racial Laws of 1938 (Fig. I-1). Under these laws, *Ebrei*, "Hebrews" (a distinctly Italian appellation drawn from the Biblical Hebrew word *Ivrit* in reference to the Jewish people), were not allowed to pursue professional occupations, were sharply limited in their rights to own businesses and property, were banned from schools, universities, hospitals and cemeteries and became subject to all sorts of petty and not so petty discrimination. In short they were reduced to the status of second-class citizens. As a result, my father was promptly dismissed from his job as the technology director of the telephone company and his brother and sister lost their medical licenses.

My parents chose to go into exile with my brothers and grandmother, along with about 10-20% of Italy's Hebrew population. In early March of 1939 they took up temporary residence in Lausanne, Switzerland (Fig. I-2). Later that spring they moved to Cremieux in France to join with a small group of my father's cousins who had also chosen exile as an alternative to remaining in Italy with its newly enacted restrictions on the Hebrew population. These relatives were running a small rubber reclaiming plant that one of them had just bought from the Italian tire company, Pirelli. My mother felt particularly comfortable in France as her mother had been raised in that country and the two of them generally conversed in that language in preference to Italian.

In September, 1939, when the hostilities of World War II broke out between France and Germany, my parents became alarmed. While Italy had not yet joined the war, they were certain that it would soon enough. They had seen the terrible conditions in the refugee camps that the French had set up for those who had fled there from the recently ended Spanish Civil War; they feared that the French would treat them even worse for they would be enemy aliens. Moreover, they were well aware of the atrocities that were already going on in the German concentration camps; these had been broadly publicized in multiple languages in a series of eye witness reports issued by the British government's Foreign Office (Fig. I-3). While no one imagined that France would soon collapse militarily to the Germans, they certainly did not want to take the least risk of falling into the hands of the murderous German Nazis.

So they began to search for a new place of exile. My father made the rounds of the various foreign consulates in the nearby city of Lyon looking for a new country in which to settle. When he mentioned to the US Consul General, that he was working as an engineer in a rubber reclaiming plant, the diplomat's ears perked up. Japan had cut American trade with Malaya, resulting in a massive rubber shortage in the US, and the Americans had been forced to ration gasoline as a means of reducing the demand for rubber tires. The Americans were desperate to recruit experts in the rubber industry to help stretch their limited supplies further. Consequently, the consul granted my parents, brothers and grandmother immigration visas for entry into the United States despite their lack of passports valid for travel to that country.

Their harrowing and chaotic escape from France in May, 1940 as that country was collapsing militarily and just before the region around Cremieux was occupied by Italy which had by now joined the war, included crossing France by train on a rail system which was operating only erratically, moving my very young brothers and all their luggage by pushing an abandoned hearse through the streets between Bordeaux's rail station and its port, boarding a ship that the Germans promised to sink on its way to America, and a ten-day ocean voyage dodging U-boats and ice bergs. Two weeks after their arrival in New York, they learned that the Germans had sunk their ship when it returned to France.

My parents landed in New York in June 1940 and quickly learned that life in their new home would be very difficult. Their academic credentials were not recognized and my father was unemployed for the next three years. As Italian subjects, they were deemed to be enemy aliens and even though the

US did not enter the war until the end of 1941. Consequently my parents were not allowed to work in sensitive industries such as chemicals, rubber and telecommunications, their areas of expertise. They soon lost access to the few assets they had been able to sneak out of Italy and France when Roosevelt froze the bank accounts of Italian and German nationals. Thus my family came to the US, not as immigrants seeking a better life but as refugees who had been exiled from a comfortable life in Italy and who now had to start anew with very little.

My family knew almost no one in New York. They did not fit in with either the Jewish or Italian immigrant communities. The former were mostly from the impoverished, Yiddish speaking shtetls of Eastern Europe, a culture totally alien to my parents. These were people who came from countries that were barely out of the middle ages and had experienced neither the Renaissance nor the Enlightenment. Most of them seemed to have studied little besides religion while the others tended towards radical leftist politics, and by then my parents had had their fill of political extremism. In any case, New York's Jews did not recognize them as co-religionists, for they were all convinced that all "real" Jews came from Eastern Europe and spoke Yiddish.

New York's Italian immigrant community was no more welcoming. Most of these people were uneducated peasants from the very poor Italian south, many with Fascist leanings. Coming from the bottom rungs of the highly stratified Italian society of the early 20th century, they were not about to embrace an educated upper-middle-class Italian Hebrew family. About the only people with whom my parents fit in were the few dozen families of other Italian Hebrew exiles who had ended up in New York during the second half of 1940. Some had come directly from Italy and France, while others had come via more circuitous routes such as through Portugal or Cuba. About half of these families were relatives of ours. And it was with this group that my parents developed their social network.

It was into this exile community that I was born in 1945. In the early post-war years, many members of this community returned to Italy, including my grandmother and several aunts, uncles and cousins. My father wanted very much to return as well. But my mother was absolutely opposed to returning, and her opinion ultimately prevailed. Nevertheless, my father's extensive business interests in Italy often took us to Italy, where most of our extended family lived, and we wound up living a bifurcated existence. I grew up in the US, but was almost as Italian as I was American. At home we spoke mostly Italian except when we spoke French. Most of our family friends were Italian. My father returned one or more times every year to look after his affairs. And I spent many summers there at our family's villa in the hills above Torino (Turin), Italy.

Until the spring of 2010 when I participated in a conference in New York on the Italian Jewish Diaspora in America sponsored by Columbia University and the Primo Levi Center I had felt very much alone in my experiences. As I spoke and listened to the other participants, I came to realize how much we had all been shaped by similar experiences on both sides of the ocean and had all developed very similar outlooks on life.

This is the story I want to tell. My story is only one in many. But it represents the lives of this Italian Jewish Diaspora in America. We have a dual background: Americans but also Hebrew sons of Italy; Italians but also informed Americans. In these essays I draw parallels and contrasts between a bygone Italy of forty or fifty years ago and the equally bygone America of the second half of the twentieth century. And in so doing, perhaps I have also captured a bit of the experiences of many of my compatriots of this small but strikingly accomplished community of Italian Hebrews who have settled in America.

As you read this volume, feel free to skip around among the individual essays. Although they are divided into six groups and those in a given group address a common theme, each can be enjoyed on its own.

Figure I-1. The Fascist Racial Laws promulgated in 1938-39

Figure I-2. My brothers, parents and grandmother Elvira:
Lausanne, Switzerland, March 1938

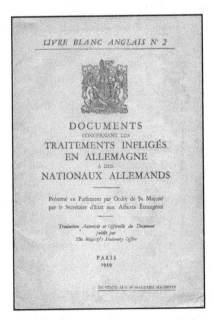

Figure I-3. In 1939, the British Foreign Office published a series
of widely-distributed documents detailing eye-witness accounts of
German atrocities

PART 1 EVOKING THE PAST

Chapter 1

Memories of Memories

A friend of mine — a psychiatrist — once told me that all beginning psychiatry residents are taught to ask their patients to recall their earliest memories, and, in particular, their earliest awareness of having had memories of prior times. My friend admitted that he was not sure what value this line of questioning might have, though he did allow it would provide a good beginning point for a broader discussion of the patient's life. In most cases, where these events had little to do with the issues that had brought the patient in for therapy, this discussion would provide a nice, non-threatening topic with which the patient and therapist could begin to develop a trusted relationship. In the exceptional cases where these early events had a profound influence on the patient, the therapist would have gotten them into the discussion early and they could lead to a quicker resolution of the patient's problems. While I have never consulted a psychiatrist professionally, I have on occasion asked myself about my earliest memories and when I first became aware of my ability to recall events from the past. And I believe that these early events really have shaped my life in very profound ways.

* * * * *

When I was just shy of five years' old, in 1950, my mother and I sailed to Europe on the Queen Elizabeth. We were on our way to Torino, Italy, to spend the summer at my grandmother's country villa. It was just my mother and me—my father had flown ahead and my brothers stayed behind at summer camp—and I was terribly seasick all the way across the Atlantic. I recall spending all my waking hours sitting on a deck chair, hoping that the fresh air would calm whatever it was that so upset my stomach. About the only things I could keep down were the strong, milky tea and the bland biscuits that a steward would bring me every hour or two. When we finally arrived at the French port of Cherbourg where we would take a train to Torino, it was almost sunset. The Queen Elizabeth required a deeper draft than that shallow port could accommodate, so getting ashore entailed clambering down a ladder from the rocking ship while it was anchored off-shore before being ferried into port in a smaller very unsteady boat. This last step did not help my digestion one bit.

But we were on shore at last and found ourselves in a crowd of more than a thousand people all picking through a jumble of suitcases, steamer trunks and packing crates, each trying to locate his luggage in this mad disorder. My mother kept a firm grip on me fearing that I might get lost in the shuffle as she searched for our bags. (As I write these words sixty-five years later, I can still feel her tight grasp on my wrist.) Then she frantically shouted in French to get the attention of one of the scarce porters and engaged him to move our luggage through customs and get it loaded onto the boat train waiting just beyond the quay so that we could continue our journey to Torino. Once on the train but before it left the station, she leaned out of the window of our compartment to buy some bread, cheese, fruit and mineral water from one of the hawkers on the platform, so that we could eat supper on our way to Italy. This was the first meal that I was able to keep down since we had left New York.

The train to Torino was supposed to get us there the next afternoon but the combined inefficiencies of the French and Italian national railway systems in the early post-war years resulted in our not arriving in Torino until about one AM. By the time we had gotten our luggage and ourselves loaded into a taxi and had ourselves driven out to our family's country villa in *Val Salice* on the outskirts of Torino, it was about two AM. It was pitch dark and the house was shut up tight for the night. My mother tried to rouse the family servants by knocking on the kitchen door. I remember how anxious she was not to make too much noise lest we rouse not only the rest of the family but also the farmers and the other tenants on the property.

As we stood there in the dark, my not quite five-year-old mind suddenly remembered the place from when we had visited there two years previous when I had been about two-and-a-half years' old. While my mother was knocking on the door and throwing pebbles at the top floor windows in 1950, I ran off to find the hand pump in the garden that I remembered from 1948—the hand pump the farmer used to water the flowers and that my grandmother's maid, Camilla, used for rinsing the laundry. I was disappointed to find that it was lying on its side, awaiting the arrival of an additional length of pipe to make it a reliable water source even during dry spells. Then I ran into the formal garden, looking for the palm trees, potted lemons and standard roses. Realizing that I had disappeared, my mother ran after me and brought me back around the house to the kitchen door just as a light came on. Camilla, dressed in her nightshirt, opened the inner door and peered through the slats of the bolted outer door to see who was making such a ruckus in the middle of the night. As soon as she recognized us, she threw open the outer door and let us in, all the while grumbling about our showing up in the middle of the night. And so we were home again in Italy, and I was on familiar ground after that miserable week's journey.

After having been up until the wee hours the night before, I slept to the unheard-of hour of nine AM. I was awakened suddenly by the crowing of one of the farmer's roosters and by a shaft of sunlight shining on my face through a crack in the wooden shutters that covered the easterly window of my bedroom. Fearing that I had missed breakfast, I washed and dressed hurriedly and ran downstairs to the dining room.

I was greatly relieved to see that Camilla had left a place set for me at the table. She then brought me a pot of hot chocolate, a bowl of cornflakes and a pitcher of peculiar-tasting warm milk. The cornflakes were incredibly stale and had probably been in the house since my previous visit in 1948—my grandmother thought that as an American child I would require cornflakes, a product that at the time was considered very exotic in Italy and that she associated with the several disagreeable years she had spent in exile in New York during the war. The odd taste of the milk came from its having been boiled. Milk was supplied daily by our farmer and boiling took the place of the pasteurization process used in commercial dairies. Fortunately, there was still a basket of rolls, toast and crisp *grissini* (thin Torino-style bread sticks) on the table together with two jars of home-made fruit preserves that my grandmother's cook, Teresa, had put up the preceding summer—I don't remember now what kind they were, but I remember vividly lots of cherry, apricot, strawberry, and black currant jams. The latter were much nicer than the old stale cornflakes and boiled milk and became my staple breakfast for the rest of my life.

After breakfast, I went looking for my mother and grandmother, Elvira. My mother was in the day room, reading, and my grandmother was in the garden just outside the day room window, knitting. My father was at work, though what sort of work he did was not something that I as a four-year-old knew or cared about. After I greeted my mother and grandmother, I was sent out to play. And so I set about rediscovering the *Val Salice* that I had known two years before.

My first stop was the hen yard, home of the roosters that had so rudely awakened me earlier that morning. There I found the farmer's kindly wife, also named Elvira, and their daughter Annunziata busily gathering the morning's production of eggs. I followed them on their rounds and was very excited to find several eggs before they did. Elvira had a broad smiley kind of face. It was heavily lined from years of hard work in the sun even if she was still only in her thirties. Annunziata was a few years older than I and was the classic pretty farmer's daughter. I am not sure how we communicated because I spoke only English, French and Italian, and they only Piemontese dialect, but somehow we managed.

I then wandered past the stable; the two cows were out to pasture, but the dozens of guinea pigs with whom they shared the stable were darting about, burrowing in the cows' straw bedding, and gathering up seeds and bits of grain that the messy cows had scattered about. Little did I know that these cute and playful creatures were all destined for the farmer's stewpot.

I was careful to stay well away from the far end of the stable where Fido, the scruffy watchdog, was chained up. He was likely to bark, growl meanly at me, and knock me down if I got close to him. Fido was the latest in a series of identically named watchdogs whose dynasty stretched back at least to when my father had been my age before World War I.

My next stop was the small formal garden, where the farmer, Giuseppin, was busy weeding the flower beds (Figures 1-1 and 1-2). One of his duties was to maintain the garden, in exchange for which, he was allowed to sell the excess flowers in the public market in central Torino along with the rest of the farm's produce. Giuseppin was a few years older than his wife and his heavily tanned face was even more deeply lined than hers. Also he lacked more than a few teeth as became evident every time he smiled, which he did often. The garden was much prettier by day than it had been during my explorations the previous night, with its serpentine paths paved in white pebbles, its pair of tall palms and its standard and bush roses that towered over me. Giuseppin kept it wonderfully with its many beautiful and aromatic roses, carefully raked white gravel paths, and nary a weed.

My final stop for the morning was to return to where my grandmother was knitting (Figure 1-4). She was always knitting. Some of her production of gloves, heavy socks, and warm sweaters was destined for various family members, but much of it was donated to the poor. I must have sat with her for quite a while for I next remember her looking at her watch and telling me to wash up for lunch. Just at that moment, my father's car pulled in though the big iron gates that opened onto the public road beyond the high brick wall that protected our villa from the outside world.

In the Italy of those days all offices closed from one to three PM. Everyone was expected to go home for a leisurely lunch, the main meal of the day. At my grandmother's a typical such meal would begin with soup, risotto or pasta, followed by a modest amount of meat, fish or poultry, copious quantities of vegetables, a salad, and finally, fresh fruits and coffee. On Fridays, the main course always was fish. In those days Catholics were supposed to abstain from meat on Fridays and, even though we were *Ebrei*—"Hebrews"—we followed the practice because my grandmother did not want to make Teresa cook separate meals for the servants and the family. On rare occasions we would also have sweets, but that was usually reserved for days when we had guests for lunch. There was always a decanter of wine on the table, and even as a four-year-old I was expected to have some. Teresa would prepare these meals on her wood-fired stove, and her sister Camilla would serve at the table. My mother admonished me in English to make sure that I left plenty of food on the serving trays, as Camilla and Teresa would be having their lunch after we finished ours. All the fruits, vegetables, milk and eggs that went into the meal came from the villa's farm, and the flowers on the table came from the garden.

The culmination of the meal was a short post-prandial nap. Accordingly, I was sent to my room for a nap. As an American kid who was almost five years old, I thought I was too grown up for such things. Nonetheless, when I saw that everyone else seemed to be nodding off, I acquiesced and followed suit.

My father generally stayed home in the afternoons unless he had pressing business that required him to return downtown. This particular afternoon, after our naps, he took me for a walk to introduce me to the villa's farming operations. Our first stop was an enclosed storage area just beyond the stables where our farmer kept many of his farming tools such as rough wooden rakes and pitchforks, scythes, pruners, massive ox yokes, and hand-made tapered ladders that were essential for picking fruit. Our second stop was the former carriage house that now doubled as our garage and as a storage place for the large wooden farm wagon, to which the farmer would yoke his cows to carry tools and materials back and forth from the fields and transport farm produce to the open-air market in the city center.

As we came out of the carriage house, we encountered Giuseppin near a well that he used to draw water for the animals. Giuseppin had just strapped a galvanized tank onto his back. This tank had a long handle on one side that projected in front of him and a small rubber hose on the other side. As Giuseppin adjusted the position of the heavy tank on his back a few drops of a bright blue liquid sloshed out of the top. My father explained that the liquid was a solution of copper sulfate, a naturally occurring mineral and the only pesticide used on the farm. Giuseppin was going to spray the solution on the grape vines to keep them from moldering. He would walk up and down the rows of grape vines, pumping the long handle with his right hand and directing the resulting spray emanating from the hose with his left hand.

My father and I then set off for a walk in the fields down the steep hill below the flat terraced area around the main house. To get there we descended on an outdoor staircase made of stone immediately adjacent to the billiard house and passed through a rusty wrought iron gate into the orchard. Off the stairs was the entrance to the small apartment on the lower level of the billiard house where there lived a toothless old woman who dressed only in black; at the time I was terribly frightened of her, thinking her a witch ... or worse. As best I could tell her only means of making a living was to wad up old newspapers and sell the wads as fireplace fuel, although she probably had a small government pension.

My father showed me the different types of fruit trees. The orchard was planted with multiple varieties of each species of fruit so that they would ripen at different times and the farmer would have additional fruits to bring to market each week of the summer and fall. At this time the first cherries called *amarene* were ripening. These smallish cherries were bright red, with a tart flavor; in *Val Salice* we would eat some of them fresh, but Teresa would preserve most of them as jam and syrup. A couple of weeks later a sweeter, darker variety would ripen, to be followed in another couple of weeks by cream-colored cherries with a red blush. Just as the cherries were finishing, the apricots would ripen, followed by four different varieties of plums, and then three varieties of peaches. Later in the summer there would be figs, and as summer gave way to fall, grapes, pears, walnuts and filberts. The filberts grew on tall shrubs that were planted as hedges along the northern side of the farm, protected from the north wind by a brick wall. The final fruits of the season were the persimmons, which ripened in November, after the leaves had fallen from the tree, leaving the bare branches festooned with large red globes.

As my father and I walked on, we came out of the orchard to the strawberry beds. These fruits had already all gone to market. Beyond the berries there were assorted vegetables and currant bushes. We continued further down the hill we came to a couple of acres of where the farmer was growing wheat. In addition to producing the edible grain, wheat was important to him for its straw, which Giuseppin used as bedding for his cows.

Next we passed Giuseppin's dung heap, a mass of accumulated manure and crushed straw from the stable floor that he raked up each morning, loaded into his cart to which he had hitched is two cows, and had them pull it down to the fields before turning them out to pasture. Later that day he would spread fresh clean straw on the floor of the stable as new bedding for the cows. Each day he would pile the day's new mass of dung and straw on the top of the heap, where it would begin the process of decay. Periodically he would shovel out fully decayed manure from the bottom of the heap for use as fertilizer on the fields and flower beds. My father explained that this was the only fertilizer he ever used. He and hundreds of generations of his ancestors were organic farmers long before the "discovery" of this approach as an alternative to chemical fertilizers late in twentieth century.

As we continued on our walk we neared the bottom of the property with its hay meadow. Earlier that day Giuseppin had cut the summer's first growth of hay with a scythe, and left it out in the sun to dry. My father explained to me that this was the first of two summer-time hay cuttings. He then told me that in a few days Giuseppin would rake up the dried hay, load it into his oxcart and have his cows pull it up to the stable, where he would pitch the hay into the loft over the stable with his home-made wooden pitchfork.

Along our walk we crossed the hay meadow, my father took me to peer through the hedge beyond it to see the main house of the next villa down the hill. That villa belonged to my father's first cousin, Ada Treves, *née* Sacerdote. Both villas had been acquired by my father's and Ada's common grandfather, Cav. Emanuele Sacerdote, in the late 1800s. Because Ada's husband, Angiolo Treves, was my father's business partner, and we both had houses on either side of the Atlantic, we tended to see them very often, both in Italy and the United States.

My father and I returned to the main house from our little walk around 4:30, when it was time for *merenda*, afternoon tea. My grandmother admired all things English, especially tea time. In fine weather, tea was served in the garden, though on rainy days, tea was served in the living room. And, tea was *always* accompanied by English biscuits. My favorites were the Huntley and Palmer's biscuits that came in a richly illustrated tin. The biscuits were much less sweet than American-style cookies and came in a variety of shapes. Each shape had its name, *Marie, Nice, Rich Tea, Digestive,* and the like, impressed into its center. As a child I was generally offered hot chocolate to drink instead of tea, but could have either. On especially warm days I could have cold *amarenata* instead of tea or chocolate. *Amarenata* was prepared at the tea table by mixing a few spoonfuls of Teresa's tart cherry syrup into a glass of cold water.

After *merenda* it was more play time. Sometimes my father or grandmother would play *bocce*, a type of lawn bowls, with me. Our *bocce* pitch was under the horse-chestnut trees that lined the driveway from the villa's main gate to the coach house at the back of the property, beyond the stable. Sometimes Annunziata, the farmer's daughter or Renzo and Emma, the children of the two families that rented the apartments over the coach house from my grandmother, would join in the game. In *bocce*, the first player would roll a small white cue ball towards the far end of the pitch. Then the players would alternate rolling larger balls towards it. Because the winner was the person whose ball ended up closest to the small ball, the key plays were either slow rolls, tightly targeted towards the cue ball or harder rolls whose aim it was to knock away an opponent's well-placed ball.

Around 7:30 in the evening we sat down to supper, which was generally a lighter meal than the early afternoon dinner. After supper we might read, play board games, or listen to the radio—at that time my grandmother did not yet have a television. And finally it was bed time for me.

And so went our days that summer. Sometimes we would vary the routine, with dinner, tea or supper guests, generally old friends of my parents from before the war or any of the dozens of my parents' aunts, uncles or cousins and their children. At other times we might go to their friends' and relatives' city apartments or country villas. One such visit was to our Treves cousins who owned the next villa down the hill from ours, the one I had glimpsed through the hedge separating our property from theirs. There I had a second occasion of remembering earlier times while we were having supper with Ada and Angiolo. As we sat in their very formal dining room, being served by Ada's white-jacketed butler, I became acutely aware of having had a similar experience two years earlier in 1948.

We had been in Paris on our way to Le Havre for the return journey to America after my family's first post-war visit to Italy. My parents, my older brothers and I had been invited to a very formal dinner at the home of my mother's uncle, Oncle Raoul, a Parisian financier and the brother of my maternal grandmother. We were all seated very stiffly in a room paneled in dark wood as Oncle Raoul's butler served us our dinner. At one point, my oldest brother Albert nodded toward the butler and whispered to my mother in English "Isn't he going to sit down with us to eat dinner?" My mother's relatives overheard his comment and then began asking "In what manner are you raising your children in America? Don't you have servants? How can your children grow up properly in that uncivilized country?" They clearly had little idea about the informality of the American lifestyle and even less of an idea about the toll that exile, my father's subsequent three years of unemployment when he was declared an enemy alien, and the war-time damage to our Italian real estate had taken on our family's financial circumstances in the early post-war years. Many years later I learned that Raoul and his wife Frida had somehow escaped from the Nazis and their Vichy French collaborators after being arrested in Marseilles early in the war.

A week or so after the dinner at Ada's I meandered down into the orchard and happened upon Giuseppin's family. They were picking cherries. They had several tapered ladders with which the three of them would climb the trees to gather the ripe fruit. They put the cherries into well-worn baskets woven from thin strips of wood. They carefully lined each basket with leaves to keep the fruit from bruising. I asked if I could help and they enthusiastically accepted my offer. Since I was much smaller and lighter than they were, I could pick the fruits growing on the thinner branches. Of course, a non-trivial fraction of the fruits I picked ended up in my mouth instead of the baskets.

On another occasion my daily wanderings brought me near the stable, where I saw Giuseppin seated in the morning sunshine next to a massive wooden contraption that held his upturned scythe. The contraption had a foot treadle and a heavy wheel made of cream-colored stone. When I asked him what he was doing, he said he was sharpening his scythe to get it ready to harvest the wheat. That afternoon I met him again, this time standing in the wheat field. I sat down to watch him as he cut the wheat. He would take a few broad sweeps of his scythe. Then he would set it down and gather up the stalks of wheat into a sheaf which he would bind with some twine he had brought for the purpose. Finally, he would stand the sheaf up in the middle of the area he has just cut and repeat the process. By the time for *merenda*, he had cut and bundled all the wheat, and the field was dotted with sheaves. These he left for several days so that the sun could dry the grain.

On the day when Giuseppin judged the grain to be sufficiently dry, just before lunch time, he loaded his sheaves of wheat onto his large wooden wagon and hauled the lot of them back up to the farm house. That afternoon I was drawn back to the stable area by an odd ka-chunk, ka-chunk, ka-chunk sound. When I got there I found Giuseppin, his family, and his brother Pierino's and brother-in-law Gioanin's families, the tenants in the apartments over the coach house, together with a stranger, all gathered around a red machine which was the source of the sound I had heard. The stranger was the area thresher. At harvest season he made the rounds of the farms in the vicinity with his machine which he rented to each farmer for a day or two. Giuseppin would untie a sheaf of wheat and drop it into a hopper at one end of the machine. In the middle was a bin that was rapidly filling up with grain and at the far end out came rectangular bales of straw bound with wire. Every so often Giuseppin would stop loading the hopper in order to empty the grain bin or to hoist the bales up to the hay loft, where his wife would stack them neatly. While all this was going on, Gioanin's wife lit a wood fire in a small brick oven built into the stable wall and began to bake *grissini* from dough she had prepared earlier in the day. As the *grissini* came out of the oven, everyone munched on them in celebration of the wheat harvest. As it turned out, this was the last year that our villa produced wheat; after that Giuseppin planted the grain field with maize because it gave him a bigger yield and did not require him to rent a threshing machine. That afternoon I had witnessed the passing of a long tradition.

Occasionally my parents would vary my daily routine and take me down the hill into the urban part of Torino, either to go shopping or else to visit one or another of the city's sights, such as the former royal palace with its collection of suits of armor, or Palazzo Madama, the traditional home of the queen mother of Italy, with its eclectic mix of architectural elements ranging from a 2000-year-old Roman tower to its ornate baroque façade on the side facing Piazza Castello. One of my favorite excursions was to go to the *Borgo Mediovale* in the *Parco del Valentino*, a large park along the river Po. The *Borgo Mediovale* was a nineteenth century replica of a medieval village and castle from the Valle d'Aosta region in the Alps northwest of Torino. Another favorite of mine was to visit the Torino's Egyptology museum with its great collection of statues and mummies; this museum had as its origin a load of war booty that Napoleon had dumped in Torino in the 1790s during his retreat from his ill-fated attempt to conquer Egypt.

In one of these forays into the city, I accompanied my mother and one of her friends to their dressmaker, where they each picked out fabrics and styles and had dresses made for themselves. At tea time I was given my reward for behaving despite my total boredom with this activity; I was taken to Talmone, a fashionable *gelateria* in Piazza San Carlo and indulged with the first taste that I remember of truly superb Italian gelato. I believe that I had one ball of chocolate gelato and a second of *gianduja*, a hazelnut and chocolate flavor that is very characteristically Piemontese.

On one of the rare rainy days, when wandering in the garden and fields would have been unpleasant, my grandmother opened a cupboard near the central staircase that was filled with enormous iron keys. She pulled out a particularly large one, and then urged me to dash out of the house to the billiard house in the garden; she followed with the key and opened the billiard house. Judging from the musty smell, it was probably the first time that it had been opened that season. Despite the rain, we opened the windows and doors to air the place out. She then taught me a couple of simple billiard games. Because I was not even five years' old, I was not allowed to use a cue stick lest I mis-aim it and rip the table fabric. Instead I was instructed to roll the heavy ivory cue ball with my hand, a bit like playing *bocce* on a green felted table.

Some weeks later, my grandmother took me into a dark storage room where we found toys that she had kept from when my father had been a boy in the years before World War I. My favorites were a special set of wooden blocks that could be stacked up to form a battleship and a set of wooden tiles that one could arrange in many attractive geometric patterns, including the patterns on the floor of the house's oversized bathroom (see Fig. 1-6).

Later that summer, my mother and I took a long train ride from Torino to Rome to visit my maternal grandmother, Nonna Ghit, Zio Ruggiero, my mother's younger brother, and Ruggiero's daughter, my cousin Gianna. The train ride was both hot and endless, but we were finally in Rome. Nonna Ghit was an imposing and rather stern woman, much the opposite of my warm and kind Nonna Elvira. At Ghit's house it was clear that while I might be seen, I was not to be heard. My mother and Ghit conversed mostly in French, a language that I understood reasonably well, but not nearly so well as Italian and English.

Zio Ruggiero's personality was the antithesis of Ghit's and my mother's. He was an easy-going man who smiled a lot. An engineer by profession, Ruggiero worked as the manager of a glue factory. He teased me that his factory was one that turned old horses into glue, though I learned many years later that in fact their products were casein-based glues, similar to Elmer's. Gianna was about one year older than I and took that as her cue that she should boss me around, an approach that I resisted as mightily as a four-year-old could, which was not all that mightily.

When my mother and I were alone, I asked her where Gianna's mother was, and my mother abruptly changed the subject. Many years later I learned that Gianna's parents had found refuge in a Red Cross camp in Switzerland after the Nazis invaded Italy in 1943. Gianna was born there, but her parents' marriage did not survive the war. Because Italy lacked a divorce law until the 1970s, Ruggiero was never able to remarry and had to raise Gianna alone.

While we were in Rome, my mother and I stayed at the *Pensione Laura*, near Ghit's apartment. Breakfast at the *pensione* always included *cotognata,* quince jam, and I became quite fond of it and have been ever since. My mother also took me to see some of the sights of Rome. Although we visited many of its most famous monuments, my strongest memory was of *La Bocca della Veritá. La Bocca* was a round slab of stone that had been carved into a face in Roman times. It was reputed to be a magical lie detector; the claim was that if liars inserted a hand into the mouth, it would be cut off, while truth-tellers would suffer no harm. I was greatly relieved to be able to insert and withdraw my hand intact despite the numerous fibs I had told. And many years later I was decidedly disappointed when I learned that *La Bocca's* original Roman purpose had been to cover a drain leading to the ancient Roman sewer system.

After we had returned from Rome to *Val Salice*, on a particularly clear morning, my mother led me through her room to the balcony overlooking the city to our west. Above the city we could see the snow-covered peaks of the high Alps that mark the boundary between Italy and France. Directly opposite us were the large snow fields that are the source of the River Po, the main river of northern Italy. She asked if I would like to go to the mountains. The question was phrased in such a way that it was clear that my answer was supposed to be "Yes."

To prepare for the trip to the mountains, my mother took me into Torino to buy a pair of mountain boots. When we got to the shoe shop, the owner indicated that because it was summer she had her stock of such boots in storage in a spare room in her apartment. It seemed that such boots were mostly sold in the winter and used for skiing. The owner suggested that we return to the shop just before one o'clock and then we could accompany her back to her apartment as she went home for lunch and try on boots there, which we did.

When we got to her apartment, we discovered that she lived on the third floor in a building that had not yet been repaired after the war. Half the building was a pile of broken bricks in a weedy lot, while the other half contained her apartment. To get to it, we had to climb what had originally been an internal staircase, but was now open to the elements, attached precariously to what had now become the outside of the remaining half-building. The staircase no longer had a railing; that feature was evidently somewhere among the piles of broken bricks down below. Although both my mother and I suffered from vertigo, we somehow got up to the shop-owner's apartment. The woman then disappeared into a back room and reappeared shortly thereafter with several pairs of mountain boots. These were square-toed leather boots that came up over the ankles; the boots had laces and Vibram™ soles. At that time such boots were worn for both hiking and skiing. As ski boots, they clamped into the "bear trap" bindings on heavy wooden skis.

After we selected a pair of boots that fit me, my mother and I went out for a most indulgent lunch ... in a very elegant pastry shop. Torino's centuries' old tradition of superb confectionary dates back to when it became an important center for the processing of chocolate. We each selected three different pastries and ordered beverages, tea for my mother and hot chocolate for me, both served in little silver pots. Even as a small child I felt very naughty with this lunch, but I so enjoyed it. Many years later when I proposed a similar lunch to my wife, she was aghast at the idea. "How can you suggest such a meal?" she asked. "After all it would be loaded with fats and sugar and totally lacking in fruits and vegetables!"

About a week later my mother and I set off by car for Courmayeur, at the very head of the Valle D'Aosta facing the Mont Blanc for a week of hiking and relaxation. Along the way I noticed the enormous number of castles that seemed to top every hillock in the Valle d'Aosta. Equally impressive was the extensive terracing of the mountain sides in the lower valley to increase the amount of arable land. Most of the terraces on south-facing slopes were planted with grapes, while those on the north-facing side of the valley were used to grow grass for hay.

One of the days that we were in Courmayeur, my mother decided that she wanted to take the cable car to *Rifugio Torino*, a climbers' hostel above 10,000 feet. Because my mother thought young children should not be taken to high altitudes, I was left in the valley in the care of one of my mother's many cousins who had a vacation house there. And so I stayed below with this woman and her very whiny daughter. Even at four years' old, I was appalled by this child's complaints about everything. And besides, she was a full year younger than me and therefore not worthy of my attention. In short, I was as domineering towards her as Gianna had been to me.

As I stood on the balcony of our cousins' house, watching my mother's cable car rise up the very steep eastern slope of the Mont Blanc, I had another flashback to a much earlier experience. I suddenly recalled having been to Plan Maison at Cervinia, about thirty miles east of Courmayeur, with my parents and brothers two years previous (Figure 1-3). After lunch the rest of the family was going to take the cable car the rest of the way to Plateau Rosa, the dividing line between Italy and Switzerland on the shoulders of the Matterhorn. I was to remain behind at Plan Maison because my mother thought Plateau Rosa was too high for a child under three years old, and so I was left in the charge of the waiter at the restaurant.

The waiter showed me to a small room with a couch on which I was supposed to take a nap. He also pointed out a push-button hanging on a wire from the ceiling and told me to press the button if I needed anything. After a few minutes, I decided to try out the push-button, and indeed the waiter came running, stuck his head in the door and asked what I needed. Of course, I did not need anything, and so he went back to work. After ten or fifteen minutes, I pushed the button a second time, and again the waiter came running, and again I did not need anything; the waiter looked none too pleased. A little while later, I pushed it again, finding this a jolly game, and this time the waiter came and called me *sciocco*. Subsequent button pushes caused the ever more exasperated waiter to call me *scemo*, *stulto*, *idiota*, *cretino* and, finally, *imbecille*. Italian has a seemingly endless number of ways to call someone a jerk, with each indicating a slightly different aspect of that jerkiness. Finally, my family arrived back from its trip to Plateau Rosa, much to the relief of the waiter. I hope my father tipped him well.

This idyllic summer in Italy finally came to an end. My father flew home, and my mother and I reversed our trip of the beginning of the summer, taking the long train ride from Torino to Cherbourg, and then making the five-day ocean crossing. Such summers reinforced and expanded a collection of memories that would inform and direct much of my later life. *Val Salice* continued to exert a peculiar draw upon us, and we always returned.

Figure 1-1. My mother Luciana in Val Salice's formal garden
with my brother Albert, 1938

Figure 1.2. George, Albert and Peter at Val Salice, 1949

Figure 1-3. Albert, Giorgio, Peter, Luciana and George
Plan Maison, Cervinia 1949

Figure 1-4. My grandmother Elvira, 1960

Figure 1.5. One of my favorite games at Val Salice

Chapter 2

Val Salice Through the Years

As I grew up, I regularly returned to *Val Salice*. Over time I gained a progressively more mature understanding of it and what it represented in our family. It became a center to which our extended family returned from the distant parts of the world to which we had been scattered. It became a mechanism for my grandmother to maintain contact not only with her children and grandchildren, but also with her broad extended family in Italy. The stories of adventures and misadventures in and around *Val Salice* have become some of my fondest memories. And, as I grew older, *Val Salice* became a vehicle through which I learned about our family's privileges and obligations.

* * * * *

One afternoon when I was nine years' old, my father and I were walking through the orchard and I noticed that the pear trees were much smaller than those bearing other fruits. My father explained to me that during the war, the Nazi German officers who had occupied our house with its strategic view over all of Torino had forced the farmer to cut down many fruit trees for use as fireplace fuel to heat the house, which lacked central heating. The Nazis were not interested in the better wood available from our woodlot further up in the hills, and cared not a whit that the fruit trees represented the farmer's chief means of earning a living. After the war, our family had to replace the lost trees with new ones, all pears, which explained the smaller size of the pear trees. As owners of *Val Salice*, we rented out the orchard, vineyard, and farm fields with their hay meadows as well as the stable and farmer's cottage to Giuseppin and his family. It was our obligation as his landlord to maintain these all in good order.

Farming, of course, is a risky business. In some years crops fail and there is little to sell, while in others there is a plentiful harvest, but prices might be so low as to generate no profit. Our rental agreement with Giuseppin allowed him to share this risk with us, so that his rent was tied to the revenue he realized from his farming work. Some of this rent we would receive in the form of produce for the table. He supplied all the fruits, vegetables, eggs, milk, and table flowers for the main house. But the rest of our share of the rent was only occasionally forthcoming. There always seemed to be an excuse. One year the peaches were small and fetched a poor price. Another year the tomatoes all rotted on the vine. And so it went. But we so enjoyed *Val Salice* that these matters tended to be overlooked.

We had other tenants on the property as well. They were holdovers from the immediate post-war years when the city officials forced landlords to take on tenants into any vacant rooms they might have because so many houses had been destroyed by the war-time bombing raids. Fearing that the city might place tenants not to our liking in various empty spaces in the outbuildings of *Val Salice*, my father filled them with tenants of his own choosing. Their extremely modest rents were much less important than having the place occupied by people we trusted.

In a single room in the basement of the billiard house lived an old woman who had a modest government pension. Her rent was set by the city at the pre-war rate of sixty lire per month, and this rent could not be raised during her tenancy. In the years before the war, sixty lire was worth about $10, the equivalent of perhaps $200 in 2015 dollars. But in the post-war inflation, the lira lost 99% of its value, so she lived essentially rent-free. We had similar arrangements with two other families who lived in the lodgings over the former coach house that now served as a garage. Giuseppin's brother-in-law Gioanin lived in one apartment with his wife and son Renzo, who often played *bocce* with me. Gioanin worked in the Fiat auto plants in the city. The other apartment was occupied by Giuseppin's widowed brother, Pierino, with his daughter Emma. I never knew their rents, but suspect that they were almost as low as the sixty lire paid by the old woman in the basement of the billiard house.

* * * * *

At some point during that summer, my cousin Gianna came to visit from Rome. Gianna was a year older than I and a rather jolly sort; she was no longer as domineering as when I had last seen her and had developed a warm personality similar to her father's. In the afternoons we took to playing *bocce* with Renzo. Renzo had a very vivid imagination which he would use liberally to invent tall tales of various exploits that he surely never had. And each day he would come up with ever more fantastic stories that he would try to pass off as fact during our games of *bocce*.

Gianna and I both understood that these stories were all lies. Our fondest wish was that we could invent even more outlandish stories and use them to counter his balderdash, but we never could muster up any good tales. At one point she and I developed a fantasy that a certain cabinet in my grandmother's living room was really a machine for creating great lies with which we could outdo Renzo. We would put "raw materials" such as old papers and dried leaves into this "machine" with the expectation that it would then produce the be-all and end-all of wild stories, though we were constantly disappointed by its lack of output. My grandmother's maid, Camilla, could never figure out why this cabinet was constantly filling up with the useless bits of junk that constituted our "raw materials."

After a couple of weeks, Gianna's father, Uncle Ruggiero, came up to *Val Salice* to visit with us, especially my mother, with whom he carried on a copious correspondence but whom he had only rarely seen since my parents left Italy in 1939. My mother and Ruggiero decided to take us kids up to Gressoney, an Alpine village in the Valle d'Aosta, for a week of hiking and relaxation. Gressoney is at the head of a side valley that ends in the Monte Rosa, a massive, heavily glaciated peak astride the Italian border with Switzerland. Our days would consist of a light breakfast at our inn followed by a hike up into the alpine meadows for a picnic lunch with magnificent views of the surrounding mountains. Ruggiero's good humor had a softening impact on my mother's generally severe demeanor. And he impressed all of us with his manly toughness when he splashed icy water from the alpine lakes on his hairy chest. After lunch we made our descent back into town in time to see the rosy alpenglow for which the Monte Rosa was named. After a hearty supper at our inn—typically a thick game stew with polenta or pasta and grilled meat and vegetables— we would play an Italian card game, *Scopa*. While I do not recall the rules of this game, I do remember that the loser of each hand had to make a forfeit, typically by submitting to having his ears, nose or hair pulled. As the youngest at the table I was most often the loser, and I recall Gianna taking particular delight in exacting forfeits from me, her younger cousin.

* * * * *

One weekend morning my father and I were standing in the formal garden admiring the beautiful view of the city and the high Alps beyond it. I noticed a very tall building that stood hundreds of feet above low-rise Torino where few buildings exceed five stories. "Papà," I asked, "What is that building?" My father looked at me with an expression suggesting embarrassment and replied, "You don't really want to know." So, I dropped the subject.

I did not, however, lose my curiosity about that building, which I learned many years later was called the *Mole Antonelliana* (Antonelli's Pile, Figure 2-1). In 1864 the Torino Hebrew community had wanted to celebrate its increasing prosperity since being freed from the ghetto sixteen years earlier. It commissioned the well-known architect Alessandro Antonelli, to design a fine new synagogue to replace the cramped quarters of the three synagogues which they had been using for religious services in the old ghetto. The community asked him to design a two- or three-story building for the purpose.

But the Hebrew community did not realize that they were dealing with a madman. As soon as the plans had been approved and construction begun, Antonelli began to change his design, making the building larger and grander. The community then went through several cycles in which Antonelli would revise his plans, the community would more and more reluctantly agree to the new designs with their added expense, and then Antonelli would expand his plans yet again, making the building ever larger, taller and more elaborate. At one point a community leader asked in jest, "To speak with God, do we need a building that touches Him?" After eight years, the community called a halt to construction, as it became clear that Antonelli's unbounded ambitions would soon lead it to bankruptcy. The Hebrew community then engineered a trade with the city, in which the former would receive a parcel of vacant land on which to build a proper synagogue, and the latter would take over Antonelli's project.

When Antonelli's building was finally completed in 1887, it stood 500 feet tall, about half the height of the future Empire State Building. It was built entirely of masonry, with not a single steel supporting member. The city engineer refused to give it a certificate of occupancy because he feared that it might collapse at any moment. And so the building stood vacant for over a century; it was vacant on the day when I first noticed it from the garden in *Val Salice*. For the normally reserved Torino Hebrew community, the building was a continuing reminder of what happens when you over-reach or show-off too much, which is why it so embarrassed my father that morning. Finally, the city had the *Mole* strengthened with massive reinforced concrete pillars, and opened it in 2000 as a museum of the Italian Film Industry. It had finally found a use after 113 years. It subsequently became the symbol of the Torino Olympic games.

* * * * *

During the summer of 1957, our visit to *Val Salice* coincided with a visit from my uncle Paolo, my father's brother, and his family from New York. I had known Paolo's children, my cousins Marc and Alan, quite well from our regular visits in America. Marc was my age, and Alan three years younger, but our visits to *Val Salice* and theirs had not coincided before. Marc, Alan, and Paolo's American-born wife, Pearl spoke little to no Italian, which often cast me in the role of translator between them and my grandmother and her servants and tenants.

One evening we were just sitting down to supper when Pearl noticed that Alan was missing. She stepped outside for a moment to call him in from wherever he was playing. As soon as he entered the dining room and sat down, we were all overpowered by a very disagreeable and unappetizing odor but no one said anything. Aunt Pearl then asked Alan, "Where have you been this afternoon, and what were you doing?" He replied, "I

43

was in the stable visiting the cows. They wanted someone to keep them company. I sat under the larger one and kept watch over her sister in the next stall." That explained everything about Alan's dinner-time aroma. His mother then picked him up by the shirt collar and seat of the pants and hauled him off to the bath for a hard scrub, while the rest of us ate a pleasant dinner minus pungent bovine emanations.

At one point Paulo and Pearl decided to go to the Riviera for a brief vacation, leaving Marc and Alan at *Val Salice* in my parents' care. With 20/20 hindsight, I am surprised that they did so. While Paolo got on well with both of my parents, there was little that Pearl and my mother agreed upon. Both were strong-willed women and each was convinced that her approach to raising children was much superior to the other's. In any case, my mother was now in charge of Pearl's children as well as her own.

In the absence of his parents and as the youngest of us three cousins, Alan fell victim to quite a few pranks. On the first night after Paolo and Pearl had left, Marc put his deep learning from summer camp to good use and short-sheeted his brother's bed. Alan, however, countered with a powerful weapon of his own, whining to my mother. Alan ran to my mother, complaining about what his older brother had done. Marc was soon on my mother's bad side, not a good place to be.

A couple of afternoons later, Marc and I went for a ramble in the hay meadow. We discovered that it was absolutely teeming with enormous grasshoppers, and we proceeded to catch and release dozens of them. Then we had the brilliant idea for another prank to play on Alan; we brought a whole sack full of the insects back to the house and put them into his bed.

All through supper and beyond, Marc and I secretly enjoyed the prospect of seeing Alan's bed-time reaction, and we had to fight down our urges to laugh and give away our secret. At last, it was bed time, and the three of us went off to bed, they in their room, and myself in my own. Suddenly I heard a kerfuffle from Marc and Alan's room as Alan climbed into bed and began to feel the bugs crawling all over him. He jumped out of bed and ran to my mother complaining that something had gotten into his bed. When she came to inspect, she pulled down the covers, revealing all the jumping grasshoppers. She quickly put two and two together and was decidedly not amused. She summoned Marc and me to remove all the offending creatures from Alan's bed and the rest of the room, to which many of them had escaped. Finally, to exact punishment for this prank as well as the short-sheeting, my mother forced Marc to swap beds with Alan, just in case there were still a few grasshoppers we had left behind.

* * * * *

Later that summer, after Paolo's family left, my cousins Emanuele and Piera Levi-Montalcini came up from central Torino to stay with us at *Val Salice*. As is common in the small Italian Hebrew community, I was related to them through both of my parents. Their grandmother Adelina Montalcini was the older sister of my grandmother Elvira, the owner of *Val Salice*, and their grandfather Adamo Levi was an older brother of my maternal grandfather, Leone Levi. Emanuele was a year older than I. Because his family had stayed in Italy during the war, he was born while they were hiding from the Nazis in German-occupied Florence, living under assumed names. His sister Piera was two to three years younger, born after the war.

Because my grandmother's children and grandchildren all lived in the Americas, she "adopted" Emanuele and Piera as her Italian grandchildren. Every summer she would have them out to *Val Salice* for at least a month. During the winter months, they all lived in the same apartment house

45

on Corso Re Umberto that Elvira, Adelina and their brother (also named Emanuele) had purchased jointly in the early 1920s. In this way, Emanuele and Piera both became deeply attached to her, *Val Salice* and Corso Re Umberto. In middle age, Emanuele bought his own villa in the hills above Torino, not far from *Val Salice*. He now owns the apartment building that used to belong to our grandmothers, and several of the apartments in it are occupied by his children and their families. His grandchildren are now the fifth family generation to live there.

Emanuele and I discovered that we shared the same love of *Val Salice* and in the course of that visit; we became life-long friends just as our fathers had been before us. We both enjoyed the simple pleasures and seasonal rhythms of country life. We loved to wander in the fields, to harvest fruit, to gather eggs, and to play in *Val Salice's* small but beautiful gardens. We were both determined to catch the small lizards that came out onto the garden walls to bask in the sun, but of course, neither of us was ever fast enough to get one.

One afternoon, Emanuele taught me how to make tiny round cages, using thin slices of cork cut from wine bottle stoppers as the tops and bottoms and pins from my grandmother's sewing basket as bars. Soon we set about catching assorted insects and confining them to our cages to create a private insect zoo. At first most of our catch consisted of flies, grasshoppers, ants and other common bugs, but soon we began to compete to see who could find and cage the most unusual specimens. Each afternoon we would bring our zoo to Elvira for her review and approval, and then we would release all of our specimens back into the wild. And the next day we would assemble a new zoo, always looking for the rarest or most colorful insects we could find. Many years later, when my wife and I were visiting the Murano glass works in the Venetian lagoon, we entered a workshop producing marvelous glass insects. I was sorely tempted to buy a small collection to send to Emanuele in little cork-and-pin cages, but I was afraid they would not survive shipping. So we left them in the "wild" in Murano.

* * * * *

One day that summer, my grandmother sensed that I needed a new toy. She unlocked the door to a large storeroom where she kept assorted old things that were not in regular use. In one corner she kept some toys that used to belong to my father when he was a boy, and one particular object caught my eye. It was a large wooden hoop with a smaller stick, the beater. My grandmother offered it to me and then showed me how to strike the hoop with the beater, forcing it to roll forward. I then spent many hours driving this hoop all over the garden and up and down the long earthen driveway from the front gate to the garage at the back of the property. I was absolutely enthralled with my "new" toy.

At the end of the summer, I had to leave my hoop and beater behind when we left to return to America, and I did so with a heavy heart. When we got home, I was astounded to see hoops, albeit plastic ones, in every shop window and driveway. "Wow!" I thought. "American kids have discovered the hoop too!" But they did not seem to be using it right. Instead of striking it with a beater and chasing it about, the kids were putting the hoops around their middles and making them go around their bodies. "Didn't they understand how you are supposed to do this?" I thought. Of course, what I had come home to was the Hula Hoop craze of the mid-1950s.

* * * * *

At one point during that summer, my parents invited me to go out for a ride to visit two other farms that my father owned on the north side of Torino, in the general direction of the airport. My father, grandfather and great-grandfather had all been in the business of buying agricultural property on the periphery of the growing cities of Piemonte (Piedmont), and then selling off bits of the land to developers as the cities expanded.

Our first stop was at *Cascina Città*. We drove into the central courtyard which had the farmer's cottage on one side, large stables with a remarkable barrel-vaulted brick ceiling housing dozens of cows on the second side, and storerooms for hay, animal feed, and farming implements on the third. The fourth side, facing the road, was simply a high brick wall surfaced with stucco. Running about in the courtyard were dozens of chickens, and the watch dog, stereotypically named *Fido*, Latin for "I trust."

The farmer's wife invited us in to share a glass of wine with the family and discuss the current state of agriculture. I remember her husband as having a large red nose and little to say. Most of the talking was done by his wife and his thirteen-year-old son. After the visit the group of us went for a walk through the fields. The farmer's son was talking excitedly about how the crops were growing, and my father was focusing on whether or not the property was being well-maintained by our tenants. Our last stop during the tour was an irregularly-shaped fallow field bounded by a road on one side and a meandering shady brook on the other.

After we got into the car my mother explained to me that the farmer at *Cascina Città* was an alcoholic and could do little to no work. His wife and thirteen-year-old son were running the farm in his stead. Effectively, the boy was the head of the household, and had to do all of the hard labor in the fields. In addition to looking after her smaller children and doing all the household chores, his mother had to take care of the farm animals, including milking the dozens of cows by hand twice a day. Given that I was nearly the same age as that boy, I could not imagine having to labor so much or having such responsibilities.

As we continued on our drive, my father explained a plan he had developed for the fallow field by the brook. It seems that most of the farm was in the so-called Green Belt around Torino. As such it could not be developed but had to be preserved as agricultural land. The only part that was not in the Green Belt was the fallow field. The Green Belt law had an interesting twist to it. While you could not build within the Belt, you could accumulate its development rights and apply them to adjacent land not in the Green Belt. My father was already negotiating with a developer to build a block of five-story apartments in the fallow field. These apartments would supply much needed housing for some of the thousands of rural families who were migrating to the cities for their greater economic opportunities.

Our next stop was *Cascina Barale*, a somewhat larger farm several miles further from town. As on our previous visit, we pulled into the courtyard full of regular chickens and also a more exotic variety called guinea hens, large roundish dark grey birds with white speckles all over them. We were greeted by our tenants and then invited in to share an obligatory glass of wine with them. While we were talking with the farmer, his wife disappeared briefly, and then returned with an irregularly-shaped bundle wrapped in newspaper, which she handed to me. I carried it unopened as we went for the usual walk through the fields, which my father noted were particularly well tended.

Beyond the far end of the farm was an industrial building. We took leave of our tenants, and my parents and I walked up to that building and entered. It turned out to be a steel mini-mill, where scrap steel is melted down and recycled into useful products. The mill had an electric arc furnace, essentially a two-story-high brick-lined steel bucket with two enormous carbon electrodes that supplied the energy to melt and purify the rusty steel scrap. When a load of molten steel was ready, the bucket would tip and pour its contents into large molds. I was at once fascinated and terrified by this bucket full of white-hot molten steel.

We then got into the car for the drive home. I was seated in the back with the farm-wife's newspaper-wrapped parcel in my lap, still unopened. As we drove back to *Val Salice*, my father told me a bit of the history of the steel mill. It belonged to a cousin of his. The land on which it stood had once been an unproductive field belonging to *Cascina Barale*. My father had sold the land to his cousin the mill owner two years before.

As he finished his story, I noticed an ominous red stain leaking through the newspaper bundle in my lap. "Papà?" I asked, "What's in this package?" "Two guinea fowl, for tonight's dinner," he replied nonchalantly. "Uh...Uh...Do they still have feathers?" I asked hesitantly. "Oh, yes" he replied. "Teresa will be delighted to have really fresh, free range poultry to cook." He replied. "What about the feet? Are the feet still on?" I asked slowly. "Probably," was my father's reply, to which my mother added, "The feet can be used to make a rich chicken soup." "And the heads...do they still have their heads on?" I asked even more hesitantly. "No" replied my father, "The farmer's wife chopped them off with a heavy knife when she killed the birds." I was relieved about the heads. "I promise you will find these the best chicken you have ever eaten." By this time I was pretty well revolted. But of course my father was right. Teresa's skill turned these birds into a fine dinner, with *tortellini in brodo* as the first course, and roast guinea fowl as the *seconda portata* (main course). Even though I had no illusions about what had gone into the broth and onto the platter, this was one of the tastiest dinners I had ever had.

* * * * *

My grandmother Elvira died in 1963, shortly after I graduated from high school. After that our visits became less frequent, though I stayed there twice more, in 1964 and 1968. At some point when I was home for vacation from college, I overheard my parents discussing some new issues about *Val Salice*. It seemed that our long-time farm tenant, Giuseppin had died suddenly. The official version was that he had fallen from his ox-cart and struck his head on a rock. I later learned the real story was that he had committed suicide after his daughter and only child, the pretty Annunziata who had often joined us when we played *bocce*, had become pregnant without benefit of matrimony. Giuseppin was so shamed by this family dishonor that he became deeply depressed and then took his life. Giuseppin's wife could not manage the farm on her own and so she had given up her family's several-generation tenancy at *Val Salice*.

* * * * *

My father found new farm tenants to run its operations day to day, the Battaglia family, but they lacked the same multi-generational bond that our family had had with Giuseppin and his family. The Battaglias replaced the cows with swine, even though their lease explicitly prohibited the raising of pigs on the property. After the change in farm tenants, neither the gardens nor the orchards were as well-tended.

My last stay at *Val Salice* was in 1968, when I brought my new bride Carol to meet some of our Italian relations. By that time, our long-time family servants, Camilla and Teresa, were becoming quite elderly. Camilla's gruffness had softened somewhat and she told me many stories of much earlier times when my father had been a boy, stories about hunting for mushrooms, about serving morels for Passover, and about some of his juvenile misadventures. Teresa was beginning to show early signs of senility, though she was still a very able cook.

In *Val Salice* nothing was ever wasted or thrown away. Vegetable parings and other kitchen scraps were fed to the farm animals. The rinse water from the weekly laundry was used to water the flowers. Even the table crumbs were swept up after each meal and fed to the birds. At one point during my last stay in *Val Salice*, I threw out a piece of cardboard packaging from one of my shirts. The next morning I discovered the same cardboard in a drawer in the hall cupboard where Camilla kept things that might someday be useful. Several days later, I broke a shoelace and asked Camilla if there might be a spare somewhere. She went to the same drawer and brought forth a lace that had been left behind when the Germans had retreated from our house in 1945. I found using that Nazi lace to be an intensely disturbing reminder of a very dark time, but I had to acknowledge that it kept my shoe on my foot.

On our second day there I took Carol for a walk in the orchards and fields. I soon discovered that she did not share my passion for country life. When we passed Battaglia's dung heap and she wrinkled her nose in disgust, though to be fair, swinish manure is much nastier than bovine. But Carol did enjoy meeting my Italian family, and we had many delicious dinners with Aunt This and Cousin That, full of lively banter back and forth in English and Italian.

* * * * *

In 1974, my brother Albert died suddenly, an event that devastated my parents. In the following years my father's health went into a rapid decline and my mother underwent a surgery to remove an enormous tumor from her bowel. At the same time, Torino's Communist city government made moves to seize *Val Salice* by eminent domain for use as a public park. My mother feared that my father would die shortly and that she would not have the strength to fight the city over *Val Salice* or to manage our other Italian properties. She began to pressure my father and his younger brother and sister to sell off our Italian holdings. In the fall of 1976 *Val Salice, Cascina Città, Cascina Barale*, and all our other rental properties in Italy were under contract to be sold, and our interest in the apartments at Corso Re Umberto were sold to our Levi-Montalcini cousins. After a couple of quick changes of hands, *Val Salice* became the property of Vittorio Lodi, an entrepreneur who owned a company making auto parts.

By this time, Teresa was quite senile and needed more care than her younger sister could give her, even though Camilla continued to be sharp as a tack. My parents arranged for Camilla and Teresa to live out their final years in a rest home operated by an order of nuns; I am sure that the arrangements included a substantial donation to the nuns' convent. There they would get the loving care they needed for their remaining days. Those two women had been in loyal service to our family since the births of my father and his brother in 1905 and 1908, respectively. They had effectively raised my father and his siblings when Elvira's energy was completely taken up with caring for my grandfather during his five-year battle with cancer, ending with his death in 1920 at age fifty. They had endured the German occupation of *Val Salice* during the war, when they had to serve as virtual slaves to the Nazis and were forced to live in the unheated billiard house. And they protected our house and our property during this time, convincing the German officers to disobey their orders that it all be burnt to the ground during the final days of the war.

* * * * *

Even after its sale, *Val Salice* continued to exert a peculiar draw upon us. My brother Peter was the first to return. In the late 1980s, he brought his family there so that they might catch a glimpse of our family's life in an earlier time and see where he had spent his earliest days.

A couple of years later, while my nephew Dean was a business school student at Boston University, he struck up a conversation with a fellow student. That classmate turned out to be the son of the then owner of *Val Salice*, Vittorio Lodi. Dean subsequently returned to visit his grad school buddy.

In 1995, my mother informed us that she would be unable to attend my son David's high school graduation because she had already planned an extended trip to Central Europe. After her death, we found pictures in her files of a final visit to Torino in which she called on *Val Salice's* new owners, the Lodi family. She had never told us about that part of her trip.

Around that time, my cousin Emanuele Levi-Montalcini bought a smaller villa in the hills above Torino, about two miles north of *Val Salice*. There he planted extensive gardens and numerous fruit trees, in an attempt to recreate the beauties of the *Val Salice* of his youth.

In the mid-2000s, I returned to *Val Salice* with my wife and son Michael. As Vittorio Lodi showed us around, I noticed the many changes he had made. The house now had central heating and was used year-round. The farm was no longer functioning and the orchard was overgrown with weeds. The farmer's cottage had been renovated and was now the home of his mother-in-law. The stable and hayloft had been transformed into a ballroom. The billiard house was no longer used for gaming; instead it had become a storeroom for cast off furniture. The formal garden with its palm trees, rose beds and serpentine paths paved with white gravel had been replaced by a plain lawn. When I asked him about the enormous walnut tree that used to stand in the bottom of the property, he motioned me into his dining room. He pointed at the dining room table and chairs and said, "There is your walnut tree."

A few things had not changed. The exterior of the house looked just as I had remembered it, with its yellow stucco walls; the historical commission had decreed that these had to be preserved. And Lodi told me about a terrible storm the previous year, in which lightning had struck the huge Lebanon cedar in the woodland garden. But that tree had survived the lightning, much as it had survived a similar strike when my father was a boy, nearly a century earlier.

In 2009 *Val Salice* came up for sale. For a couple of weeks I seriously toyed with the idea of buying it back. In the end, rationality convinced me of the impracticality of the whole project. My family was firmly rooted in America. My wife and children spoke only limited Italian. I would be able to use it at most a few weeks a year. And the cost and labor of restoring the gardens to their former beauty and the farm to serious production would have been prohibitive. It was time to reduce the past to nostalgic memories and family lore.

Figure 2.1 The Mole Antonelliana and
the Alps north and west of Torino

Figure 2.2 Peter's children Alisa, Alex and Laurence, in what
used to be Val Salice's formal garden on a revisit, 1980s

Figure 2-3. Val Salice's western façade

Figure 2-4 Val Salice's southern façade and the billiard house,
with my mother and the Lodi family

Chapter 3

The Big Wooden Crate

Some years after the death of my grandmother Elvira, when my parents were emptying *Val Salice* in preparation for its sale, they decided to ship to America some of the furniture they had inherited from her. In effect, they were bringing a bit of *Val Salice* to America. They contracted with a large freight forwarding firm, Gondran, to pack up the goods and ship them from Torino to New Jersey where they lived at the time. The goods arrived at the port of Newark during the summer of 1973, when I was a research fellow at the Institute for Advanced Study and my parents had gone to out of the country on vacation.

When I received the notice from the shipping company that my parents' belongings had arrived, I hired a truck and drove down to the Newark docks with my documents to collect their goods. My wife Carol had offered to come with me, but I figured that the Newark docks with their well-earned reputation for tough people and tougher ways of dealing with strangers were no place for a lady, no matter how spunky.

When I drove through the gate designated on the shipping company documents, I found myself by the open door of an enormous warehouse, perhaps fifty yards wide and three hundred yards long. I walked in and looked for someone who might be in charge. On one side was a line of idle fork-lift trucks, with their operators seemingly asleep in their seats. Near the door was the US customs office, where duty would be assessed on incoming goods. Occasionally, a fork lift would bring a pallet of goods up to the customs office, where someone would then show his papers, sign some documents, and then have the fork lift operator load the goods onto his truck. Near the customs office an armed guard wandered about, more or less aimlessly, taking no notice of me or of any of the trucks going in and coming out. I poked around for about an hour, but could not discern anyone in charge. And no one seemed interested in me or what I was trying to do.

Finally, desperate to get my task completed, I turned to the guard and asked him,

> "Who do I have to talk to locate my goods, get them inspected and loaded onto my truck?"

> "Youse gotta find Tiny. Tiny'll help ya." he replied.

> "So how do I find Tiny?" I asked.

> "Youse'll know 'im when ya sees 'im. Youse can't miss 'im."

So, I began to wander the warehouse again, looking for somebody who might be called *Tiny*. When I spied a guy who was about five feet tall and four feet wide, with a loud gravelly voice.

"Are you Tiny?" I asked, almost pleading.

"Yeah! Whaddaya want?" he growled back.

"Tiny, can you help me find my goods and get them out of here. I've already been here for a couple of hours. I don't want to have to come back tomorrow and lose another day's pay."

"I'll make sure ya don't lose anudda day's pay!" he roared back into my ear. "Lemme see da papers."

I showed him the documents the shipping company had sent me. Tiny looked around for a second, and then led me down the full three-hundred-yard length of the warehouse. I felt like I was living a scene from the Marlon Brando movie *On the Waterfront*. Sure enough, right near the end was a tall stack of huge wooden crates, one of which had numbers matching my documents. Suddenly Tiny let out an ear-piercing whistle, and one of the sleeping fork-lift operators woke up and drove down to where we were standing. Tiny motioned to tell him which crate to pick up, and off he went with my crate. The full time that it took us to walk back the length of the warehouse, Tiny shouted in my ear, "He done you a fayva! He done you a fayva! He done you a fayva!"

When we got back to the front door of the warehouse, a customs inspector reviewed my documents and then waved me through without assessing any duty. While he was doing his inspection, I asked the guard,

"How much am I supposed to give Tiny?"

"Youse don't gotta give Tiny nuttin'. Give a twenny to da guy wid da fawk-lift, an' he'll split it wid Tiny."

Then Tiny turned to me and barked, "Where's ya truck? Bring it here!" Within a minute, my enormous crate was loaded onto my truck, I paid off the fork lift man, and was on my way. I was relieved to be out of that place with my life, ego and wallet all more or less intact.

When I got to my parents' house in Englewood, I was now faced with another problem. How could I unload this crate from the truck into their garage? The crate was roughly an eight-foot cube, and probably weighed half a ton. I no longer had Tiny and his fork lift operators to help me for a suitable bribe. I rooted around in the basement and turned up a heavy crowbar with which to pry open the lid and one end of the packing case. I was then able to unload some of the smaller pieces fairly quickly, while littering the driveway with excelsior and other packing materials.

I was now faced with the three heaviest pieces, two enormous locking dressers and a marble topped wash-stand. Each weighed more than a hundred pounds. I discovered that the marble slab was removable from the wash-stand, though even just that part was about as much as I could lift without help. I struggled to move the stone into my parents' garage and laid it down on top of the lid from the crate. The body of the wash-stand was then just light enough for me to move it into the garage as well. I then remembered that my mother had shown me where she had hidden the keys to the dressers; she had brought them back from Italy separate from the furniture for fear that they would get lost if she shipped them. I found the keys, which mercifully she had not moved to another hiding place, unlocked the dressers, and removed their bulky drawers. This rendered the bodies of the dressers light enough for me to shift them into the garage as well, where I reinserted the drawers into each piece, relocked the chests, and returned the keys to my mother's hiding place.

One of the chests matched the washstand and also a small table, with all three in a faux Chinese style that was much in fashion in the 1840s (Figures 3-1, 3-2, and 3-3). They had originally belonged to my great-grandmother Emilia Perla Levi Sacerdote. Over the years, my parents had given these to me, and they now grace my house, reminding me daily of my earlier years at *Val Salice*. Many years later when Carol, Michael and I toured the royal palace in Torino, we discovered similar pieces in the Palace's Chinese Suite. The other dresser, perhaps the most beautiful of the pieces my parents sent to America went to my brother Peter, and is currently in his widow's New York apartment (Figures 3-4 and 3-5). Years later, I discovered a matching piece in my Aunt Eugenia's apartment in Buenos Aires.

A few weeks after my adventure with Tiny and the Newark docks, I was sharing my story with the director of the Institute for Advanced Study. He responded with an even scarier tale of the same Newark docks. At one point a very distinguished European scientist had arrived at the Institute to take up residence on the permanent faculty. His household effects were stuck on the Newark docks and could not be retrieved because the longshoremen's union was in the midst of a nasty strike in which there were numerous incidents of vandalism and physical threats to those who tried to breach its picket lines. The Institute's director managed to negotiate a deal with the union to allow the professor's personal effects to be picked up, but the director had to go personally to oversee the operation. He hired two burly bodyguards to accompany him. As they crossed through the union picket lines, they were subjected to considerable jeering, pushing and shoving. But eventually he was able to get the local strike leader to honor the union's deal with him and supply a couple of laborers (no doubt for large under-the-table payments) to move the professor's goods through customs and out of the warehouse. I am sure I would not have had the guts to face down striking dockworkers. They are the toughest of the tough guys, and, when on strike, the meanest of the mean.

Figure 3.1 The chinoiserie desk

Figure 3.2 The matching marble-topped dresser

Figure 3.3 The matching wash stand and mirror

Figure 3.4 Top view Jacob's Ladder Chest

Figure 3.5 Front view Jacob's Ladder Chest
Both figures courtesy of Bonnie Sacerdote

Chapter 4

A Collection of Antique Judaica

Over the years I have assembled a modest collection of antique Judaica, mostly Italian, and mostly comprised of pieces that have been handed down in my family. The oldest pieces, a pair of books, date back to 1542, and the remainder is spread over the ensuing several centuries, with the newest pieces dating back to the early 1900s. Many of the pieces have interesting stories associated with them, and for me they make tangible my family's Italian past and Hebrew present, things that to many others are seemingly ancient history.

The first piece, and perhaps the most beautiful of all, is a silver Kiddush cup with a floral cover that had been in my father's family since the late 1700s (Figure 4-1). My father gave it to me after he sold his mother's houses in Italy, in the mid-1970s. We have used it to celebrate Passover ever since, and also for my grandsons', Nathan's and Daniel's, *Brit Milà* (ritual circumcisions). For a number of years I tried to find a suitable book of Italian silver hallmarks in order to date the piece, but all without success. In 2005, when I was visiting the extraordinarily beautiful 400-year-old synagogue in Casale

Monferrato, I found a nearly identical cup in the synagogue museum. The museum cup bore the same hallmarks as mine, including the stamp of the silversmith and the initials GV of the royal assayer who certified the purity of the silver. According to the museum, their cup was made in 1792, which suggests that ours was made at the same time. I subsequently found a third cup in the same style and with the same hallmarks at the home of my cousin Maurizio Mayer who lives outside of Tel Aviv; Maurizio's grandmother was my father's first cousin.

My guess is that Maurizio's and our cups were acquired by my great-great-great-grandfather, Leone Sacerdote, around the time of the first liberation from the ghetto during the reign of Napoleon I. Revolutionary France under Napoleon abolished laws restricting Jews to ghettos in the early 1800s. Leone would have been in his late forties at the time, and presumably at the prime of his career. He was well-to-do (and therefore had the means to acquire elaborately worked silverware) and a leader of the Chieri ghetto. During the civil unrest when Napoleon's troops reached the town, Leone saved the ghetto from a group of ruffians bent on no good. He invited the ringleaders of the mob into his cellar to sample some of his rare vintages. While they were drinking, he sent a messenger to the officer in charge of the French garrison camped just outside of town, asking him to send a squadron of soldiers to arrest the mob's leaders and restore order. Sometime later, when the French officially lifted discriminatory measures imposed on Chieri's Jews, Leone and several partners acquired a disused convent in the town for use as a textile factory. One of the Napoleonic reforms had been to close monastic institutions that served no social purpose (i.e. those that did not operate schools, hospitals, orphanages, or almshouses) and sell off their property. That former convent now houses the Chieri textile museum.

When my father gave me our cup, he also passed to me a tiny silver case containing an even tinier leather scroll with a biblical passage written in

Hebrew. The case has a small silver ring at one end, suggesting that this case was supposed to be worn on a chain around the neck. Neither my father nor I had any idea what the purpose of this case and scroll might have been, nor when they had been acquired; he only knew that his father had owned it before him. He also gave me a couple of Shaddai amulets whose style suggests that they were made in the early 1900s. Italian Jews used to attach such amulets to babies' cradles to invoke divine protection for the newborn child, a practice that does not appear to have any analog among the Eastern European Jews.

When my mother was on her deathbed, she kept on telling us to make sure we found her Shaddai amulet. We had never in our lives seen it and had no idea what she was talking about. Perhaps she was a bit delirious, though that seemed unlikely as she was otherwise perfectly lucid right up to the end. Indeed, she made very little use of the opiates that Hospice had provided to ease her last weeks.

After her death, Carol and I searched her apartment looking for things she had stashed. My mother had a terrible fear of thieves, and indeed she had hidden things in all sorts of odd places. In her bedroom, we found several small envelopes containing cash stuck inside books on her bookshelves. She had never trusted ATM machines and evidently she did not want to be caught short if she needed to shop on a day when banks were closed. In her kitchen we found silverware stashed inside little used pots and pans in the back of her cupboards, including a small silver cup I had used as an infant.

Finally, as we sorted through her linens, we found the Shaddai to which she had referred (Figure 4-2). It is of finely worked filigreed silver and evidently very old. I suspect that it had been in her family for a long time, though how long was anyone's guess. I examined the Shaddai very closely, hoping to find hallmarks that might indicate when and by whom it had been crafted, but I could not find any.

Although it showed significant signs of wear and tear and was quite fragile, the Shaddai was very beautifully worked. On one side the word Shaddai was inscribed in Hebrew, and on the reverse side were the four Hebrew letters יחכח, which perhaps abbreviated a Biblical phrase with which I was unfamiliar. I asked our local rabbi if he could enlighten us on its meaning, but he indicated that the phrase in question did not appear in any of the references he checked. I subsequently found the phase through an online search and discovered that it stands for "Wisdom, Crown, Kindness, Foundation."

The mystery of the Shaddai's age continued to vex me for several years and was only solved by a chance occurrence. In 1995, when Carol and I visited the beautiful 1500s synagogue of Casale Monferrato, we found a very similar object in the synagogue's museum. Their catalog dated it to the late 1600s or early 1700s. So the piece dated to the reign of King Vittorio Amadeo II, the king who forced the Piemontese Jews into the ghetto.

The next item in my collection was a Passover Haggadah that we found among my mother's books. It told the Passover story in Hebrew and Italian, and was richly illustrated with copper engravings of the principal events in the text as well as related stories form the Bible and the Talmud. I remembered this Haggadah from my childhood and had always loved its pictures.

When I examined the book after my mother's death, I ascertained that it had been published in Livorno (Leghorn) by the Belforte publishing house, probably in the 1880s. Belforte had issued a series of Haggadot during the 1800s, always using the same illustrations, but with the vernacular text sometimes in Italian and sometimes in Ladino (Judeo-Spanish) for the export market to North Africa, the Balkans and the Middle East where at that time Ladino was spoken. (Judeo-Spanish is a derivative of the 1500s Spanish of the Jews who once lived on the Iberian Peninsula and is written using the Hebrew alphabet). I subsequently learned that the illustrations were reproductions of the illustrations from a Haggadah first published in Venice in the early 1600s, and that such illustrations had been regularly reproduced in Italian Haggadot in the succeeding centuries.

In comparing this Haggadah to Ashkenazi (Eastern European) versions I began to notice small differences. For example, the four questions appear in a different order and come at a different place in the service. Also several of the blessings and psalms, are recited at different times, and parts of the text are altogether different. I later compared this version of the Haggadah to one of the earliest printed Italian Haggadot and found it faithful to the original text.

Because of the book's fragility, I had it reproduced with copies for my own use and to give to my sons and grandchildren. I pull it out every year at Passover to enjoy it for another year.

In addition to this Haggadah, I found an assortment of other Hebrew books in my mother's library. These were mostly nineteenth and twentieth century prayer books. I used one, a Sephardic (Spanish-rite) prayer book published in France in 1853 in Hebrew and French, to organize my mother's funeral. Others were daily or holiday prayer books for use according to the Italian rite.

The largest part of my collection of Judaica, however, was a by-product of my writing my first book, *Remembrance and Renewal*. I had wanted to give a copy of this book to my cousin Gianna, my mother's brother Ruggiero's only child, whom I had known quite well when I was a child. On several occasions, my mother and I had gone to Rome to visit Ruggiero, Gianna, and my maternal grandmother Nonna Ghit. Gianna had also come up to Torino, and on one occasion, Gianna, Ruggiero, my mother and I had all gone on vacation together at the Alpine village of Gressoney in the Valle D'Aosta. Also, Gianna had come to stay with us in New Jersey for several months when we were both in our early teens. Finally, Carol and I had a congenial dinner with Gianna and Ruggiero in Florence in 1968.

However, since 1968, I had lost touch with Gianna and I did not know where to send the book. I knew that she had married and I found among my mother's papers an old letter that included her married name, Costanzo, and the town in which she lived, Frattamaggiore, near Naples. I then tried to look up her home address on the Internet, and discovered to my horror that there were dozens of Costanzo families in Frattamaggiore. Not knowing how to proceed, I decided to telephone each one of them, expecting that I would ultimately find her. Unfortunately, none of the families I called had any clue as to who I was, so I gave up.

A couple of weeks later I came home from a business trip to find a message from Gianna on my answering machine saying that she was returning my call but leaving no return telephone number. Not having any way to call her back, short of repeating the process of calling all the Costanzo families in Frattamaggiore, I once again did not know how to proceed. After another couple of weeks I suddenly received an email from Gianna—she had been able trace me through the Internet because I am the only George Sacerdote in the United States. In our initial exchanges of messages, she sent me her correct address so I could send her a copy of my book, and from there on we were in regular contact by email and Skype.

Our initial calls covered the basics about our families, our grown children and our hopes for grandchildren. But soon I began to ask her questions about my mother's family. I had hardly known my maternal grandmother, Nonna Ghit, whose autocratic disposition meant I knew her even less than my limited contacts might have allowed. And, as little as I knew Nonna Ghit, I had never known my maternal grandfather, Leone Levi. He and Ghit separated when my mother was a girl, twenty years before I was born and my mother had had no contact with him since.

It turned out that Gianna had a wonderful collection of old family pictures of Leone, Ghit, their siblings, Ghit's parents and Leone's mother that Ruggiero had kept after the death of Ghit. She scanned these pictures and sent them to me over the Internet, giving me a much greater sense of connection to that side of the family.

At about this time, I found Leone's hand-written will in a folder of old papers that my mother had kept. In it he indicated that as an old man (he died in the 1960s, when he was in his mid-eighties) he had few possessions left, most of which were to go to his long-time consort, a woman who had hidden him from the Nazis at great risk to her own life during the German occupation of Italy. However, his books and the marble bust of his father were to go to his son Ruggiero.

In my next message to Gianna, I asked, "Do you know what became of these things?" "Oh" she replied, "the bust is on a table in my living room and the books are in my bookcase." Dying of curiosity I asked, "Would you be willing to send me some pictures of the bust and the title pages of some of the books?" She readily agreed, and over the next few days I received images of this bust and the title pages of about twenty volumes.

The books all seemed to be in Hebrew but beyond that I could not really make out what they were about. Thus began many months of detective work to determine what they were and thereby gain a bit of insight into the life and interests of my grandfather. The first clue came from one of the title pages which had the city of publication in large Roman letters near the bottom of the page. I guessed that those with a similarly placed word in Hebrew also indicated the city of publication, and soon I read *Amsterdam, Venezia* (Venice), *Bologna, Mantova*, and so on, all rendered into Hebrew characters. Excitedly, I wrote back to Gianna that these books appeared to be very old.

Having done the first piece of deciphering the story of these books, Carol and I then began to work through the title pages to determine just what they were. Here are a few of the more unusual books:

1. *Machzor*, with commentary (1542) (Figures 4-3 and 4-4): Two volumes with ornate red leather covers; these were a rabbinical *machzor*, that is a volume with all the prayers and biblical readings for the annual cycle of Sabbaths and Holidays, together with commentary by a certain Rabbi Johannan Treves. The final page of this book, which Gianna had copied and sent me, had the signatures of two Inquisitorial censors, who must have reviewed the books and excised whatever comments or prayers they found violated Catholic precepts. These two volumes were published in Bologna in 1542 and were the books that standardized the Italian rite for Jewish religious services.

2. A Hebrew Bible in four volumes with commentaries (1568, 1618): The commentaries were by learned rabbis from the first through the fourteenth centuries of the Common Era. Three of the four volumes were published by Joan DiGara in Venice in 1568 while

the fourth volume (the books of the later prophets) was published by his successor Lorenzo Bragadin in 1618.

3. *Pirke Avot (The Sayings of the Fathers)* (c. 1600): A volume of the *Pirke Avot* in which each verse was repeated twice, once in Hebrew and once in Judeo-Italian (Italian written, in Hebrew characters, much as Ladino is 1500s Spanish written in Hebrew characters): This book was also published by Bragadin in Venice in the 1600s.

4. Kabbalistic lore by Joseph ben Abraham Gikatilla (1561): Two volumes of Kabbalistic lore bound together; these had been originally written by Joseph ben Abraham Gikatilla in the 1200s in Spain. This volume was published in Riva di Trento in the Bishopric of Trent in 1561 under the patronage of the Bishop. The odd part of the story is that at this time the Council of Trent (which the Bishop hosted) was plotting the Counter-Reformation, two of whose actions were to demand the enclosure of Jews into ghettos and the burning of Jewish books such as the Talmud as heretical tracts, as happened in Cremona—an important publishing center for the Hebrew press—in 1559.

5. A Commentary on the Book of *Zohar* (*The Book of Radiance*) (c. 1700): The title page of this Commentary on one of foundational books of the Kabalistic tradition indicated that it was published in Amsterdam by Nathanial Foa. The Foa family had been publishers in a number of cities in northern Italy including Mantua, Cremona, and Venice in the 1500-1600s. They repeatedly ran afoul of the Inquisitorial censors forcing them to move from city to city and ultimately to Amsterdam in the early 1700s. Because Amsterdam was a Protestant city, the Inquisition had no power of censorship there.

6. *Sefer Raziel HaMalakh* (*The Book of the Angel Raziel*) (1701): This is a first edition of Kabbalist lore, published in Amsterdam in 1701 by Abraham Mendes. Possessors of this book were supposed to be protected from house fires and assured that their wives would have easy deliveries, in addition to various other elements of magic. The practitioners of this book's black arts did not want it published. Apparently they did not want their secrets opened to the general public.

After this work of decipherment, I wrote Gianna that she should definitely keep the books in the family. She replied that her children had no interest in them and asked if I wanted them. At that point I offered to buy them from her, and thus they came into our possession. Unfortunately, Gianna developed cancer at about this time and died with a year of my buying the books from her, though I have kept up a correspondence with one of her daughters.

Although Gianna and I never knew our grandfather, Leone Levi, he gave these books to his only son, and in this way they came into Gianna's hands. I am grateful that we were able to reestablish our communication before she died. Through her I also discovered something of the history of Grandfather Leone's parents and how these books came into his possession. His parents had all been born in the ghetto. His mother, Benedetta Debenedetti, had married twice. Her first husband, also named Leone Levi, had been trained as a lawyer, but his early career was as the professor of Hebrew and Middle Eastern Languages at the University of Torino. As his family grew—he fathered eleven children—he could no longer support his family on an academic salary; he then resigned his chair at the university and took up legal practice with his younger brother, Samuele Levi. After the elder Leone died in the early 1870s, his widow married Samuele and produced three more children, including my grandfather, the youngest of her offspring. My guess is that the elder Leone acquired this small library of antique Hebrew books and passed it on to his younger brother, who then passed it to his only son, my grandfather, the younger Leone. It was through his hands, then, that these books reached my uncle and then my cousin Gianna and subsequently me. In holding these books in my hand, I hold a tangible element of my maternal family's history. Overall the entire Judaica collection gives me great pleasure, more for the ways in which it reminds me of my forbears and the vicissitudes of their distinguished lives than for its moderate intrinsic value.

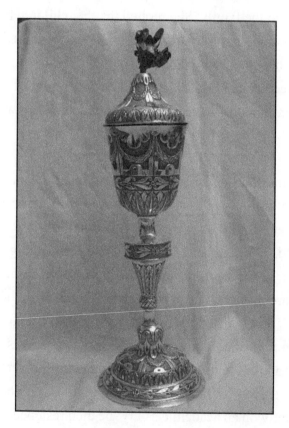

Figure 4-1. Silver cup of Elijah, 1792

Figure 4-2. Silver Shaddai amulet, early 1700s

Figure 4-3. Machzor Vol. 2, title page, Bologna, 1542

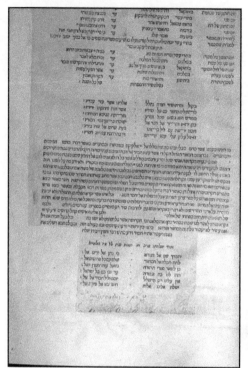

Figure 4-4. Machzor Vol. 2, final page with Inquisition censors' signatures

Figure 4-5. Shulchan Orech, Mantova, 1722

PART 2 ON FAMILY

Chapter 5

A Search for My Family's Roots

My mother died in September of 2003 at the age of eighty-eight. She had lived through tumultuous times. She was a small child when the armed militias of the Italian left- and right-wing extremists were having fist-fights and gun battles in the streets. She was in elementary school when the Italian Fascists staged a *coup d'état* and overthrew the democratically elected government. When she was a university student, a number of her professors and classmates were arrested for anti-Fascist activity. After just three years of marriage, when she had two small children, Mussolini's Fascist government passed its racial laws banning Hebrews from schools, universities and the professions, forcing my parents into exile. Less than a year after the family settled in France, they were forced into exile a second time as France fell to Nazi Germany in May of 1940; the family caught the last ship to leave Bordeaux for the United States. The Germans promised to sink the ship as it sailed, and made good on their promise on its return voyage from New York. And once my parents had made it to New York they had to rebuild their lives with no friends, no community and no support network. But rebuild it they did.

After my mother's funeral my brother Peter turned to me and said, "We are the last ones in our family to speak Italian. We are the only ones who can read all the old family documents that have found their way to America. We need to write down the family story for our children — and grand-grandchildren." After my father had died in 1979, my mother had attempted to write a family history, but she had produced only a slim volume in extremely simple language for *her* grandchildren, all of whom were still quite small at the time. Now my mother, who had been my last close link to my Italian past, was also gone, and while I agreed with my brother's observation, I did not know where to begin the project, and thus it remained something that I would get to someday when I had time to deal with it.

As a child I knew little about my family's roots beyond knowing that my parents, brothers and paternal grandmother had left Italy in the late 1930s, and came to America in 1940 after having settled first in Switzerland and then in France. What came before was total void. Over the years we had acquired a number of tangible mementoes such as the furniture from *Val Salice,* which had arrived in a big wooden crate after my grandmother Elvira had died, the diamonds on our wives' fingers that had been part of a necklace that my parents had smuggled out of Italy before they left for good, and a few objects such as my mother's Shaddai amulet from the late 1600s and my father's Cup of Elijah from the late 1700s, which later became the start of my future Judaica collection. However, these constituted a sparse foundation upon which to build a story.

About a year later, I began to sort through some of the old pictures and papers that my parents had saved over the years. There were many that were very interesting, such as my grandparents' and great-grandparents' dowry contracts, old real estate transactions from the 1800s, and family pictures going back as far the 1870s. Perhaps the most interesting document in my family's collection was a copy of the 1838 census of the Hebrew ghetto of Chieri, the town where my paternal grandfather Alberto Sacerdote was born and where I later learned his ancestors had lived since the 1500s. That census listed his father as a boy of twelve, his grandfather as a man in his late fifties and his great-grandfather, Leone, the man who had saved the Chieri ghetto from mayhem during the Napoleonic invasion, as an old man of eighty-seven. I was simply astounded by the thought that this single document took my family back to the time when George Washington was president and George III was king of England.

Sometime after that, my wife Carol and I made our first trip to Argentina to attend the wedding of our oldest niece in that branch of the family. The Argentine branch of the family had left Italy shortly before my parents and had settled in Buenos Aires where my uncle, Zio Maurizio, ran Pirelli's rubber business and his wife, Eugenia, my father's sister, did cancer research. While my parents had kept up a long correspondence with them, I had met them in the flesh only once or twice when I was a child. At a dinner during our visit my aunt Eugenia showed me a brief history of the family of my paternal grandmother, Elvira Montalcini, written by Michele Luzzati, a second cousin of mine on the Montalcini side. Luzzati, a professor of medieval history at the University of Pisa, traced the Montalcini back to Rome in the 1300s and documented the family claim to be descended from a Hebrew family that was already established in that city at the time of Julius Caesar. She also shared with me a genealogy back to 1700 of my grandmother's family assembled by my great uncle Emanuele Montalcini.

My next break was when my friend, Enzo Falco, showed me a three-volume set of books that contained documents relative to the Hebrew communities of Piemonte for the 500-year period 1297-1797. It turns out the Italy abounds in official documents which are a wonderful resource for historians; unfortunately, they are scattered in dusty and forgotten archives all over the country. The collector of these three volumes of documents, Renata Segre, had spent thirteen years digging through royal archives, courthouse basements, and old municipal files to assemble some 4000 documents. Some of these documents were simple statements, "So-and-so was fined ten lire," with little indication of why. Some were more interesting, such as commercial licenses, lawsuits and legal judgments, and appeals to the duke to undo the damage caused by Inquisitorial raids looking for heretical literature or to seize Jewish children who had supposedly been baptized. Others entailed detailed census data, extensive records of the meetings of the Hebrew community, or royal decrees concerning rules governing the Hebrews, including the discriminatory Jewish tax levied against so-called "foreigners" for the right to live under the protection of the duke and practice their religion.

The surnames appearing in many of these documents were identical to the names of several of my great-grandparents: Sacerdote, Segre, Montalcini, Levi and Debenedetti. One group of those documents concerned a certain Vitale de Sacerdotibus, a sixteenth century banker, diplomat, and economic adviser to the Piemontese ruler, Duke Emanuele Filiberto. The most important of those particular documents was the duke's 1572 invitation to Hebrews to settle in his domains. The document explicitly described the invitation as being in response to Vitale's personal request. I began to wonder if Vitale was an ancestor of mine, though I had no evidence to support that thought. I decided that I had to trace as much of my family as far back as I could in order to write its story. Thus was born the research project which culminated in the publication of *Remembrance and Renewal* (Figure 5-1).

The research to develop the content of the book had many interesting twists and turns. The first problem was to determine the ancestry of five branches of my forbears. I had five important documents that tracked my ancestors back to the late 1700s or early 1800s.

1. The census of the Hebrew ghetto in Chieri that was already mentioned (Figure 5-2).

2. A history of the Chieri Hebrews written by my cousin Sergio Treves as his doctoral dissertation.

3. A genealogy of the Montalcini family back to 1700 researched by my great-uncle Emanuele Montalcini with additional data unearthed by Luzzati to bring the record back to the 1300s.

4. The wedding contract between my great-grandfather Salvador Montalcini and Eugenia Segre, giving the names and birth cities of their fathers.

5. A genealogy back to around 1820 of the Levi and Debenedetti families, my mother's paternal grandparents, assembled by my mother's first cousin, Giovanna Dompé.

Using these documents, I was generally able to posit links between my recent ancestors and individuals mentioned in documents towards the end of Segre's collection.

My next step was to identify the earliest documents in Segre's collection that mentioned people with the right surnames. Two families were easy: The Piemontese Montalcini and the Debenedetti. The Piemontese Montalcini were all descended from a certain Emanuele Montalcini, a banker resident in San Damiano Monferrato, who became Piemontese when San Damiano was transferred from the Duchy of Mantua to the Duchy of Savoy in 1628. From him we reached the 1700 start of my great-uncle's genealogy in a couple of generations. And Luzzati had carried the family's ancestry back to Mantua, Tuscany and Rome.

The Debenedetti were all descended from one Benedictis de Benedictis, a Spanish banker who settled in the Piemontese town of Cherasco in the 1530s. While there were several branches of this family, we were able to work forwards from his sons and backward from my great-grandmother Benedetta Debenedetti, born in Alessandria, to pin down that branch's genealogy.

I found three Sacerdote families in the mid-1500s, headed by three men whom I suspected of being brothers, sons of a certain Abram Vidal de Sacerdotibus. Abram Vidal left Spain in 1490, two years before Ferdinand and Isabella's infamous expulsion of the Jews in 1492. He settled in Alessandria, a border town and commercial center now in Piemonte but then in the Duchy of Milan, and opened a bank.

The Segre clan, also Spanish bankers, was a more complex problem. They appear to be descended from one Elia de Segre, who was active commercially in the mid-1400s. In any case, I ultimately traced Eugenia Segre, one of my great-grandmothers, to one of his presumed sons, Bellavigna Segre, born around 1470, whose Piemontese banking career was well documented in the early to mid-1500s. In the next generation or two, some of descendants settled in the town of Savigliano. To connect these descendants to Eugenia, we began with her marriage contract, which indicated that her father was from Torino. We then found a couple of Segre men who moved from Savigliano to Torino during the Napoleonic opening of the ghettos in the late 1790s, and only one of whom had a son; he was almost certainly Eugenia's grandfather.

The most complicated family to trace was the Levi. There were numerous Levi families that ended up in Piemonte in the mid to late 1500s. Most of them transferred to that duchy from several different, but nearby towns in the Duchy of Milan. The close proximity of their geographical origins suggests that some or all of them were part of the same clan. They moved to Piemonte in the mid-1500s, when Milan came under the control of the Spaniards with their venomously anti-Semitic policies. Two keys to which of these Levi families were my ancestors came from Dompé's genealogy: In the early 1800s our Levi ancestors lived in the small market town of Nizza Monferrato and they had a tradition that they were Ashkenazim who had originated in Hungary. As I hunted through the documents, I worked backwards from the handful of Levi families in Nizza Monferrato and found one that 150 years earlier had petitioned a local bishop for the right to open a German-rite synagogue. Bingo! I could then trace them back to the mid-1500s.

One of the keys to tracing these families were three naming conventions peculiar to the Italian Hebrews. First off, unlike the Eastern European Jews, the Italian Hebrews all had surnames dating back at least to the Middle Ages, following the Roman tradition of using surnames and people's birth cities to more accurately determine the populations of different parts of the empire so they could be taxed accordingly. In the case of the Montalcini clan, their original surname was *Min-ha-Knesset* in Hebrew, which was later translated into Italian as *da Sinagoga*. This original name was already in documented use by a Hebrew family in Rome at the time of the Caesars. This family name was changed to *da Montalcino* when our branch of the family left Rome in the late 1300s and opened a bank in the town of Montalcino in the Republic of Siena. The reason for the name change was to distinguish it from another branch of the same Roman family that operated a banking group based in Pisa and took the name *da Pisa*.

The second naming convention was the tendency of Italian Hebrews to name their sons after their living grandfathers and uncles, so that one could easily link generations—similar to the Roman tradition of using surnames to link to important historical figures. This convention was opposite to the practice of the Eastern European Jews, among whom there is a strong taboo against naming children after living relatives.

The third naming convention was to translate names literally from one language to another. Thus the surname *Cohen* (Hebrew for "priest", the name traditionally borne by the male descendants of the Biblical Aaron) became *de Sacerdotibus* (Latin) which later became *Sacerdote* (Italian). Similarly, *Baruch* (Hebrew for "blessed") became *de Benedictis* (Latin) and later *Debenedetti* (Italian). The same happened with given names: *Chaim* (Hebrew for "life") became *Vidal* (Spanish) and later *Vitale* (Italian). Likewise, *Shmuel* (Hebrew for "God heard" from the Biblical story of the birth of the prophet Samuel) became *Intendadeo* (an archaic Italian name that literally means "God listens") and later *Samuele* (modern Italianization of the original Hebrew word). In a similar vein *Nathaniel* (Hebrew for "given by God") became *Donato* (Italian for "given"). A few of the name changes required a bit more Biblical knowledge. For example, *Yehuda* (the name of the one of the sons of the Biblical patriarch Jacob) became *Leone* ("lion" in Italian) because of Jacob's deathbed prophecy that his oldest son Judah would be the Lion of Israel. These name changes were constantly sending me back to the Bible and my Hebrew and Italian dictionaries.

Once I had sorted out the genealogies of these five families, I could identify which documents in Segre's book spoke about them. The first thing that struck me was the importance of their banks in the Piemontese and European economies of the sixteenth and seventeenth centuries. Each of their banks had capital in the tens of millions of current dollars. They made loans to sovereign governments ranging from small countries like Piemonte to the greatest power in Europe, Spain. The loans to Spain were so large that when Philip II defaulted on his debts after the sinking of the Spanish Armada, my ten-greats uncle, Simone de Sacerdotibus, was able to negotiate, as part of the price for rolling over the loans, an agreement to allow Alessandria to keep its openly practicing Hebrew community, the only one in the global Spanish empire for the next 120 years. These bankers also had extensive loans to local and regional governments. And these were in addition to their commercial banking to finance industry, agriculture, and international commerce.

Furthermore, we could begin to develop pictures from particular documents of how changes in government policies affected individuals in their daily lives. When the Piemontese government began to de-emphasize banking and focus on developing a stronger commercial and industrial economy, these families shifted their investments from banking to manufacturing and trade, opening businesses making and distributing cotton and silk fabrics, distilling spirits, running the state lottery, and the like. When government policy was to assert its independence from the papacy, these families had their religious freedom protected from the predations of the Inquisition. When the government subordinated its sovereignty to the Church in the 1700s and the post-Napoleonic reaction, these same families were segregated into crowded and unhealthful ghettos. And when government policy turned against the Church again, as it did in the early during the Napoleonic occupation and again during the *Risorgimento* (Italian unification), these families were freed from the ghetto and immediately took leading roles in public life and the learned professions.

This tight linkage between the traditional view of history as the story of kings and politicians and of wars and conquests and the modern historical view of the changing lives of ordinary folk became the central thesis of my book. In each chapter, after I developed the picture of what my ancestors in these five families were doing, where they lived, and what business dealings they had, I developed the parallel picture of the larger political context in which the tiny Duchy of Savoy (Piemonte) and its subsequent larger incarnations, the Kingdoms of Sardinia and Italy, were operating in the power politics among the papacy, Spain, France, Austria and England and Germany.

At one point I found references to a number of scholarly articles about the Piemontese Hebrew community that I wanted to read as background information for my research. These articles were all in obscure Italian research journals. My wife Carol had a graduate degree from Harvard allowing her lifetime use the university's libraries and so offered to use her library privileges to help me find some of these articles. We spent an afternoon at Widener Library retrieving the articles and copying them for study at home. One article, however, did not appear in the journal volume cited in the original reference. On the assumption that someone had miscopied a volume number, I suggested to Carol, "Why don't you try the nearby volumes?" "Maybe I should ask a reference librarian," she replied. "They are so good at finding things. What's the article about?" "It's about the diary of an eighteenth century circumcisionist," I answered nonchalantly. Carol looked at me in horror and blurted out, "I can't ask for *that!*" I laughed and said, "Well do what you can." She went off and returned fifteen minutes later with the relevant article. "How did you find it so quickly?" I asked in surprise. "I asked a reference librarian, just like I said I would." "I thought you didn't want to ask for an article about a circumcisionist." "I didn't. I asked her for an article about birth records."

As I was writing, I continued to be a bit uneasy about the ancestral linkages of my "modern" family documents from the 1800s and Segre's document collection that ended in 1797. A few of the connections, such as those of the Sacerdote family of Chieri were iron-clad, thanks largely to the 1838 census document, which included my great-great-great grandfather, as an eighty-seven-year-old. Likewise, I was sure of my genealogy of the Montalcini clan in that period because of the family tree back to 1700 constructed by my great-uncle Emanuele Montalcini. The third family of whose linkages across the divide between the Segre documents and my own were rock-solid was that of my great-grandmother, Benedetta Debenedetti; I easily tied her father to the single Debenedetti family with surviving sons in her birth city of Alessandria in the late 1700s.

Some of the other family linkages were a bit more tenuous, especially the Levi from Nizza Monferrato. This problem was causing my writing to bog down to such an extent that I feared I would never finish the book project. The Levi family had moved several times in the 1600s and 1700s, and appeared to have roots both in Nizza Monferrato and in the larger nearby spa town Acqui Terme. So in 1995 I went on a research trip to Italy. I figured that during this trip I could also collect some photographs of sites and people with which to illustrate the book.

My first stop was at Torino's Hebrew cemetery. It is made up of three walled areas, each containing tombs from a different period. It is immediately adjacent to the cemetery of the Waldensian Protestants and the enormous Catholic cemetery. I quickly located the Sacerdote family tomb which I had visited several times with my parents when I was a boy.

Nearby was the Levi family tomb. With some hunting I found the tomb of my grandmother Elvira's father, Salvador Montalcini. And, in the course of my hunting I found the tombs of the Levi-Montalcini, Segre and Treves families. The Treves were cousins with whom I am particularly close; Ada Treves was my father's first cousin and almost exact contemporary. In Torino, her family villa was next door to ours, and in America, her husband, and later one of her sons, were business partners of my father's. We continued to have close relations with her sons, grandchildren and great-grandchildren.

On the second day, Carol and I visited Chieri, the city where my Sacerdote ancestors had lived from the mid-1500s until the end of the 1800s. Chieri had traditionally been a center of textile manufacturing. Indeed, my nine-greats grandfather had acquired a license to manufacture cotton cloth in the 1590s. At that time, much of the local farmland had been given over to the growing of mulberry trees and woad. Mulberry leaves are used to feed silkworms, and woad is the source of the dark blue dye, indigo. Our initial stop was at the museum of the textile industry, which was housed in a former convent that Napoleon had decommissioned in the 1790s and that my three-greats grandfather had bought in partnership with a David Levi (the Chieri Levi families were unrelated to my mother's Levi relatives) for use as a textile factory.

At the museum I met a descendent of that David Levi. He was the last practicing Hebrew left in town; the rest of that town's Hebrew families had migrated to larger cities in search of better economic opportunities, much as my great-grandfather had done in the 1890s. Our guide then offered to take us on a tour of the former ghetto of Chieri and the two Hebrew cemeteries of the town. When my brother Peter had visited the ghetto some twenty years earlier, it was very run down, with many of the buildings occupied by squatters. To my great surprise, the building where my family had lived and that also housed the former synagogue was undergoing a beautiful restoration. Parts of it had already been made over into elegant commercial offices and apartments. The building dated to the 1350s and had originally been the palace of the noble Solara family; on the side facing the main street, there is a plaque commemorating a visit by the French king Charles the VIII in the 1400s and his love affair with one of the Solara women. In the ghetto days, the building was cut up into apartments for different families. The rabbi had the front rooms, facing onto the main street that formed one side of the ghetto. The room that served as synagogue was in an interior courtyard, since the royal rules prohibited synagogues from being visible or audible outside the ghetto.

I remember from my brother's pictures that there had been a sign over the main entrance indicating that my great-grandfather had donated a statue that stood over the doorway to the Torino Civic Museum in 1875. The sign was no longer there. When I asked the developer about it, he took me into his office where the sign now stood on the marble mantelpiece. I resolved to find the statue, though a quick check of my guide books showed that the Torino Civic museum no longer existed.

As we left the ghetto, our guide took us up Chieri's main street where he pointed out a nineteenth century apartment house with the initials DS in wrought iron over the main entrance. That building had been built by a certain Davide Sacerdote who was a cousin of my great-grandfather. Our last stop was at the two cemeteries where I examined and photographed several old family tombs.

That evening, I had dinner with my cousin, Piera Levi-Montalcini. I knew she had a substantial archive of documents and photographs relative to the Levi and Montalcini families. This archive was marvelously well-organized. Looking though her pictures and photos helped my research immeasurably. Piera is also active in Torino politics. When I told her about my quest for the statue from Chieri and the problem of the no-longer-existent Torino Civic Museum, she told me that she served on Torino's Cultural Council. Perhaps another councilor knew what had become of it.

The next morning she called me on my cell phone.

> "One of my colleagues knew about your Torino Civic Museum. It merged with the Museum of Antiquities in the 1920s."

> "Oh", I replied. "I know that museum. Isn't it in Palazzo Madama in Piazza Castello? I could go there this afternoon."

> "Not so fast," she replied. You have the right museum, but it has been closed for the last thirty years 'for renovations.'"

> "So, now what do I do?" I asked unhappily.

> "Let me ask around some more and see if there is a solution. Call me again tomorrow morning."

The next morning I called Piera again and learned that the entire collection of the Antiquities Museum was in a warehouse on the outskirts of Torino owned by the Gondrand Company. (That same company, which specializes in shipping and storage, had been the one to ship a big wooden crate of *Val Salice* furniture to us in New Jersey decades earlier after my grandmother Elvira died.) I was also told that the curator of that part of the collection was a certain Professor X. If I called him, he might be willing to let me see my statue. I called him at once and he agreed to help me find "my" statue. We made an appointment to meet several days later at a specific loading dock of the Gondrand Company's warehouse.

While we were waiting for the appointed day to arrive, Carol and I went on three more excursions out of Torino. The first was to the town of Casale Monferrato. Its ornate synagogue is one of the most beautiful in the world and it has been designated a UNESCO world heritage site. The synagogue has been in continuous use since 1595 and was originally built as an indoor tennis court. At one time Casale had the second largest Hebrew community in Piemonte, and that community was very well-to-do. It is said that the Nazi's stole several tons of silver and gold from that town's synagogue. Now only a handful of Hebrew families remain in the town. These days the synagogue holds services only on the major holidays and for special occasions such as weddings and Bar Mitzvah services for families that originated in Casale. One of my second cousins once-removed, Anna Giuli del Monte was married in that synagogue.

As we wandered through the little museum in what used to be the women's gallery, I spotted a large silver chalice. It was very similar to the one that had been handed down through our family since the 1790s and that became a core part of my Judaica collection. This trip to Casale Monferrato enabled me to date my Kiddush cup. Their cup and ours bore the same hallmarks; they had both been made by the same silver-smith in 1792. Then I found a silver Shaddai amulet from the late 1600s or early 1700s that was nearly identical to the one we had found among my mother's effects when she died—the one she had not told us that she owned until she was on her deathbed.

The next day we traveled to Acqui Terme and Nizza Monferrato. In Acqui we quickly found the old Hebrew cemetery. It was surrounded by a high brick wall and had a locked wrought iron gate at one end. As we peered in through the gate we could see many old grave stones, some broken or fallen down and others still standing. Here and there we could discern relatively new stones, marking the graves of individuals who wanted to be buried in their ancestral city, even if their families had had left it two to three generations previously. I desperately wanted to enter the cemetery but did not dare to climb over the gate or wall. I might fall or get trapped inside. How could we find the key? Carol suggested that we go to city hall to see if we could find someone who had the key, to which I responded, "Yeah! Sure! Dream on!"

However, lacking any other ideas, I agreed to go to city hall which I noted was on Piazza Abramo Levi, perhaps a good omen; I was looking for an ancestor of that name. We entered the courtyard and discovered that city hall was locked up tight: it was lunch time. We sat on a bench to figure out what to do next. Suddenly a young man asked, "May I help you?" We explained our interest in going into the old Hebrew cemetery, to which he replied, "I work for the city. I am my way home for lunch. If you come back after three PM, I will be in my office and I will see what I can do." So Carol and I went off to find a restaurant for lunch, and returned to the man's office at the appointed hour. He then made half a dozen telephone calls and learned that the keeper of the Catholic cemetery had a key to the Hebrew cemetery—one of his duties was to mow its grass once a month.

We then drove to one end of town to collect the key from the Catholic cemetery, and then drove back across town to the Hebrew cemetery. Amazingly, the key worked and Carol and I entered. We began to wander among the tombs, reading the inscriptions and looking for some connection to my Levi ancestors. At one point I wandered off into a corner to examine a broken head stone. A few of the letters were no longer legible but I could clearly read Giuseppe Ottolenghi, born 1745, died 22 March 1820, and a few particulars about his life (Figure 5-3).

I shouted to Carol, "Come here! I know this man!"

She hurried over, looked at the stone, and said "What do you mean?"

"Carol, I know this man."

"How could you possibly know him? He died 200 years ago."

"He was the uncle and guardian of one of my Levi ancestors from Nizza Monferrato," I replied. "My ancestor Abramo Levi had been orphaned as a teenager. I read a court case in which this man defended the child's property rights from encroachment by one of the neighbors, a certain Debenedetti family."

Others of Segre's documents had detailed Ottolenghi's life. He had been a wealthy and important banker. He had witnessed and documented the civil disorders in the ghettos of Acqui and surrounding towns with the impending arrival of the Revolutionary French Army. The ghetto residents were refusing to pay the Jewish taxes and demanding that the ghetto be opened. These taxes were to go directly to the king, but since the local Hebrew community was responsible for generating the revenue to pay these taxes, Ottolenghi had quickly left town for fear *he* would be assessed for the unpaid taxes of the entire Hebrew community of Acqui.

We then searched about for the other half of the headstone which we found lying face down, about five feet away. We turned it over and read a brief synopsis of the man's life story. "He lived in the turbulent times of the French occupation. He suffered much during the civil disorders when he was taken hostage for six months by the revolutionary army. Subsequently he became a town councilor." And here I was touching a piece of my family's history, a very tangible representation of my central theme of how the large-scale politics of kings and armies affected the day to day lives of ordinary folk.

Our next stop was to go to Nizza Monferrato, a much smaller town a few miles from Acqui. In the central square of the town, we found an imposing building, Palazzo Debenedetti. My Debenedetti great-grandmother's family had come from Nizza, and one branch had moved to Alessandria in the late 1700s. This building had been put up in the years following the second opening of the ghettos in 1848. We then went to the municipal cemetery. In this case the Hebrew cemetery was simply a walled-off corner of the Catholic cemetery. There we found grave markers of various lateral branches of my mother's ancestral Levi and Debenedetti families.

While Carol and I had been in Acqui and Nizza, my aunt Eugenia and cousins Mauro and Livia from Argentina showed up in Torino, coincidentally staying in the same hotel as we were. We were all there to attend the forthcoming wedding of Piera's daughter Paola. At dinner that evening Carol and I told them about our earlier visit to Chieri and my tortuous quest to find the statue, a quest which was due to be completed on the morrow. Mauro and Livia quickly agreed to join us for the warehouse visit the next day.

Early the next morning the four of us set out for the Gondrand warehouse. At the appointed hour, Professor X showed up on the loading dock, and we all went inside. All about us were locked shipping containers containing the museum's collection. Professor X then took us to an open container, packed floor to ceiling with furniture, paintings, statuary and tapestries. Next to this particular container was a wooden crate, and on top of the crate was an old wooden statue of an angel bearing a shield with the coat of arms of the Solara family, the original owners of my family's house in Chieri (Figure 5-5).

He then told us a bit about the history of the statue. It seems that in the 1400s an itinerant Flemish sculptor had stopped in Chieri. The Solaras commissioned him to create a suitable decoration for their front door as a way to project their importance. Then Professor X said, "By the way, your great-grandfather also gave several other items to the museum. Would you like to see them?" We readily agreed. The professor motioned to a couple of workmen to pull out two other objects. The first was an elaborately decorated baroque table clock with a red enamel casing. I found it beautiful even though my taste generally does not run towards such fussily over-decorated objects. The second item was more interesting. It was a large, dark wooden chest with inlaid designs in lighter woods and mother-of-pearl. Carol looked at the lid of this chest and immediately spotted a repeated pattern of finely worked mother-of-pearl *Magen David* symbols. (The *Magen David* is the six-pointed star commonly used as a symbol of the Hebrew people.) On the face of the chest we made out light wooden inlays of trees, which in Hebrew symbology relate to the Torah, often described as the Tree of Life. Perhaps this chest had once held ritual objects, prayer books, or perhaps Torah scrolls. This linked the chest to the Chieri synagogue which had been in an interior wing of our family house. These objects made us feel as if we were touching our ancestors, people who had been born in the ghetto in the 1820s and who had died before our parents were born. Since that time, the Museum of Antiquities has reopened and both the statue and the chest are on display.

The next day Carol and I took our Argentine cousins and their ninety-five-year-old mother, my aunt Eugenia, on an excursion to Ferrere, a small town well outside of Torino. Our great-uncle Emanuele Montalcini, Zio Manno, had been mayor of Ferrere for many years between the world wars. He also owned a great country house there, Castel Rosso, which he had bought before World War I from a bankrupt nobleman, Count Gromis (Figure 5-4). Eugenia had fond memories of her visits there when she was a girl and young woman, before she was driven into exile by the racial laws of 1938. A family portrait from 1913 taken on the front steps of the house is on the front cover of my *Remembrance and Renewal* book.

We turned off the two-lane highway onto Viale Montalcini, the side road leading up the hill to the town and soon we were soon in the main square of the town. On a hill a couple of hundred yards above the center we saw a large house, perhaps Castel Rosso. Just at that moment, a fellow stopped us and asked,

"May I help you?"

"We are looking for Castel Rosso" we replied. "It used to belong to my uncle, Emanuele Montalcini," added my aunt.

"Oh. Yes! He is well remembered around here. My name is Giovanni. I am on the town council. I'd be glad to show you around."

And so we went off with Giovanni to Castel Rosso.

We discovered that the main house was vacant and boarded up, with police tape blocking access to the outside staircase. We wandered through what remained of the garden. We asked Giovanni if there was any way we could peek inside, but he said the house was unsafe to enter. When Mussolini decreed the racial laws in 1938, Zio Manno lost his political offices. He sold Castel Rosso to another Torinese family who used the property as a small boarding school for their daughter's classmates during the war when relentless bombardment made the city unsafe. After passing through several hands, title to the property ended up with the local Catholic diocese. The Church had several failed schemes for the property including using it as a community center and movie theater, a pre-school, a school for handicapped children, and a rest home for the aged. After some years, they built a modern rest home in the garden and left the main house vacant, slowly rotting away. It has since been given over to a commercial provider of services for the aged.

Giovanni then asked, "Would you like to see the school that Mayor Montalcini built in 1925? It is only a short distance down the hill." We all agreed and walked down to the school. As we entered the vestibule we saw the dedicatory plaque thanking Zio Manno for bringing the first secondary school to the village. On the plaque was noted that the architect had been Gino Levi-Montalcini, my cousin Piera's father, and Zio Manno's nephew. I believe that the design of this school had been one of Gino's first major projects after completing his architectural studies.

Posted on the wall were a series of oversized photographs showing the groups of dignitaries and townsfolk who had attended the school's dedication. One of these pictures was partially obscured by a sliding bulletin board. When Carol shifted the bulletin board to one side, she found herself face to face with a picture of my father as a young man, my uncle Paul, my grandmother Elvira, and many other family members, most of whom were dressed in dark suits and dresses. In the middle of the picture, wearing a stark white dress was my aunt Eugenia as a girl of fifteen. And now Eugenia was looking at this picture for the first time at age ninety-five, when she was nearly blind. We were moved almost to tears by this scene. That evening we told Piera of our adventures in Ferrere. She told us that she had the original of that picture in her archives; she would have it digitally scanned for us.

On Friday night of that week, Carol suggested that we go to services at the Torino synagogue. It was the first night of the festival of Sukkot. She thought it might be interesting to see such a service in the Italian rite and to hear the ancient Italian-rite melodies for the principal prayers. For me this was to be a new experience. While I had walked by the synagogue many times, I had never been inside. The service was held in a small chapel in the basement that had been designed by a cousin of mine, the architect Giorgio Olivetti. (Our maternal grandfathers had been brothers.) While the chapel was modern, the reader's platform and the Holy Ark were very old.

Those old furnishings had originally been the synagogue furniture in Chieri. When the synagogue in that town fell into disuse in the 1920s, they became Sacerdote family property since the synagogue was in a wing of the ancestral family house. When my great-uncle Leone Sacerdote died, he had left these items to the Torino synagogue. They were then placed in storage off site, so they were spared when a British bomb landed on the synagogue during the war, causing extensive damage. When Olivetti designed his chapel in the early 1970s, these furnishings were dug out of storage and became the central elements of his design. So here I was yet again faced with tangible elements of my family heritage, both ancient and modern. My book just had to be completed!

When I returned home to America a couple of weeks later, I began writing furiously and organizing the many illustrations that went into the book. As book designer, I hired Joe Moore, a graphic designer I had used in my business. I had seen the beautiful job that he had done for the books his wife had written about the Cambridge Skating and Garden Clubs. In about eight months we were done, and the book appeared in late summer of 2006, around the time of the third anniversary of my mother's death. When I was done, I had documented a five-hundred-year history of five Hebrew families and the impact of kings and armies on their daily lives.

The publication of this book had a wonderful and totally unexpected result. Initially I presented copies of it to those relatives who were named in it. They talked about the book to other relatives, many of whom I had never met. (My mother, for example, had about three dozen first cousins whose children, my second cousins, number over one hundred.) Soon I was receiving requests for copies from the several continents to which my family had scattered as a result of World War II. Copies of it have gone to Argentina, Mexico and Canada, to Italy, France and Switzerland, and also to Israel and India. *Remembrance and Renewal* not only became the vehicle through which I reconnected with my cousin Gianna—from whom I ultimately purchased my great-grandfather's library of antique Hebrew books—but it also became a catalyst for knitting our extended family back together again, and the Internet has made it possible for us to personalize our newly-formed family relationships.

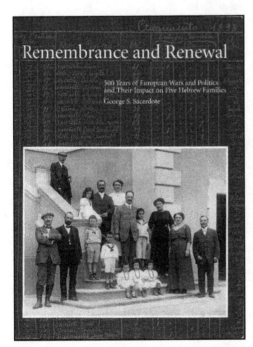

Figure 5-1. The front cover of *Remembrance and Renewal,* featuring a 1913 family portrait on the steps of Castel Rosso in Ferrere, the town where my great uncle Zio Manno was mayor for several decades

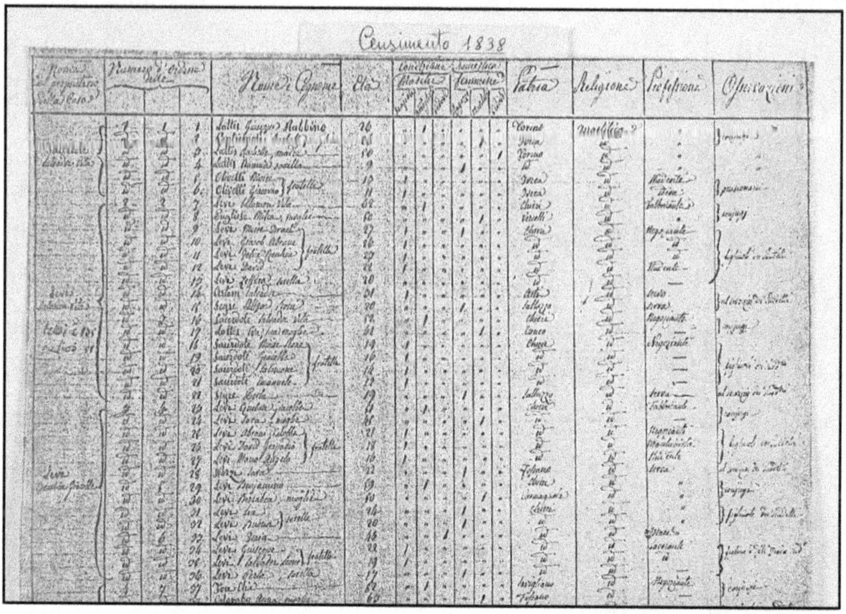

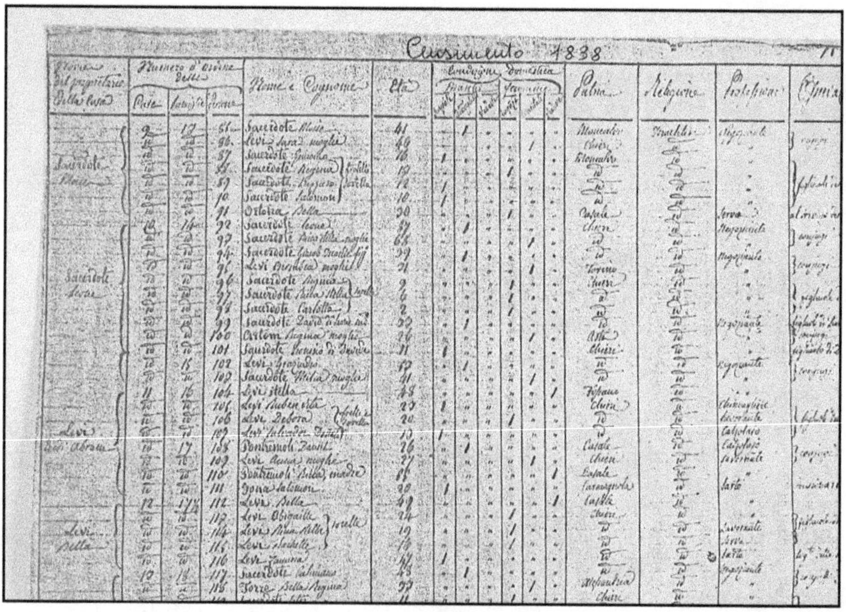

Figure 5-2. Extracts from the 1838 census of the Chieri ghetto in which my great-, great-great-, and great-great-great-grandfathers were listed at ages 12, 52 and 87 respectively

Figure 5-3. The broken headstone of my great-great-great-great uncle, Giuseppe Ottolenghi, Aqui Terme Hebrew cemetery

Figure 5-4. Castel Rosso, the country house of my great uncle, Zio Manno

Figure 5-5. The 14th century statue of an angel bearing the arms of the Solara family that originally stood over the doorway of the Sacerdote house in Chieri. My great-grandfather donated it to a predecessor of Torino's Museo d'Arte Antica.

Chapter 6

Why Is this Kid Different from All Other Kids?

Sometime after my ninth birthday I became aware that I was very different from most of my friends and schoolmates. I certainly did not understand why I was different, though, now that I have written *Remembrance and Renewal,* I suspect in retrospect that this difference had its roots in my family background, which was so very different from the other children with whom I grew up.

All I knew as a nine-year-old was that my friends and schoolmates had cousins in the Bronx or Brooklyn. We had cousins in Italy, France, Argentina, Ecuador, Canada and Mexico. They all spoke English at home; we spoke Italian and French and used English only when we had guests who did not speak those other languages. Their fathers owned local retail stores or were suburban dentists or small-town lawyers; my father's business, perhaps no larger than theirs, made products (or more precisely had products made for it under contract) that it sold globally. Their mothers generally did not work and often had not gone to university. My mother had a doctorate and was a professor of chemistry. Their parents drove, or aspired to drive, a Cadillac, generally pronounced Cad-E-Lack; my parents owned an English car, a Humber Super-Snipe. When they went on vacation to the mountains, it meant a weekend of overeating at a borscht-belt resort in the Catskills; for my family it meant a couple of weeks of hiking in the Alps. If they went to the beach for a vacation, it was generally to the Jersey Shore; for us a seaside vacation was a trip to Cape Cod, Nova Scotia, or the Riviera. If their family owned a second house, it was a rough cabin by a lake in western New Jersey; we owned a villa in Italy. For them a great day was to go the ball game; for us it was a trip to an art museum or an evening at the Philharmonic. They all loved to watch the Milton Berle and Jackie Gleason shows on television, and I was not allowed to watch either. When they talked about the future, they thought in terms of days, weeks and months; we worked on a much longer time-frame. And, while my Jewish friends of Tsarist Russian extraction thought *gefilte fish* to be the culinary *summum bonum*, I found it revolting and could never force myself to eat it; even our cat put her nose up when we put some of it in her dish.

It was not that we were a lot richer than they were—indeed, I do not believe we were. We lived in a more modest house than many of my friends' families, and most of my friends were indulged with many more *things* than my brothers and I. And we certainly were not smarter than they were—the crowd I grew up with was absolutely remarkable for how many really brilliant kids it included. But my family tended to have very different values from most of my friends' families, with more of a focus on world affairs, intellectual matters and high culture. In short, we were Western European *haut bourgeois*, and they were part of the great American lower middle class.

I first realized how different I was from the American mainstream at summer camp the summer after the fourth grade, when I was not quite ten years' old. The camp I attended was Camp Greenbrier in the Blue Ridge Mountains of West Virginia. The family connection to that camp dated back to my brothers' childhoods, and I believe that my parents first heard about the camp from a teacher in the Teaneck schools who worked there as a camp counselor during the summers. About two thirds of the boys in this camp came from various states of the American South, including Mississippi, Alabama, the Carolinas and the Virginias. They all seemed fixated on regional collegiate football rivalries, typically between a university in their state and the equivalent institution in an adjacent state. I was not even dimly aware of these particular rivalries, but they seemed to be terribly important to the majority of the other boys. Almost every day at lunch or dinner, one table or another would begin chanting some taunt to another which proclaimed the strength, power, and athletic superiority of its favorite team, and the corresponding feebleness of its hated rival.

At Greenbrier, the campers were housed in large tents erected over permanent wooden platforms. A typical tent would house four to six boys in bunk beds who were overseen by a counselor. One of my tent-mates that summer was a boy named Jim from the small city of Galax in southern Virginia. I had been to Italy for the early part of the summer and was at Greenbrier only for the second session. One afternoon, Jim asked me why I had not been there for the first session, and I made the mistake of telling him that I was in Europe visiting my relatives. He then began telling everyone that my name was *Sassadonte the Forrinnahh*, a name that he would make sure he pronounced as mockingly as possible. About a week later, I was cornered by Jim's older brother Bill, a tall thin fellow about five years older than me and a yahoo who was even more ignorant that his little brother Jim. Bill put his hands around my neck and snarled, "Hey, Sassadonte. I hear yer a *forrinahh* and a Yankee to boot. This is what we do to people like you back home in Galax!" And then he lifted me by the head at least one foot off the ground. For a moment I thought I had breathed my last, but then he put me down again. That day I learned a lesson to keep my differentness to myself. And I made a studied effort to avoid Bill for the rest of the summer.

The highlight of the summer at Camp Greenbrier was a musical revue called *Moot's Minstrels*, organized by the field and track counselor, Mr. Moot. This show was presented in the assembly hall, a large barn-like wooden structure with a stage at one end, during the last weekend of the camping season. The show's company consisted of an assembly of counselors, led by Moot, pretending to be southern blacks. The actors dressed in rags and blackened their faces with burnt cork. They sang songs and staged skits that mocked those downtrodden victims of Jim Crow. Most of the other campers howled uproariously at the "jokes." I found them to be in terrible taste and was revolted by the whole affair. Even as a mere nine-year-old in the days before the civil rights movement, I could not imagine what was so funny about being dirt poor, uneducated, and denied any sense of personal dignity. Perhaps it was my Jewish upbringing with its emphasis on education and justice for all that gave me this sensibility. Or perhaps I remembered snippets of stories from the time of my great grandparents who had been born in the ghetto where they were segregated from the rest of the population and locked in every night. Whatever it was, I had by then learned to keep my different thoughts to myself, so I kept my mouth shut and just nodded politely when the other boys repeated the "jokes" after the show.

From then on I discussed such matters only with people whose backgrounds and outlooks were more or less like those of my family. It was often safer to blend in and keep a protective wall around myself. Of course, the 1950s in America were a time that prized petty conformity, and the American South, where most of my camp-mates came from, prized it even more than the rest of the country. It was the time of the *Organization Man* and *The Man in the Grey Flannel Suit*. Nonetheless, even today, I find it better to avoid arousing resentment when I am working in the broader society than to call too much attention to myself, my abilities or my accomplishments. The damage caused by the attendant jealousies often more than offsets the higher status or admiration one might expect to accrue from those differences. There is no better example of the pervasiveness of this issue than the model common in many schools and children's athletic programs in which every child gets a trophy independent of achievement. It is seen as better to hide competency by giving the same awards equally to those with and without distinguishing ability than to call attention to those who excel in a given area.

That lesson was hammered home very forcefully in an early scene in Steven Spielberg's movie, *Schindler's List*. This scene centered on a German-Jewish woman who was a slave laborer in a Nazi concentration camp during the 1930s. This woman had been detailed to a group that was building a barracks building. The woman made the mistake of approaching the SS officer commanding her work team, offering to use her engineering training to make the work more efficient. She thought that by making herself useful she would be more valued. The SS man turned to her and sneered, "What have we here? An educated Jew?" He then drew his Luger and murdered her on the spot.

It is commonly said that women need to hide their intelligence and abilities to be accepted in the broader American society. Actually this issue applies to both sexes to about the same degree. In situations in which wealth, intelligence or ability are highly prized and valued, and one should use all of his or her gifts. But there are also situations in which these capacities are more of a source of envy and resentment than a benefit. The trick is to know what set of rules apply in a given circumstance. As I write this essay I wonder if I am betraying my own advice in calling out many aspects of my own differentness.

Chapter 7

My Family's Sports and Games

Our family tended not to be accepted by either the American Jewish or the Italian American communities. Most of them had arrived in this country a generation earlier than my family and their social and educational backgrounds were completely different from ours. The Jews in our town were largely from Eastern Europe and the other Italians were from Catholic working-class families out of southern Italy. Part of what made us seem so odd to both the Jews and the Italians in Teaneck, New Jersey, in the 1950s were the sports and games we played. The Eastern European Jews in our neighborhood tended not to do sports, and most of the Italian kids reveled in American football, boxing, and other sports that my parents deemed violent and disapproved of. As an Italian Hebrew family that had much more recently arrived in the US, the sports and games taken up in our family reflected our roots in northern Italy, Switzerland, and France and were generally seen as a bit off beat by most of the other families in my crowd.

For example, sometime during the winter of 1950-1951, I learned to ski. Almost all of my parents' Italian friends and relatives grew up in the shadow of the Alps. Alpine sports were all the rage during their youth in the 1920s and 1930s, because such sports had been favored by the Italian crown prince, Umberto II who resided near our ancestral home of Torino in those days. The lone exception to this family interest in skiing was my father who was lame in one arm and one leg as a result of a terrible automobile accident in the 1920s, although he had continued to ski through the 1930s, including the time when he and my mother had skied across the Alps to spirit assets out of Italy just prior to their going into exile. Each year there was a complex swap among these families to reassign outgrown skis, boots and poles to smaller children as the families grew up.

Skiing at the time was not cleanly divided into Alpine and Nordic skiing. There were a couple of ski areas within an hour or two's drive from Teaneck, New Jersey, which had simple rope tows to pull the skiers uphill with perhaps thousand feet of elevation, and we would visit these occasionally. But just as often we skied over hill and dale at golf courses and other areas of open terrain. Our skis were long, straight, heavy slabs of hickory wood to which our leather lace-up boots were bound with metal contraptions evocatively known as bear-traps (Figure 7-1). Safety bindings had not yet been invented, let alone perfected, and there was always a continuous stream of people carted off from the downhill slopes in ambulances, though I do not recall anyone we knew breaking a leg at this sport. Skiing was another family sport that was viewed as out of the mainstream in our town. My school friend Fred Schauer was the only other kid I knew outside my parents' circle of Torinese friends who grew up skiing, and in his case, it was my family that interested him in the sport. His parents were certainly not skiers, notwithstanding their Austrian heritage.

During that winter I also learned to ice-skate. There was a fair-sized pond that had been dammed off from the Hackensack River near the house of my schoolmate, Michael Brown. In those days, this pond would freeze over in December and remain solidly frozen until early March. My first skates were clamp-ons. That is, the blades were riveted to clamps that could then be attached to any sturdy shoe (Figure 7-2). For this purpose, my mountain shoes acquired the previous summer in Italy filled the bill. Within a few weeks I could skate well enough to tag along with my older brothers when they played ice hockey, a sport that had not yet degenerated into its modern violent form. More important, I could skate well enough to be able to escape with impunity after pelting the girls with snow balls. Almost every afternoon after school and every weekend during the winter we would all go down to the pond to skate. After snow storms, we would take snow shovels down to the pond to clear off areas for skating. On particularly cold days, we would build a bonfire on the shore and use it to warm up whenever we got cold. While some of my friends also skated, the skaters were definitely in the minority in our circle.

And then there was the walking. Walking was an important family pastime. On weekend mornings my father would often walk the mile to the shops in West Englewood just to buy the newspaper or pick up a loaf of bread for the simple pleasure of a walk on a fine day. Neighbors who would pass him in their cars would offer him rides and shake their heads in disbelief when he turned them down, explaining that he preferred walking to driving. On warm evenings, we would go out for a neighborhood walk after dinner in memory of the Italian rite of the post-prandial *passeggiata* where entire towns turn out for an hour's walk after the evening meal; of course, in Teaneck in the 1950s and 60s we would be the only ones out for a walk. In summer, we would often go to Bear Mountain Park in New York or to Highland State Park in New Jersey for a day of walking and a picnic. And we would often take hiking vacations in the Alps. Our Teaneck friends could not imagine our spending an entire day *walking* when we could get to where we wanted to go by car a lot faster and with a lot less exertion.

In addition, around 1950 my older brothers, Albert and Peter, took up fencing with strong encouragement from my father. This interest was probably the direct result of our older cousin, Alex Treves, becoming NCAA sabre champion in 1950 and 1951, and then joining the US Olympic team in 1952 in that event. I certainly knew no one else who fenced.

And about this time Peter joined the high school soccer team. Although soccer has become the kids' sport of choice today, to the point that the term *soccer moms* is synonymous with suburban mothers of school-aged children, it was barely known in the US in the early 1950s. At that time, our town's high school was one of the few that competed in that sport. Peter then taught me how to play the game, and I in turn introduced it to a few of my friends. Soon there was a small group of us who would meet periodically on warm afternoons in the spring and fall to play soccer either in our back yards or, less often, in public parks. As a child, I always preferred soccer to the more mainstream kids' sports. I was totally inept as a baseball or basketball player and never found much pleasure in being slammed to the ground, which seemed to be the main point of football.

Our family games tended to be equally eccentric from the point of view of our neighbors. At one point my mother brought home a game of Bird Lotto—a matching game featuring pictures of birds. While it helped me learn the names of common songbirds, I do not recall ever seeing a copy of this game being played by anyone else. For all I know, we owned the only copy ever sold. As a child I also played *Monopoly*, but generally only in Italian where it was called Monopoli. The street names were all of major thoroughfares in our native city of Torino and the currency was different, but the rules I believe were largely the same.

My father taught me early on to play what he called by its Piemontese name *Terim Balin*, a game on a beautiful wooden board (Figure 7-3). The game consisted of two players alternately placing their nine counters on the vertices of three nested squares and then sliding them from one vertex to an adjacent one. Whenever a player could get three of his pieces in a row, he was entitled to remove one of his opponent's pieces. The game would continue until one player was reduced to only two pieces and therefore could no longer capture any of his opponent's pieces. Although this game also exists in English under the name *Nine Men's Morris,* and some claim that this game was brought to Britain by Roman soldiers when Rome conquered that province. I was certainly the only one of my friends to play this game. According to my father, in his day, every school desk in Italy had a *Terim Balin* board scratched into its surface and the standard way to not pay attention in school was to play this game with the child seated next to you.

The only family games that seemed to fit the norm in Teaneck were the card games—Bridge, which my brothers brought home from college, and Canasta, which seemed to be the standard of the PTA's fund-raising card parties in the 1950s. We sometimes played Scrabble, but my father would always soundly beat the rest of the family; he had a seemingly endless supply of high-scoring Latin- and Greek-rooted words from his many years' study of those languages as a schoolboy in Italy.

While at some level this differentness in recreation further isolated us from the town in which we lived, it also helped to strengthen my bond to my family and my Italian heritage, a heritage that I touched regularly with visits to *Val Salice* in my youth, and one that I came to understand deeply only much later in life as I delved into our family's roots and sought to transmit it on to the next generation.

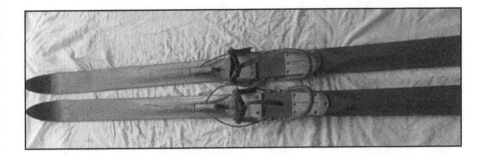

Figure 7-1. Wooden skis with bear trap bindings

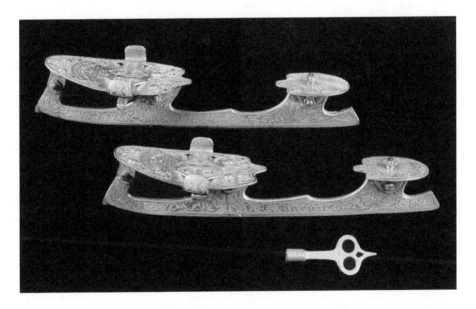

Figure 7-2. Clamp on ice skates,
Courtesy of Annette LaMond and the Cambridge Skating Club

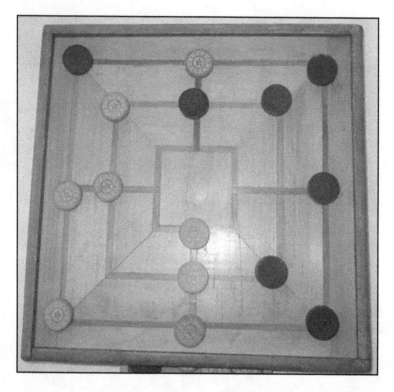

Figure 7-3. A terim balin board

Chapter 8

From the Past to the Future

It has often been noted that one does not generally get to choose one's parents. I was indeed fortunate in the ones I acquired through the accident of birth. My father (Figure 8-1) was very gentlemanly and sort of old school, having descended from families that had been comfortably off since the Renaissance. After earning a doctorate in engineering, he rose through the ranks of the Italian telephone company, STIPEL (*Società Telefonica Italiana di Piemonte e Lombardia*), eventually becoming the company's technology director. My mother (Figure 8-2) was a striver, first for her own precocious academic achievements, earning a doctorate by age twenty, and then for her children's successes, both academic and in life in general. She too had grown up in comfort though her childhood was scarred by her parents' separation when she was ten years old. Their first son, my brother Albert was born in mid-1936, exactly nine months after they were married, with a second son, my brother Peter, arriving less than16 months later.

My family was driven into exile twice, first from Italy by the Fascist Racial Laws and a year later from France as the French army collapsed in the face of the German blitzkrieg. In the United States, our differentness had resulted in a significant degree of social isolation outside of the very small circle of Italian Hebrews in the New York area. These repeated forced displacements caused my nuclear family to develop a very tight-knit internal cohesion. We could not depend on anyone but each other.

I was born in 1945. Between my mother pushing me to excel academically and my father setting an example of refined and cultured behavior, I grew up focused on academic success and desiring to live up to my family's high standards, following the examples of my older brothers' achievements. I was especially close to my brother Peter from whom I learned many lessons about what is truly important in life and family, while also absorbing the lessons that my brother Albert exemplified of duty and obligation.

Where one does get to choose family is in the choice of a spouse, and here I was fortunate indeed. I met Carol, the love of my life, when we were students, I at MIT and she at Wellesley College. We met on a blind date organized by one of my fraternity brothers and his girlfriend, one of Carol's Wellesley classmates. One never knows how a blind date will work out, and I certainly had had a number of rather disastrous ones before this time. The occasion for this particular date was a barnyard-themed party at my fraternity house in which we had transformed an elegant Back Bay townhouse into an agrarian setting with six inches of straw on the floor and rabbits and chickens running about. I went to Wellesley to pick up Carol for this party dressed in my costume for the party, a 1930s suit that I had bought for $3 at a second-hand clothing store in Cambridge. What she thought of this outfit she has never told me. I guess it did not put her off too much because we had a great time at the party. We were soon dating regularly. Initially our dates were just conventional events—dinners, movies, concerts, and museum shows. As time went on, we fell deeply in love and became "an item" as they say in the tabloids.

In the winter of my senior year at MIT and her junior year at Wellesley, I proposed to Carol, though we had to withhold announcing our intentions for several weeks as protocol dictated that my brother Peter announce his intention to marry Bonnie first as they were older. In due course all became public, and I gave Carol a diamond that my parents had given me many years previously—from a necklace they smuggled over the Alps shortly before they left Italy. We took our diamond to the old-line Boston jeweler Shreve Crump & Low (founded in 1796). With this ring we formalized our relationship and were officially engaged. We then set about making wedding plans for the following year, when Carol would have graduated from Wellesley. As it happened, we had to accelerate our wedding plans when it appeared for a time that the United States Army wanted to give me a one-way ticket to Vietnam around the time we had originally chosen for our wedding.

Over the next nine years Carol and I enjoyed the itinerant scholarly life, first as graduate students in Urbana-Champaign at the University of Illinois and subsequently in Oxford, Princeton, and Amherst. Along the way we had a series of adventures some of which are detailed in other essays in this volume. We were deeply in love and sharing these experiences made them ever so much sweeter than having them alone.

After we had been married for about eight years, Carol and I decided to attempt a novel biological experiment—producing a child—which resulted in the arrival of our older son, David, in April of 1977 (Figure 8-3). The day before David was born, Carol and I were to host a lunch for my parents who were up from New Jersey. My father was already quite sick

119

with his final illness and we were anxious that all go well. As Carol was organizing lunch, we had a succession of disasters. The drains all backed up and we discovered that we had both ants and mice in the house we were renting from my employer, Amherst College. By some means or another we managed to prepare and serve a most pleasant lunch. We went for a walk around town with my parents after lunch, keeping it short to accommodate my father's health and Carol's very late stage pregnancy.

That evening, Carol went into labor, and it kept us up most of the night. I remember switching on the television in the wee hours and finding a channel that was showing some dreadful old Italian movie about an infant who was miraculously found under the proverbial cabbage leaf. What could have been more fitting? At about six AM the next morning Carol thought it was time to go to the hospital. I remember that it was a brilliantly sunny morning and the forsythia were in full bloom; I have ever since associated forsythia with the miracle of childbirth. As I was driving Carol to the hospital, I suddenly began to talk to her only in Italian; I guess the excitement had dropped me back into my first language.

When we arrived at the Cooley-Dickinson hospital in Northampton, Massachusetts, we were escorted into separate rooms to change from our street clothes into hospital attire. Another couple arrived at about the same time we did. As the other woman was shown into the changing room, her husband turned to leave. A nurse stopped him and said, "Tom, aren't you going to stay for the delivery?" Tom paused briefly and looked down at his shoes. Then Tom's wife spoke up, "I don't think Tom is up for this". Tom turned again towards the exit, and the nurse shouted after him, "You chicken-shit!"

As soon as Carol and I had changed we were reunited in the labor room where I was detailed to time her contractions and reminded her of the lessons from our Lamaze classes on how to manage the birthing process. After many more hours in which her contractions gradually increased in frequency, our delivery nurse called the obstetrician to the hospital. Now things were beginning to get serious. Soon Carol was wheeled into the delivery room and the pace of activity sped up dramatically. When the time to push arrived, Carol was straining so hard she nearly pulled herself off the delivery table. I was instructed to hook my arms through her armpits to keep her in place lest she fall and hurt herself or the baby. With one more heroic push, Carol finally delivered David, who was promptly taken aside by one of the nurses to be cleaned up, measured, weighed and swaddled. No matter what we had been told during our classes, nothing prepared us for the intensity of emotions that we felt during the delivery. It was without doubt the most overwhelming thing either of us had ever experienced.

An hour after the delivery we telephoned our parents with the news of David's arrival. Carol's mother was incredulous we were talking with her only an hour after the delivery. In her day, women in labor were put under total anesthesia and then presented with their child several hours later when they reawakened from the effects of the anesthetic.

Carol and David were kept in the hospital for another couple of days, and then they were released and we all returned to our house on Amherst's Pleasant Street. We tried to settle into a routine, but the baby kept on waking us up at odd hours, causing us both to become quite exhausted. After few weeks, just as we were about to go crazy with exhaustion, we fell very deeply in love with this little person who had entered our lives. We started feeling an intense attachment to the baby that way more than compensated for the nightly wake-up calls. Whatever evolutionary process had designed babies and their parents had done a marvelous job. In the following months we watched David grow and develop, seeming to learn new things almost every day. With each passing day our bond to each other and to him grew ever stronger.

In 1979 we repeated our biological experiment, with the ultimate result of the arrival of Michael. His arrival was just as dramatic as David's but totally different. The evening before Michael was born Carol was meeting with a group of other women who were sorting and labelling donated baby clothes to be sold to raise money for charity. When her contractions began, the other women suggested that she should go to the hospital. Remembering the long drawn out eighteen hours of labor that she had had with David, she saw no reason to hurry.

When she finally got home around ten PM, her contractions were already quite frequent, so I bundled her off to the Newton-Wellesley Hospital, concerned that the baby would arrive en route. When we arrived at the hospital, the admitting nurse rushed us through the admissions process for fear that the baby would arrive while Carol was still her responsibility. Carol was then taken directly to the delivery room; the baby arrived before either of us had finished changing. After all was finished, the obstetrician arrived, and despite his not having done anything as part of the delivery, he billed our insurance company for his customary charges.

Michael's early development was just as amazing as David's though, as old hands at this baby raising stuff, we were less awed by the process. Nonetheless we were soon as fully in love with him as we were with David and delighted in watching him learn about the world he lived in (figure 8-4).

During Michael's infancy, Carol and I had a terrible scare. At some point the continually interrupted sleep wore Carol down terribly. She had a couple of rounds of mastitis and eventually contracted pneumonia. At first the pneumonia seemed like a serious but otherwise routine ailment, but she seemed not to be recovering. Then the disease worsened quite rapidly. We sent the children to stay with their grandmother and I tended to her day and night. I remember one night falling into despair as I could feel her life slipping away from me minute by minute. I called her doctor late that evening to ask what further we could do. He suggested that all she needed was total bed rest, which was what I thought I was providing. Finally, he and I agreed that perhaps she needed a few days in the hospital where she would have round the clock nursing care. This might finally arrest the course of her illness. It turned out that the hospital where her doctor had admitting privileges was a decidedly second-rate institution. (It has since been closed.) Despite that hospital's shortcomings, Carol did begin to rally and was soon well enough to return home. After several weeks of further recovery, she was finally strong enough to resume most of her normal activities, though she still tended to tire easily. Finally, I took her for a vacation in Hawaii so that warm sunshine and fresh sea air would help her to complete her recovery.

Raising our children then became our main project in life, and has remained so even as they entered adulthood and formed families of their own. As our children grew we reveled in their successes and supported them when things did not go so well. One of the peculiarities in how we raised the boys was that I spoke to them only in Italian until they were fifteen years old; my theory was that even if they never learned to speak the language, they would at least understand it, feel its cadences, and capture a bit of my cultural heritage.

Figure 8.1. My father,
Giorgio, 1927

Figure 8.2. My mother,
Luciana, 1935

Figure 8-3. George, Carol, David and Michael, 1979

Figure 8.4. David and Michael, 1982

PART 3 MANY EDUCATIONS

Chapter 9

Kindergarten Babies

When we returned home to New Jersey (Figures 9-2 and 9-3) after spending the summer of 1950 in Italy, my mother informed me that I would be starting school in a couple of weeks. I was taken to the doctor to get the requisite vaccinations and a health certificate to allow me to begin school. And I was taken shopping for "school clothes." In the 1950s, the Teaneck schools had a strict dress code. Boys had to wear a collared shirt and proper pants—tee shirts and jeans were not allowed—and girls had to wear a dress or blouse and skirt. School was viewed as serious business, and children were expected to dress accordingly.

On the appointed day, my mother walked me to Whittier School (Figure 9-1) at the top of the hill on which we lived, a distance of about four blocks. She took me in to a large sunny room and introduced me to the teacher, Miss Crearie. My mother always made a point of knowing my teachers personally. She also got on famously with the Whittier School principal, Miss Hoak, an imposing woman who had held the job for many years. My mother had gotten to know Miss Hoak when my older brothers went to the school. Luciana made a point of stopping in to renew Miss Hoak's acquaintance after she dropped me off with Miss Crearie.

Miss Crearie was a treacly middle-aged woman who seemed to delight in teaching very small children. I use the word "teach" advisedly, as I do not recall learning much of anything other than the ABCs. I suspect that the main purpose of kindergarten was to civilize the children, and we seemed to spend endless hours playing with blocks. If I recall correctly, one of the main lessons was that we were all to carry handkerchiefs in our pockets. Each morning children who had these cloth rectangles were obliged to parade them in front of those who did not. I guess many children never quite 'got' the lesson, as the hanky parades continued all year.

On the second day of school, my mother again walked me to school but did not come in. Instead she stood by me as I queued up with the other children and their mothers along the walk to the eastern entrance to the school, the one nearest the kindergarten room. The kindergarteners lined up on one side of the entryway and the much more grown-up first graders on the opposite side. When the bell rang indicating that it was time to enter the school, Miss Crearie came out to summon her charges, and our mothers all left.

On the third day I was told to walk to school on my own. My mother had arranged with a certain Mrs. Brown, whose son Michael was also in kindergarten, that Michael and I should walk together. The Browns lived an additional block down the hill from us, on a small street that ran alongside the Hackensack, a tidal river that eventually emptied out into Newark

Bay. At the appointed hour of 8:30, Michael showed up at our house, and then he and I would proceed on to school. When we arrived we queued up just as we had the day before, except that our mothers were not there. Suddenly the first graders began to taunt all the kindergarteners, chanting:

Kindergarten babies

Stick your head in gravy

Wash it off with bubble gum

The kindergarteners all felt terribly humiliated by this chant. Several of us tried to organize the kindergarteners to chant back, but all we could muster was:

First grade babies

Stick your head in gravy

Wash it off with bubble gum

This aping of the first graders did not seem either to faze them or to improve our sense of self-worth.

At the time the kindergartners seemed to put a high premium on being near the head of the line, which caused Michael and me to hurry to school every day, more running than walking. The main result of this hurrying was that we had to endure more taunts than if we had walked at a normal pace and gotten to school at the normal time. Somehow we never made the connection between being near the front of the line and the daily extra dose of "kindergarten babies." We had to endure these taunts all year, patiently waiting for the time when we would be first graders and we could do unto the new crop of kindergartners as had been done unto us.

Sometime during the first few days in Miss Crearie's kindergarten I met a very bright child named George Stein, with whom I shared much of my childhood. George's father, an Alsatian refugee from Nazi Germany, was the classic German burgher. He spoke English with a heavy German accent even though he had immigrated to the United States as a teenager. The Stein family was heavily intellectual and also strongly devoted to classical music. Over time, George, and his two brothers, Sam and Fred, and sister Ada each learned to play various musical instruments; on Sunday afternoons, their father would lead the family in chamber music performances. As we grew up, George and I both became very interested in mathematics and eventually earned advanced degrees in that subject. Subsequently we both left academic careers: George became a journalist and I a management consultant.

And so the first year of school went. Each morning, sunshine, rain, or snow, Michael Brown and I would walk to school and endure the first-graders' taunts. When it rained we wore bright yellow slickers made of some sort of rubberized cloth and heavy rubber boots. The slickers came with hoods made of the same rubbery material that constantly dripped water onto our faces. The only concessions to the weather were made on rainy day, when we were allowed to queue up for school in the hallway just inside the door, and on days when the temperature was below freezing, when girls were allowed to wear pants to school under their skirts, provided that they hung the pants up in the coat closet during the school day. If we awoke and found it snowing, we all listened to the radio where there were several stations that would broadcast endless lists of schools that had been closed on account of snow, but these events were quite rare. The notion of being driven to school was one that was beyond the comprehension of any of our parents, and we children were totally unaware of such luxuries.

I recall that one Monday morning in mid-autumn, someone rang the doorbell at 7:30 AM, when my family was still dressed in pajamas. It was Michael Brown, ready to go to school. It seems that his family had missed the end of daylight savings time. So my mother invited him in and he joined us for a second breakfast. After I got ready for school, Michael and I ran up the hill for our daily dose of "Kindergarten babies."

The next year I entered Miss Werner's first grade. First grade differed from kindergarten in many ways, not the least of which was that we could now taunt the lowly kindergarteners while queuing up before the school doors opened. Whereas kindergarten only ran for two and a half hours a day, nine o'clock to eleven-thirty for some children, and one o'clock to three thirty for others, first grade required us to be there for both sessions. That meant that we had two classes of kindergartners to call "kindergarten babies," which surely was ample recompense for the humiliations of the previous year. During the time from eleven-thirty to one we were expect-ed to walk home for lunch, eat and then walk back to school.

In the first weeks of the school year we were sorted into three groups ac-cording to someone's measure of reading readiness. One group consisted of those who had been forced to repeat first grade because they had not learned to read well enough to go on to second grade. This was before the days when considerations of "self-esteem" made it mandatory that every-one be promoted whether or not they had learned anything. In any case, that group clearly knew the rudiments of reading, so I got it in my head that they must be the smartest kids in the class instead of the class dunces. I was heartbroken to learn that I had been assigned to a different group and burst into tears in class. Of course the teacher could not tell me that the repeaters were anything but the top reading group. Even at that tender age I had become very competitive academically. There seemed to be some mysterious osmotic process by which my mother's precocious competitiveness of thirty years previous in another country was transmitted to me without my ever being aware of it.

The standard elementary school readers of the day were a series of books featuring Dick and Jane, their parents, their little sister, Baby Sally, and their cat and dog, Muff and Spot. The stories were deadly, even for six-year olds: "See Dick. See Dick run. See Spot. See Spot run. Run Dick run. Run Spot run. Baby falls down. Baby says 'Oh Oh Oh.'" I still find it a wonder that children were not so turned off by this pap that they refused to learn to read.

In the early fall of that year, all the kids in the neighborhood began to troop into the house of our next-door neighbors, the Hessian family. The Hessian's two sons Mickey and Tommy were high-spirited boys a couple years older than I. But they were not the attraction that brought all the neighborhood children to their door. Rather, the attraction was that the H's owned the only television on our block, and the hottest kid's program, *Howdy Doody*, came on just as we got home from school. *Howdy Doody* was broadcast live with a studio audience of children known as the Peanut Gallery. The characters on the show included both marionettes and live actors. The main puppets were Howdy Doody, a cowboy, and Mr. Bluster, a character dressed as a 19th century banker who was the show's villain. The live characters included the host (and the show's creator) Buffalo Bob Smith, a whiskered old prospector named Gabby, a couple of Indian chiefs named Thundercloud and Chickenfeathers, an Indian princess named Summerfallwinterspring, and Claribel the clown, whose only means of expressing himself were to squeeze the bulb on an air horn clipped to his belt or to squirt the other characters with a seltzer bottle. My parents disapproved of *Howdy Doody* as so much silliness that would surely cause mind-rot, but we kids could not get enough of it. The show must have been quite a cultural icon, because most of the main live characters including Buffalo Bob and Claribel merited long obituaries in the *New York Times* when they passed away in the late 1990s and early 2000s.

Notwithstanding my reading group placement and the mind-numbing effects of Dick and Jane and *Howdy Doody*, I managed to learn to read reasonably well in first grade and also to add whole numbers. What I did not learn well was penmanship. I had a singular talent for making my block letters so sloppily that they were hard to read. And, as both my parents and children could attest, my handwriting worsened over the years until it became utterly illegible.

In first grade I was also subjected to "rhythm band", which was a key part of the curriculum. Each child was given a "musical instrument" such as a pair of sticks, some jingle-bells or a tambourine. Miss Werner would play a short piece on the phonograph and then cue the players of the various "instruments" to make noises in time to the music at specified places in the music. Even as a six-year-old I knew that that these were not "real" instruments and felt like our teacher was a phony when she claimed we were making music. "Real" instruments were things like clarinets (which my brother Peter played), trumpets, pianos, drums and violins. Many years later, I was horrified and totally uncooperative when I had to relive "rhythm band" as an adult; similar instruments were handed out one Friday evening in synagogue, and we were expected to beat them in time to our chanting of the prayers. UGH!

My second-grade teacher, Mrs. McKinney, was a very jolly heavy-set woman with a big head of curly white hair. Because the morning session in second grade ran to noon, half an hour longer than first grade and leaving only an hour to go home for lunch, she would hand out candies to the children at 11:30 every morning, "to give us extra energy." She also handed out candies whenever someone answered correctly a question she posed to the class. This habit of hers made her immensely popular with the children and probably contributed substantially to the prosperity of the town's dentists.

Second grade reading classes had a major step up. Dick and Jane now came in four word sentences and occasionally the words had more than one syllable: "Dick can run fast." "Mother bakes sweet cookies." Oh, give me a break! Fortunately, our town library had a wonderful children's librarian. My parents would take me to the library every week and this woman would supply me with books whose humor or adventure stories I found irresistible. Thanks to this gifted librarian, I truly learned to enjoy reading. At about this time I also taught myself to read Italian; that language is much easier to read than English because its spelling is completely phonetic. To practice my Italian reading, I would read the copies of the Torinese newspaper *La Stampa* that my parents received in the mail every couple of days.

In second grade we were also introduced to the mysteries of English spelling. This subject was introduced to us as something we simply had to memorize, but I soon learned that there were patterns to English spelling, for example: night, light, might, and sight; or lotion, notion, motion, nation, and ration. As I gathered a large inventory of these patterns, I became a whiz at the weekly spelling bees that Mrs. McKinney held to reinforce the weekly list of spelling words. I also found that I could often guess at which pattern would apply by thinking of the equivalent word in Italian and translating the Italian pattern back to English. The method worked fine for words with Latin or Greek roots such as *nation* or *bicycle*, but I soon learned not to try it for words with Germanic or Celtic roots such as *night* or *pumpkin*.

Mrs. McKinney also introduced to the mysteries of subtraction of whole numbers. I quickly figured out that this operation was the opposite of addition and soon could do substantial problems in my head. The final subject we studied in second grade was cursive penmanship. In no time I learned that I could write even more sloppily in cursive than I could using the block letters that we had learned in first grade.

My third-grade teacher, Mrs. Dukes, was perhaps twenty years younger than Mrs. McKinney and much more energetic. She began to introduce us to books other than Dick and Jane, although that moronic family remained at the heart of the reading curriculum. I believe that the major step in third grade reading was to introduce verbs in the past and future tenses, and the interrogative voice in addition to the declarative: "Jane broke the dish. What will Jane do? Mother saw the broken dish. She said 'Oh, dear!'" In arithmetic we progressed to the multiplication of whole numbers.

All through the primary grades there was a great deal of time spent on the proper ways to celebrate the various holidays that came out during the school year. Each year we would spend a month making Halloween masks, drawing jack-o-lanterns and witches, and learning the proper etiquette for going from house to house to beg for sweets. No sooner would Halloween be over than we would start with Thanksgiving. We had to learn Thanksgiving songs, read Thanksgiving stories, put on Thanksgiving plays, and make Thanksgiving drawings. Then it would be the same for Christmas. Every classroom would have a Christmas tree in it, we would put on plays full of nativity scenes and angels, and we were required to sing Christmas carols and exchange presents with the other children. This cycle would then continue with St. Valentine's Day, Lincoln's and Washington's birthdays, and Easter. Mercifully the Easter celebration focused mostly on its Pagan elements: coloring eggs, drawing pictures of the Easter rabbit and eating jelly beans--we were spared from putting on Passion plays. When I reached the fifth grade, the school added a Chanukah play to this annual cycle in December, a concession to the rapidly increasing Jewish population in the neighborhood. Unfortunately, this added celebration had the effect of suggesting a confusing equivalence between the minor Jewish holiday of Chanukah, and the major Christian and commercial celebration of Christmas.

Third grade is the age at which boys will have the least to do with girls as they can, except when there are opportunities to torment them. I was no exception to this rule. I would join with the other boys in taunting the girls as we queued up before entering the school. During the winter we all took great delight in driving them away with fusillades of snowballs. There was, however, one girl in our class, a certain Bernice, who got the better of us. She knew the one weapon that struck absolute terror in the hearts of nine-year-old boys. Whenever we boys taunted her or threw snowballs, she would chase us and attempt to kiss whomever she could catch. We boys knew of nothing more humiliating than to be kissed by a girl, and she knew it.

In that year a new child moved to Teaneck named Fred Schauer. His family lived a couple of blocks from our house. Fred joined my small circle of friends comprised mainly of the brighter students in Mrs. Duke's class, including George Stein; the group of us wound up in the same classes all through elementary school, and junior and senior high. Fred ultimately became a well-known constitutional scholar at Harvard after a somewhat circuitous career. After completing law school, he was working as a junior attorney in a mid-sized Boston law firm. One day the owner of a local movie house called with a major legal problem. The movie house owner had been banned by Boston's municipal censorship board from showing a pair of X-rated films, *Deep Throat* and the *Devil in Miss Jones*. None of the established lawyers would take the case, so it was passed to Fred to argue. Not only did he win his case based on the constitutional guarantees of free speech and freedom of the press, he succeeded in having the Boston censorship board disbanded. From there he launched an academic career in constitutional law that eventually led him to Harvard.

It was at this time in my life that my father decided I should study Italian grammar. This was no small undertaking as Italian has a rather complex, highly inflected grammar, which perhaps makes up for the fact that the language takes an extremely simple, completely phonetic approach to spelling. Nouns could be either masculine or feminine, and either singular or plural, and adjectives would change form in accordance to the genders and numbers of the nouns they modified. Italian verbs have many more tenses than do English verbs, and change form according to the person, number, tense, and, in some tenses, the gender of their subjects.

Each Sunday morning my father would sit me down in the dining room with the grammar book and my copy book. The lessons always began with his asking me to copy several sentences from the grammar book to my copy book. Typically those sentences illustrated the particular grammatical element of the given lesson. While I was busy copying my lesson, my father would read the morning newspaper. When I was done copying, he would look at my work, exclaim how terrible my handwriting was, and then begin to give me handwriting lessons. Despite the sudden change of direction which happened virtually every week, I did somehow learn most of the Italian grammar, with the exception of a few obscure points such as the conjugation and usage of the *passato remoto*, a verb tense that is mostly used in very formal writing for describing historical events. My father's handwriting lessons, however, had much less effect and I continued to be highly deficient in that dimension.

136

The summer before I entered the fourth grade was a tense one for all of the children entering that grade at the Whittier school. One of the teachers, the dreaded Miss Kitchen, was reputed to be a merciless taskmaster and a very rigid disciplinarian. My brother, Peter, had had her and he had warned me about what I could expect if I were assigned to her classroom. Peter's tales of horror were corroborated by tales about this dragon-lady that my friends had heard from their older brothers and sisters. I was greatly relieved on my first day back at school that fall to learn that my teacher was to be someone new to the school, and not Miss Kitchen. It turned out that this new teacher only lasted about three months before leaving the school and we had a substitute teacher, a very old and tired Mrs. Oshren, for the rest of the year. Academically, fourth grade was more or less a lost year. About the only thing I recall learning from these two women was the long division of whole numbers.

The one highlight of fourth grade was that I began music lessons through the school. Peter's clarinet was handed down to me now that he was a college freshman. Each week I would be excused from class for half an hour to go to a clarinet lesson with the town's elementary school music teacher, Mr. Jenney. These lessons were given in a dank room in the school basement. Every afternoon after school, my mother would work with me during my required half-hour of clarinet practice. On Saturday mornings, Mr. Jenney would assemble all of the elementary school music students in Teaneck, about one hundred children, in the auditorium of the Washington Irving School for band practice. My parents would give me two quarters and allow me to take the public bus across town for these rehearsals. At the end of each school year, the elementary school band would give a "concert" to which all the parents would come and politely applaud our squeaks, squawks, and occasional right notes. Given the singular lack of musical talent represented by this assembly of "musicians," Mr. Jenney must have had the patience of a saint or else been totally deaf to lead this band year after year.

During my fourth-grade year my mother took it in her head that she should give me formal instruction in the French language. She had grown up in a bilingual French/Italian household because her mother was French and her father Italian. She could not fathom a world in which I was not fully conversant in both languages. I already understood French fairly well as it was what my parents spoke when they wanted to keep secrets from us kids. And I had had occasion to speak it on our trips to France to visit my mother's Parisian relatives.

French turned out to be considerably harder to learn than Italian. It combined the complexities of Italian grammar with the mysteries of a spelling system every bit as illogical as English. My mother had learned from my father's experience not to make me write out my lessons. Instead she had me read little stories from a book subtitled *Lecture Sans Larmes,* (*Reading without Tears*). Each lesson session would begin with my mother having me read a story from the book. For whatever reason, I resisted these lessons. I quickly learned that I could exasperate my mother by reading the book as though French were written phonetically and would do so even though I knew perfectly well how to read the language correctly. At first she would correct my pronunciation politely but firmly, but after about ten or fifteen minutes she would lose patience with my deliberate mistakes, and soon would begin calling me an idiot in French. Thus I learned the French equivalents of the dozens of Italian words for different types of idiots. And soon there were plenty of *larmes* to go around, the book's subtitle notwithstanding.

The fifth and sixth grades in Whittier School were organized departmentally. That is, we had specialist teachers for history, English, reading, spelling, penmanship and arithmetic. Our homeroom teachers were responsible for the weekly singing lessons. In those years, I had several very gifted teachers: Miss Pierce for arithmetic and spelling and Mr. Wangler for American history [fifth grade]; Mrs. Oberg for world history [sixth grade], and Miss Bauer for reading and English [fifth and sixth grades]. Except for Mrs. Oberg, all of these teachers had had my brothers as well, and so had high expectations of me, which I endeavored to meet. They also knew my mother very well and understood her expectations of them. Miss Pierce introduced us to the arithmetic of fractions and decimals and taught the principles underlying this world, thus making it much more interesting that the dry memorization of the arithmetic of the lower grades. Mr. Wangler kindled in me a strong interest in history which has remained with me throughout my life; he succeeded Miss Hoak as school principal upon her retirement. Miss Bauer began to teach us English grammar. I immediately recognized it as a vestigial form of the much more complex Italian and French grammars I had learned earlier from my parents.

At Whittier School, the culmination of one's academic life was the Sixth Grade Luncheon that took place at the end of the pupil's final year in the school. The wait staff for this lunch was made up of fifth graders who were selected for the job by their teachers using undisclosed and indiscernible criteria. The sixth graders lorded it all over us waiters with comments such as "Work, slave, work!" and I felt as though I were reliving "Kindergarten babies." Shortly after I entered the sixth grade, a rumor swept through the class that each boy had to ask a girl to be his "date" for the luncheon that would be happening eight months later. After much hemming and hawing and lengthy procrastination, I asked a girl to be my date. Several months later, she was also asked by a fellow she must have found more appealing because she summarily dumped me, leaving me without anyone to escort to this lunch. At the last minute, my mother arranged for me to escort another girl, one whom I did not find attractive in any way. Such are the humiliations and tribulations of childhood. Many years later I learned that several of my friends including Fred Schauer had been similarly traumatized by this introduction to social relations with the fair sex.

And thus my elementary school career began and ended, both opening and closing with academic excellence, life-long friends and social trauma. Mercifully, the former two far outweighed the last item, and life went on.

Figure 9-1. Whittier School, Teaneck, NJ, where I went for grades K-6

Figure 9-2. 676 West Englewood Avenue, Teaneck NJ, where we lived during my school years

Figure 9-3. 253 East Palisade Avenue, Englewood NJ. My parents moved here when I was a college freshman

Chapter 10

Three Religious Educations

Hebrew School

One day, late in the summer of 1955, when I was about to enter the fifth grade, my father took me aside and informed me that I would be beginning Hebrew school that fall (Figures 10-1 and 10-2). I really did not know what to make of it as I had not heard about this institution from any of my friends, and my brothers, who were eight and nine years older than me, had completed Hebrew school before I was five years old. All I knew was that my father told me that it would entail going somewhere two afternoons a week after school and for two hours on Sunday mornings.

If I remember correctly, my teacher for the *Aleph* (first level) class was a Mrs. Wiesel, a colorless middle-aged woman whose job it was to teach us the basics of reading and writing the Hebrew language. On the first day we were all asked what our Hebrew name was. As the teacher went around the class, she got the answers she expected, "My name is *Mordechai*," "My name is *Avraham*," "My name is *Schlomo*," "My name is

142

Chaya," and so on until she got to me. I answered, "My name is George," which of course is not a Hebrew name at all. I was then sternly ordered to go home and ask my mother what my Hebrew name was; I could not use an English name in Hebrew school.

That evening I asked my mother what my Hebrew name was and she told me to tell the teacher that my name was George and that was that. Two days later I announced to Mrs. Wiesel that my name was George, and so for the entire Aleph year, I was the only George in a sea of *Mordechais* and *Shlomos*. Of course, what Mrs. Wiesel did not understand was that the practice of requiring separate religious name was primarily a custom of the Jews that had emigrated from the old Tsarist Russian Empire. They probably used these private names as a form of guarded protest against the practice of the nineteenth century Russian officials who had forced them to take surnames and Slavic given names. Because she and all the other teachers in the Hebrew school were from that population, she ignorantly assumed that what they did was universal Jewish practice. Among the Italian Jews, some followed this model but others, including my family, did not. This was only the first time of many that I ran afoul of the extremely narrow world view of my Hebrew school teachers.

On the first day of Hebrew school I learned that the most important words in Hebrew were "*Sheket! Sheket! Sheket!*" meaning *Silence! Silence! Silence!* or, to put it less delicately, *Shut up!* Typically, Mrs. Wiesel would yell these words at the top of her lungs several times an hour as she tried to control a room full of boys and a few girls that had little interest in being there.

Each day for the first few weeks in Mrs. Weasel's class, we would learn how to pronounce another Hebrew letter or vowel. During the second week we were introduced to the vowel ֶ , which she told us to pronounce *aw*. When I told my mother about this lesson, she corrected me, telling me that that is how the Polish Jews (her term for the Yiddish-speaking Jews from Tsarist Russia) pronounced that vowel but that we Sephardim pronounced it *ah*, and that the Sephardic pronunciation was what was used in Israel. And so I always pronounced it *ah*, resulting in my pronouncing the name of the Lord as *Adonai*, rather than *Adonoy*, much to Mrs. Wiesel's continuing annoyance. Likewise, when we learned the Hebrew letter ת, Mrs. Wiesel told us to pronounce it like English *S*, whereas my mother told me to pronounce it like English *T*, so that the word for Sabbath, שַׁבָּת, would come out *Sha'baws* from her and *Sha bat'* from me.

Once we had learned to read and write the Hebrew alphabet, she began to teach us how to read the main prayers. I soon learned that Mrs. Wiesel put a high premium on knowing how to read them quickly, but that she seemed not to care whether we knew what they meant. Reading Hebrew quickly is very easy because the language is almost completely phonetic, and I became very proficient at it. However, since I had a working vocabulary of only about fifty words in that language, reading the prayers was largely a simian exercise. While some of the words I knew such as *blessed, holy, heaven, earth, and amen* were in the prayers, many of my fifty words were just everyday words such as *boy, girl, father*, and *mother*. And the words we heard most often in class — "*Sheket! Sheket! Sheket!*" — did not appear in any of the prayers.

In addition to going to Hebrew school three times a week, we were supposed to go to Sabbath services every Saturday morning. My family was not particularly observant, and so I never went to services except on Yom Kippur. Besides, I had band practice every Saturday morning, and that was a lot more fun. Each term my lack of attendance at Sabbath services would be duly noted with a large scarlet *F* in my report card that contrasted with the black *A*s in all the other subjects.

My second year in Hebrew school was in the *Beth* (second level) class of
Mr. Wool. He was a large unattractive man in a black, ill-fitting suit. He
had a very sour disposition and smelled as though his house lacked a bath-
tub. Mr. Wool had the peculiar habit of sucking in his cheeks and pursing
his lips whenever he was displeased, which seemed to be almost all the
time. I believe that he commuted out to the suburbs from New York's
Lower East Side, as did all the other Hebrew school teachers. If Mrs. Wiesel's only understanding of Jewish practice was that of the Polish Jews,
Mr. Wool was even more so. He was determined to bully me into being a
nice Polish Jew like himself. He grew very angry that I lacked a Hebrew
name. After a few weeks he pulled me aside and told me that henceforth
I was to be called *Gershon*, a name to which I answered only grudgingly.
And he glared at me and sucked in his cheeks every time I applied the
Sephardic pronunciation to Hebrew, which seemed to happen about every
third word in the prayers that he expected us to recite at breakneck speed.

As the various Jewish holidays occurred, Mr. Wool would instruct us in
the proper ways to celebrate them. I recall that when we got to Hanukah,
we were told that we were supposed to eat latkes, and a lady came in to
fry some for the class on a small electric hot plate. I, of course, had never
eaten one in my life, so I asked Mr. Wool what they were and why we
had to eat them. His abrupt reply was, "We eat them because the ancient
Israelites fried up potato pancakes when they celebrated Hanukah!" and
then he glared at me for being so stupid, sucking in his cheeks particularly
deeply.

That evening I told my mother that we were supposed to eat *latkes* because it was Hanukah and that was what the ancient Israelites ate. She
asked me what *latkes* were, and I replied that they seemed to be some sort
of mushy greasy fritters made of potatoes. My mother then hit the roof
about Mr. Wool's stupidity, calling him almost all of the numerous Italian

words for *idiot*. She then explained to me that the ancient Israelites certainly did not eat potatoes because that vegetable was indigenous to South America and did not reach the eastern hemisphere until the mid-1500s. I then tried to look up *latke* in a Hebrew-English dictionary and discovered that it is not even a Hebrew word. What little respect I had for Mr. Wool evaporated instantly. Evidently the rest of the class had little respect for him either, as he had to yell "*Sheket! Sheket! Sheket!*" even louder and more often than Mrs. Wiesel.

In the third year I was promoted to the *Gimmel* (third level) class of Mr. Fisch, despite my record of F's in attending Sabbath services. Like Mr. Wool, Mr. Fisch was large smelly man in an ill-fitting black suit. The only difference was that at least he had a sense of humor, or so my friends told me. Most of his jokes seemed to turn on phrases in Yiddish, a language that no one in my family had ever spoken and that I knew nothing about, save three words that I had learned on the street, *schmuck, putz,* and *dreck.* I only had a vague sense of the meaning of these words, though I did know you that if another kid applied any of them to you, you were supposed to answer him with a punch in the nose.

In the course of the year, Mr. Fisch endeavored to teach us Jewish history as one of our subjects. His version of Jewish history naturally started with the stories of Adam and Eve, Noah, Abraham, Moses and the other familiar figures of Genesis and Exodus. It continued on through the periods covered in the books of the prophets, the successful revolt against the Greek rulers of Syria (celebrated at Hanukah) and the disastrous revolts against the Romans in the first and second centuries CE. Then suddenly he skipped from there to Tsarist Russia in the 1800s, as if the all Jews had gone to sleep for 1700 years and then magically woke up uneducated, poor and miserable living under the Tsars. He painted a picture of downtrodden Jews subject to seemingly daily pogroms, accusations of causing epidemics by poisoning wells, and blood libels in which Jews supposedly kidnapped and murdered Christian children to use their blood to produce *matzah*. This Tsarist history was presented as the universal Jewish experience.

Fifty years later, as I was doing the research for my book *Remembrance and Renewal*, I revisited this supposedly universal Jewish experience and found that the picture Mr. Fisch painted was far different from my family's history. I learned that the last time, if ever, my family *might* have experienced a pogrom would have been in Spain in the 1400s. As for Jews spreading the plague by poisoning wells, I found a document from the year 1600 describing the actions of the Italian city of Asti when a Jew surnamed Foa came down with the plague. The municipal officials quarantined him and his family for several weeks, just like anyone else would have been. After he recovered from the disease, city officials required the Foa family to burn all their clothes and sent in a cleaning crew to disinfect the house with alcohol. Finally, the cleaning crew was quarantined for three weeks to make sure they had not caught the disease. When famine, war and plague wiped out more than half the population of Milan, Mantua and other northern Italian cities in 1628-1630, there were no mentions of Jewish conspiracies. And in England, when the plague of 1665-1666 was followed by a great fire that killed more than 100,000 Londoners, there was no public linkage between these events and the official re-admission of Jews to England that had occurred barely ten years before. The latest reference I could find concerning blood libel in Italy was a letter from the pope to the Franciscans written during 1400s. In that letter the pope ordered the Franciscans to stop preaching the "long-discredited theory of blood libel." And the only examples of kidnappings that I found were from the 1700s when Catholic clergy were kidnapping Jewish children and baptizing them, notwithstanding royal decrees prohibiting such practices. The last such kidnapping occurred in the 1850s, when the Inquisitorial police kidnapped ten-year-old Edgardo Mortara, baptized him, and eventually brought him to live with Pope Pius IX in Rome.

Mr. Fisch's family of course came from Russia, which remained a backward, medieval country until late in the nineteenth century. That country had experienced neither the Renaissance nor the Enlightenment. He seemed to be completely unaware of the existence and history of Jews like my family, who had lived and prospered in the Mediterranean basin during the seventeen hundred years from between the Roman-era revolts and his family's life under the Tsars. Of course by this time I had learned to discount much of what we were taught in Hebrew school and largely tuned out Mr. Fisch's lessons.

One of the lowlights of my *Gimmel* year in Hebrew school was a Polish Jew in my class named Alan. Alan was a big brute, about a foot taller than I, and weighing perhaps half again as much. He was also quite dense and could barely read Hebrew, despite more than two years of Hebrew school. Alan took an intense dislike to me, although I do not recall doing anything to stimulate that dislike. I suspect that he hated me simply because I was different from him and the other kids. He began to glare at me threateningly during our classes. I took the precaution of always being with several friends whenever I was outside of the building. Unfortunately, one day I had to remain after Hebrew school for a few minutes to talk with Mr. Fisch and found myself leaving the building alone. I was suddenly aware that I was being followed and began to run towards Teaneck's main street, Cedar Lane, hoping for help from a passerby. Alan quickly overtook me and beat me viciously, leaving me lying in the street bruised and bawling. Having satisfied his primal urges towards violence, he left me alone after that. But I never again left Hebrew school alone, just to be sure that I would be safe.

During my *Gimmel* year I began to attend Sabbath services on an irregular basis. In most cases it was on days when friends of mine were having their bar mitzvahs. This attendance familiarized me with the structure of the Sabbath service, knowledge I would need to have by the following September when I too would become a bar mitzvah. It also had the side benefit that my grades in attendance at Sabbath services rose from scarlet *F*'s to black *C*'s.

About two thirds of the way through that year I began individual instruction with another Hebrew school teacher, Mr. Lauer, to prepare for my bar mitzvah. Mr. Lauer was a very short man, also given to wearing black, ill-fitting suits. He had a pimply, pasty complexion that was quite off-putting. In addition to training bar mitzvah students, he substituted occasionally for the cantor in leading synagogue services when the latter gentleman was ill or on vacation. On a personal level Mr. Lauer was pleasant enough and he never seemed to need to yell *"Sheket! Sheket! Sheket!"* perhaps because he worked with his students one-on-one. Mr. Lauer's main job was to teach us how to chant the Torah and Haphtarah (readings from the Biblical books of the prophets) portions that would be the main part of our bar mitzvah ceremonies.

One afternoon, Mr. Lauer asked me if I owned a pair of *tefillin* (also called *phylacteries*), two small black leather boxes containing a passage from Deuteronomy that are attached to leather straps. The ultra-religious wrap the straps around their right hand and head during daily morning prayers, thus fulfilling literally the commandment that one should bind the word of God upon one's hand and wear it as a frontlet before one's eyes. That evening I asked my father if we owned such things and he turned up an ancient set that probably dated back to the early- to mid-1800s. They looked as though they had not been used since. The leather straps were all stiff and dried out. The next time I saw Mr. Lauer, I showed him what my

149

father had turned up. He then instructed me in how to put them on, and thus I wore *tefillin* for the one and only time in my life.

Finally, the time for my bar mitzvah arrived. Two other boys and I shared the ceremony one Sabbath morning. We were called up to the Torah and chanted our assigned portions of the Torah and Haphtarah. My brother Peter made the arduous weekend trip home from Cornell for the occasion, a gesture that I greatly treasured. Our older brother Albert was unable to join us; at the time he was serving as a naval officer aboard a small ship bobbing in the stormy Gulf of Alaska. After the ceremony, my parents threw a low-key garden party to which most of our New York area relatives and my school friends were invited. Of course, I received a variety of gifts on that occasion. My grandmother in Italy sent me a fine Swiss watch that I still wear every day, nearly sixty years later. That evening my father informed me that I no longer needed to go to Hebrew school, perhaps the best bar mitzvah gift of all.

Even to this day I feel like an outsider when I attend services at most American synagogues because they are clearly for Polish Jews only. I cringe whenever the rabbi tells a story about the "good old days" in the shtetl, tells a Borscht-belt joke that turns on some phrase in Yiddish or defines being Jewish as exhibiting some characteristic behavior that is unique to the Polish Jews. These acts make it abundantly clear to me that I am not wanted and do not belong; they do not regard me as one of them. The other congregants have a narrow shared historical background and world view that have never been a part of my history or life. I sense that they resent my differentness, just like Alan, the Polish Hebrew school bully of my *Gimmel* class.

Home Schooling

The religious education that really mattered in my life I absorbed at home, even though we were not a very religious family. The main festivals that we observed were Yom Kippur and Pesach (Passover). On Yom Kippur we would eat a major meal just before sunset in preparation for the twenty-four hour fast required by religious custom. The next day we would spend most of the day at services in the synagogue, reciting what seemed to me to be an endlessly repetitious and tedious set of prayers, while abstaining from all manner of work, food and drink. Of course, my Hebrew school training came in handy, and I could race through the prayers faster than almost anyone else in the congregation. When sunset came, the shofar was sounded and we could return home to break the fast.

The post-Yom Kippur meal was always a cold meal that had been prepared before the holy day, since one could not cook on that day. The first course was always *bruscadella*, toasted slices of Italian bread that were covered with sugar and cinnamon and soaked in dry red wine. I always looked forward to breaking the fast with this delicious concoction, and to this day a Yom Kippur without it feels like a lot of wasted suffering. The main course was always *polpettone di tacchino*, a dish with no analog in either American or Polish-Jewish cuisine. It consisted of several different meats, usually ground turkey and veal, and various herbs and condiments stuffed tightly into the skin of a turkey and then cooked. My mother would prepare it about a week before the holiday and keep it in the refrigerator under weights so that it would become firm and easy to slice. She would then serve it decorated with chopped aspic and parsley. Along with this *polpettone* my mother would serve various vegetables, depending on what was in season, which had been cooked before the holiday and seasoned with olive oil and vinegar. And dessert alternated between *zabaglione*, a wine and egg custard, served with fresh fruits or berries, and *Monte Bian-*

151

co, a paste made of chestnuts, chocolate and rum surmounted by whipped cream, all molded to look like the eponymous Alpine mountain.

Pesach was always a very joyous time in our household. Perhaps the holiday had special meaning for us as exiles who had been forced by circumstance to leave our native land, much as happened to our Spanish ancestors in the 1490s, and to the Biblical Jacob and his family. As the Bible relates, Jacob's family went down to Egypt during a famine in Canaan and dwelt among a people of strange tongue, and thus it sets up the whole story leading up the Exodus four hundred years later. Whatever the case, Pesach was an occasion for a large group of us Italian Jews in the New York area to gather to reread the story of the Exodus in Hebrew and Italian using beautiful old Passover Haggadot (illustrated books that retell the story of the Exodus from Egypt) that our families had brought with them when they left Italy in the 1930s and 40s (Figures 10-3 and 10-4).

Our Pesach Seders largely followed a similar structure as those of other Jewish groups around the world, though the choices of ritual foods had a decidedly Mediterranean bias. As bitter herbs we used a bitter lettuce such as Romaine or endive. Our spring greens were usually parsley, which we dipped into red wine vinegar diluted with water. And our *haroset* was compounded from dates, almonds, oranges, egg yolks and white wine. After the initial half of the Passover ritual, we would eat dinner, whose opening course was a soup called *minestra dayenu* consisting of hot chicken stock in which were floated new spring vegetables, typically baby spinach, and bits of crumbled *matzot*. The main course was always roast lamb in memory of the paschal sacrifice that our ancestors ate on the night before their departure from Egypt. Alongside the main course there were always an assortment of new spring vegetables, since Pesach in Italy occurs when the first of the new season's vegetables come to market. For dessert we always had spring fruits (often early strawberries), and unleavened sweets such as *amaretti* (cookies made from almond paste and egg-whites), *matzod ascirod* (hard, unleavened sugar cookies), *pan di spagna* (literally, "Spanish bread"; a sponge cake that probably originated in medieval Spain and was brought to Italy by Jews expelled from Spain in 1492) or any of dozens of remarkable unleavened tortes such as *torta del re* (literally, the king's cake). Somehow, between adults who were sleepy from eating a grand feast and cranky children who were tired of a dinner that had gone on too long, we never got to the postprandial half of the Passover Seder.

Learning at the Table

One of the great pleasures of my life has been that my dear wife has discovered the wonderful cuisine of the Italian Jews and regularly livens up our holidays with special treats appropriate to the season. Through her efforts at learning traditional Italian cookery (Figure 10-5) I have come to observe more of the Jewish festivals, or, what is perhaps more to the point, the Jewish feasts. Among her specialties I am especially fond of the sweets: *sfratti* at Rosh Hashanah, *ginetti* for Sukkot, *fritelle di Hanukah* (a fried yeast dough soaked in a lemon and honey syrup) for Hanukah, *Orecchie di Amman* (Haman's ears, a crisp fried pastry dusted in sugar) for Purim, all of the fabulous Passover tortes, and *Monte Sinai*, a very eggy cake, for Shavuot. In the recent years, we learned about a traditional Sephardic Jewish practice of holding a special Seder for Rosh Hashanah complete with its own special ritual foods (Figure 10-6):

- Figs for a sweet year

- Squash to avoid bad judgments against us

- Fennel, that we lead meritorious lives

- Leeks to drive off our enemies

- Dates to make an end to hatred

- Pomegranate that our merits should be as numerous as its seeds

- Lamb to remind us of the binding of Isaac

- Fish, that our descendants be as numerous as the fishes of the sea

Perhaps this culinary revival to celebrate the holidays has been the best religious education of all.

Figure 10-1. The main entrance of the Teaneck Jewish Community Center where my brothers and I had our bar mitzvahs.

Figure 10-2. The sanctuary of the Teaneck Jewish Community Center; The central barrier to create a separate women's section in the sanctuary was added when the building was recently taken over by an orthodox congregation.

Figure 10-3. 1890 Passover Hagaddah

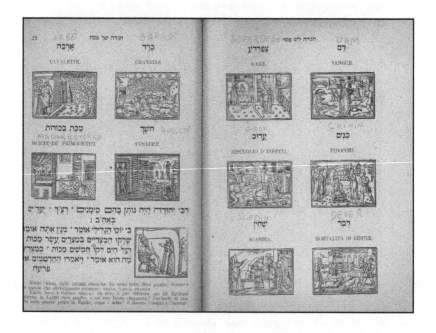

Figure 10-4 The Ten Plagues from the 1890 Passover Haggadah

Figure 10-5. Italian Jewish Cookbook

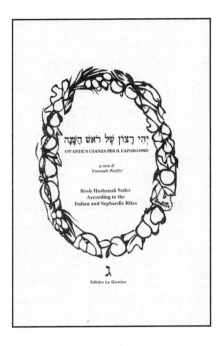

Figure 10-6. Rosh Hashanah Haggadah

Chapter 11

Junior High—Important Lessons in Spite of Going to School

When I was in elementary school, our town of Teaneck had a combined junior/senior high school atop a hill that was more or less in the center of the town. The northern half of the building covered the grades 7-9 and the southern half, grades 10-12. As the town population grew, this building was no longer large enough to house all the junior and senior high school students, so the town decided to build two smaller junior high schools and devote the central building exclusively to grades 10-12.

The two new schools, named for Benjamin Franklin (Figure 11-1) and Thomas Jefferson, were in Teaneck's northwestern and southeastern quadrants respectively. The Franklin school, the one in my part of town, was finished during the summer before I entered the seventh grade, but the Jefferson school was not scheduled for completion until the following summer. The Teaneck Board of Education decided to move all the junior high students into the Franklin school as it waited for the completion of Jefferson. To accommodate twice as many pupils as the school was designed for, we were put on split sessions. For half the year, I was due at school at 7:10 AM and was released at 12:10, while the future Thomas Jefferson kids and their teachers came to school at 12:30 and remained until 5:30 PM. At mid-year, the sessions were switched so that the inconveniences of early start times for the morning session and late release times for the afternoon session were shared equally by both groups of students and teachers.

During my junior high school years, I gave up walking to school as I had done in elementary school. The Benjamin Franklin School was a little more than twice as far from my house as had been my elementary school. Instead of walking most of my friends and I bicycled to school unless it was raining or snowing. In the latter cases we would walk because wet bicycle brakes work poorly at best. The concept of being driven to school was just as alien as it had been when we were in elementary school.

In the seventh grade I had one wonderful teacher, a certain Mr. Dublin who taught my class both English and Social Studies. He was very stimulating teacher and much loved by his students. With him we learned the fine points of English grammar, and more important, how to write compelling English prose. He introduced us to the great American writers of the early 1800s, and I remember to this day the stories and poems he had us read, especially those of Edgar Allan Poe.

In the ninth grade, I had one other superb teacher, Mr. Maisel. Mr. Maisel taught a survey course covering world history from ancient times up to the middle of the 1800s. He accomplished what seemed to be an impossible task, compressing 5000 years of the history of mankind into a single year's course. As part of that course, we learned a lot of the basic cultural heritage that I find so completely lacking in most Americans. We were expected to understand the elements of the political, military, religious and artistic achievements of the many civilizations from East and West Asia, Europe and the Americas. This was before the days of political correctness when all such studies were replaced by endless readings about African village life. I distinctly recall having examinations in which we had to compare religious ideas across cultures, identify the sources and periods of archaeological finds by their writing and/or artistic expression, and distinguish among the styles of different Renaissance painters.

Aside from these two teachers, I found junior high school to be a total waste of time. Junior high math and science were jokes. Except for the above two classes, history and English were no better. Even as a boy in my early teens, I believed that its three-year span could have been compressed into a single year with no loss of learning.

Perhaps the only other important thing I learned at Franklin Junior High concerned the ice cream cups that were sold in the cafeteria. These cups came with a dollop of chocolate syrup. We all learned that if you opened one end of the wrappers on the cafeteria's drinking straws, dipped the other end in this syrup, and then blew through the straw, the wrapper would fly up to the ceiling, and stick to it; hundreds of such straw-wrappers dangled from the cafeteria ceiling.

One area in which my education grew during that period was in foreign languages and that was as much outside of junior high as within it. The in-school part came as I started to study Latin. While the class did pick up the rudiments of Latin's very complex grammar, I doubt that our teacher contributed much to our learning. We had a very bright class who learned the language mostly on its own, while our teacher would carry on dogmatically about how Latin was not a dead language and how the world would be much improved if all were to join her favorite evangelical cult group called "Moral-Rearmament". Most of the class was Jewish and many of the kids were deeply offended by her preaching. So much for the separation of church and state!

When I entered the eighth grade, my mother arranged for me to sit in on a first-year French class so that I could learn the language a bit more systematically than merely hearing it at home. By this time my mother had given up hope of teaching me French grammar on her own. The following summer, my parents sent me to *Les Roches*, a boarding school in the French-speaking part of Switzerland. My cousins Emanuele and Piera Levi-Montalcini had been there the previous summer and my parents deemed it a good place for me to learn French.

At that school, I took formal classes in French and German. The French class solidified my speaking, reading and writing of that language. The German class was very much a beginner's class, as I had no background in that language. But it gave me an ear for the language which wound up being very helpful when I began more formal study of that language in the tenth grade. At *Les Roches* I shared a bedroom with two Italian boys and from them I learned all the words of street-corner Italian that my parents were certainly never going to teach me.

The boys at the school were an eclectic mix of Italians, Germans, and Americans with a few others such as Luis Salazar from Portugal mixed in to add spice. The Americans were almost all children of ex-pats working for the American oil companies in various Arab countries. They tended to be quite spoiled and behaved with an air of superiority to the nationals from all other countries. I found the Americans to be mostly ignorant, uncultured and ill-mannered. Many of them came from Texas and Oklahoma and exhibited the worst of the "Ugly American" stereotype. On balance, I tended to identify more with the Italian group than the Americans. Their culture, their manners, and their approach to life seemed much more in tune with the world I knew.

A second major lesson of my junior high school years was the importance of being honest and forthright in all of one's dealings. At *Les Roches* there was one American named Jimmy who did not fit the mold of the others; he was much worse. If the others were mostly ignorant jingoes, Jimmy was an out and out liar. Jimmy kept on telling us tales of his "successes" with the girls. The more he insisted that his tales were true, the more the rest of us knew they were merely hormonal fantasies. After all, how much sexual experience could a thirteen-year-old boy have had? Jimmy's lying also had a darker side. He would regularly run out of his weekly allowance of spending money before the week was over. He would then borrow money from the other boys, promising to repay them on the following Sunday evening when the school administrator, M. Bühler, would hand each boy his weekly allotment of five Swiss francs. Come Sunday evening, Jimmy would collect his allowance and refuse to repay the loans, denying that he had ever borrowed anything. If a boy insisted on repayment, Jimmy would back up his denials with his fists. Jimmy ultimately became a Philadelphia lawyer. I have little doubt about what sort of lawyer he was.

My few months' education at Les Roches certainly had a much more important influence on me than junior high school. The French and German classes substantially expanded my facility in multiple languages. My peer to peer relationship with large numbers of Italian kids gave me a broader exposure to that society than I had had at home with my parents and with my grandmother in *Val Salice*. Most important, the Jimmy experience taught to be wary of trusting people who come across as full of baloney; this was a lesson that I drew upon several times during my work life. Perhaps it is for this reason that I have had a life-long skepticism of most politicians and salesmen.

Figure 11-1. Benjamin Franklin Junior High School
Teaneck NJ

Chapter 12

High School, Oregon and Columbia

In the fall of 1960 I at last entered Teaneck High School (Figure 12-1). The school was an imposing brick structure, complete with vaguely medieval towers and battlements. It was situated atop a hill more or less at the geographic center Teaneck, overlooking Route 4, the east-west highway that bisected the town. The first two lessons imparted to us by the upperclassmen were (1) the name of the school mascot, the Highwayman, a term whose real meaning was lost on most of us, and (2) the parody version of the school song one version of which ran as follows:

On a hill she stands rejected, lousing up the view
Dishonor, defiance, and rejection—these are all her due
Fighting daily in her classrooms, students sad and blue
Forget her story and her teachers, boo her to the sky
Woe to thee our Alma Mater, woe to Teaneck High

My entering class of 729 students contained many dozens of remarkably brilliant kids. Their collective genius ultimately led a fair number of them to the highest echelons of government, academia, medicine, law, and business. Because of the tracking system in the school, I wound up sharing all of my classes with this group over the next three years. Of course, my class also its share of dolts, but the tracking system meant that I had little contact with them other than in gym class where the gym teachers used to encourage them to beat up on the smarter kids.

Most kids on the academic track in high school took five major subjects, plus the usual gym and lighter electives. My mother, who had been very precocious as a child and finished her doctorate by the age of 20, pushed me to take six majors in the tenth and eleventh grades in order to ensure that I was sufficiently challenged. (She was well aware of the flabbiness of the junior high school program and feared that high school might be just as weak.) Consequently, in the tenth grade I took the required course in English together with biology, plane geometry, and three languages, Latin 2, French 2 and German 1. My mother tried to push the school into putting me into French 3 but they insisted that I had to do one year of grammar; since I had never taken French 1, I had to go into French 2.

On the first day of school, all of the Latin 2 students were the victims of a scheduling mistake: they were told to report to an advanced French class instead of Latin 2. I, of course, was the only one of the Latin students who understood the proceedings, which were conducted exclusively in French.

Of all my studies in the tenth grade, plane geometry made the greatest impression on me, with its elegance and crystal-clear logic. I turned out to have a real knack for it. On the first exam we were asked to prove some theorem we had never seen. Initially I was totally mystified by this problem. I then reviewed in my head all of the theorems we had proved in class. When I got to Thales Theorem — that the base angles of an isosceles triangle are equal — and went through the construction that was the heart of its proof, I suddenly realized that the same construction could be used for the proof needed for the exam question. I was the only one in class to solve this problem. Thales Theorem was known to countless generations of geometry students as *pons asinorum* (Latin for the *bridge of asses*), and I had crossed over it from the land of the geometrically ignorant to the beautiful world of serious mathematics. And this initial small incident kindled my love of mathematics and logic that ultimately led to my initial career as an academic mathematician.

The polar opposite was my experience with tenth-grade biology. Despite the great microbiology revolution that was happening in just those days in the subject, our class was limited to a deadly dull study of taxonomy. Our teacher would spend each class period reading the textbook to the class and we would all yawn our hour away. One day one of the boys stole her textbook just before the start of class and we all enjoyed listening to her stumble through her lecture without it. The only two interesting highlights of this course were the dissection of large, fat earthworms and then of leopard frogs. I think most of the fun was when some of the boys wiggled the worms and frogs on the lab benches of some of the more squeamish girls. At home I talked so much about the dissection exercise that my mother obtained a preserved shark for me to dissect at home. I never quite knew the source of this shark but suspected that it came from the university where she taught chemistry. In any case, I then invited one of my best friends, George Stein, over for a Saturday afternoon and we spent the entire time dissecting the shark and finding all its major and minor organs.

My French teacher was a sadistic spinster with very crooked teeth. She was known to all the students as Toothy Ruthie. When she would return our marked exams, she would go over them in class. With each question she would humiliate all those who missed that question by forcing them to raise their hands. And if someone did not raise his or her hand quickly enough for Toothy Ruthie's liking, she would bark out, "Up with your hand Johnnie! I know you got this one wrong. And you too, Susie! We need to see the hands of all those who missed this question." Fortunately, I could generally recognize correct French usage by ear because I had heard the language spoken at home since I was a baby. So, I only rarely had to submit to the hand raising torture.

Part way through the tenth grade my parents recognized my burgeoning interest in mathematics. They suggested that I apply for a place at one of the National Science Foundation's newly organized summer programs to enrich the backgrounds of scientifically oriented high school students. The impetus for these programs had been the discovery of the woeful state of American science and math teaching in the aftermath of the Sputnik debacle.

I was accepted at a program focused on mathematics and the as-yet un-named field of computer science at Oregon State University. In the mornings we would hear lectures on linear algebra, logic and computer programming, and in the afternoons we would have labs. One lab focused on building simple programmable logic circuits using electro-mechanical devices such as relays and stepping switches. The other had us writing programs and running them on the university's only computer, an ALWAC III-E. The ALWAC was a massive room-sized machine with endless racks of vacuum tubes that always seemed to be burning out, particularly since the machine room lacked air conditioning. It had the perhaps a little less compute power than early personal computers like the Apple 2. Its only input and output medium was punched paper tape, which we would then have to print off-line. And its only programming language was a hexadecimal absolute code. It did not support an assembly language, let alone any higher-level languages.

At the end of the summer, my mother flew out to Oregon to pick me up and we took a week's vacation together. Our first stop was to drive down to Crater Lake National Park in the Cascades. The lake filled the caldera of a dormant volcano. The absolutely clear sky gave the water a haunting deep-blue color which contrasted strongly with the heaps of yellow and red pumice and lava that surrounded it. From Oregon, we then flew to San Francisco where my mother was to meet a potential publisher for the chemistry textbook she was writing. It was our first visit to the Bay Area, a region that would later become an important part of my life.

As I entered the eleventh grade, I continued the program of six major subjects. I had to drop one of my languages, Latin, in order to make room for the AP version of the required two-year course in American history, a subject I enjoyed almost as much a mathematics. My love of history has continued to this day, and was one of the drivers behind the writing of my first book *Remembrance and Renewal*. The only other change in my program was that physics replaced biology. In mathematics I studied second year algebra and analytical geometry, with perhaps the most gifted teacher of my school years, Mr. Garcia. He was both entertaining and very effective in conveying the power and beauty of mathematics. And the class, comprising about twenty very bright and motivated students, made the experience absolutely wonderful. The following year, the same group of students had Mr. Garcia for calculus as well. We all developed a deep appreciation for the genius and explanatory power of that subject.

During the eleventh grade, I also attended another NSF program on Saturday mornings at Columbia. That program was focused on physics, and their presentation of that subject was a hundred times more engaging than the supposedly equivalent class I was taking in high school. The Columbia program did a wonderful job of teaching how the power of mathematical modeling could "explain" much of the behavior of the physical world. Indeed, the Columbia program was so exciting that I toyed off and on with the idea of switching my interest from mathematics to physics. In contrast, my high school physics teacher was a weary old man, well past his prime, who was just going through the motions, teaching the same old thing as he had for the preceding thirty or forty years.

While I was in the eleventh grade, my mother's book writing project took off in earnest. At the time there was a fashion for "teaching machines." As this was long before there were desktop computers of any sort, let alone ones that were powerful enough to do computer-based instruction, these teaching machines were basically mechanical devices that presented bits of textual material followed by rounds of questions to reinforce the relevant lesson. My mother's chemistry book (figure 12-2) was designed for these systems. Her book enjoyed considerable success and was ultimately translated into several languages including Italian, Spanish, Portuguese and Swedish. She continued to receive royalty checks for more than a dozen years. Because my mother was not a native writer of English, I became her copy editor, suggesting how to rephrase some of her sentences for greater clarity and also fact checking parts of the book, to make sure that no substantive errors inadvertently crept into the text. Through this process, I learned the bulk of collegiate freshman chemistry.

The summer after the eleventh grade I did another National Science Foundation program, this time at Columbia and this time covering computer science exclusively. Unlike the program in Oregon the previous summer, the program was almost entirely focused on software, with little mathematics and no discussion of hardware. Our computer was an IBM 650, the first computer produced on an industrial scale. It had the advantage

169

of having both an assembly language and an early version of FORTRAN, which made it possible to focus less on the innards of how the computer processed information, and more on what tasks we wanted it to accomplish.

In my senior year, I dropped back to only five major subjects to allow time for the college admissions process. I studied calculus with the same gifted Mr. Garcia, took the second half of the 2-year AP American History class and continued German as my only foreign language. With my background in chemistry from editing my mother's book, AP chemistry was a breeze, though most other kids found it rather easy as well; I recall that someone nicknamed our very effeminate chemistry teacher *Tinkerbell*, and the name stuck.

The senior year was largely taken up with the college entrance rat race with its seemingly endless rounds of entrance exams and campus visits. My friends and I started receiving unsolicited letters from various colleges and universities inviting us to apply. One that stood out in my mind as singularly inappropriate was some college of mortuary science. At one point several of us hatched a conspiracy to create a fake applicant to the honors program at Michigan State. We filled out the forms they sent us under the name Marvin Schwartz with one friend's address and my home telephone number. We invented courses he had taken, of course with all As, and put down high College Board scores for him. The gag continued for several weeks until my mother answered a telephone call from someone in the Michigan State admissions office asking to speak with Marvin Schwartz. I had made the mistake of letting my mother in on the gag and she spilled the beans on us to the admissions officer, thus cutting short our prank. Some years later, another group of students succeeded in pulling off a similar prank by getting a fictitious student admitted to Princeton; they went so far as to send a kid in for the required admissions interview with copies of Plato and *Sports Illustrated* under his arm to show how "well-rounded" he was.

For the most part, I made my college visits alone or with a friend as both of my parents were working and felt that it was important that I take the initiative of setting up and going on these visits on my own. I remember visiting Princeton via a circuitous route that entailed taking a bus into New York City, riding the subway down to Penn Station, and then taking the train out to New Jersey again. At one point I flew up to Boston to see Harvard and MIT. At that time both of my older brothers were living in Cambridge; Albert was working as a chemical engineer at the Dewey and Almy chemical works that was near Fresh Pond, and Peter was in his first year at the Harvard Business School. I stayed overnight at Albert's house near Harvard Square. I remember being truly intrigued by MIT with its focus on science, and their admissions office seems to have been taken with me as well. In the end I applied to five schools and then withdrew four of my applications after being admitted early to MIT. MIT also placed me out of much of the freshman year curriculum, giving me credit for a full year of calculus, including areas I had not studied such as vector calculus. Also, my work editing my mother's book enabled me to place out of the full year freshman chemistry course with its interminable and disagreeable smelly labs. I also received credit for the two years of AP American History I had taken.

Towards the end of the senior year in high school, we were all ushered into the auditorium for an awards assembly in which the principal would announce the winners of various prizes and scholarships. Traditionally the high point of that assembly was the awarding of Good Citizenship prizes, sponsored by the local chapter of the Daughters of the American Revolution. The school faculty would select the male and female winners of these prizes, and then the president of the local DAR chapter would show up in wearing a large hat and white gloves to present the certificates and checks. In my class, the faculty awarded the prizes to a politically active Jewish boy with strong leftist leanings and a black girl active in the civil rights movement. For the first time ever, the local DAR president refused to come to the Awards Assembly to hand out these certificates and shake the hands of the winners.

High school graduation was taken terribly seriously by our teachers and largely as a joke by the students. I recall spending days lining up in alphabetical order, marching in and out of the school's football stadium in the broiling June sun, and repeatedly standing up and sitting down until we could all do it together. The tedium was occasionally relieved by some lighter moments. At one point one of the class goof-offs began to brag loudly about how proud he was of his class rank of 687th in a graduating class of 702. The measure of his stupidity was that he did not realize that this might not be something to boast about. Several of us joked that he was trying to demonstrate his qualifications for a run for public office! The low point of graduation practice was having to learn the real words to the school song. The teachers made us sing it over and over and over until they were reasonably sure that we knew the words. They were in mortal fear that we would belt out *"On the hill she stands rejected, lousing up the view..."* in front of the assembled parents and town dignitaries.

Figure 12-1. Teaneck High School, Teaneck NJ

Figure 12-2. The Spanish edition of Luciana's programmed general chemistry text book.

Chapter 13

MIT: Work Hard, Play Hard

In early September of 1963 my parents drove me up to Boston for the start of my undergraduacy at MIT (Massachusetts Institute of Technology). I will never forget the day. When we left New Jersey it was pouring rain with balmy temperatures in the 70s. By the time we got to the middle of Connecticut, the rain had stopped but a howling wind had set up and temperature began to fall precipitously. As we entered Cambridge the temperature had fallen to the mid-thirties and the biting wind made being outside hard to take. This remarkable contrast in weather became symbolic of my four years at MIT, which alternated between extraordinarily hard work and periods of great fun.

My first introductions to other students from MIT had come the preceding summer. During the day I was working as a counsellor in a day camp not far from Teaneck, a job that I found quite unappealing as one of my charges was a dreadful brat. But that job left me free most evenings, and I began to get calls and visits from various MIT upperclassmen, members of various fraternities who were scouting out the entering freshman class for potential new members. At the time MIT students could join fraternities at the beginning of their first year in school. While a few of these visitors were the stereotypical party-boy types, most struck me as fascinating guys (at the time MIT's undergraduate student body was 99% male) who were seriously engaged in studying science and technology.

Once on campus, we started the process of moving me into my dorm room. I had been assigned a room on the fifth floor of a pair of dreary buildings collectively known as East Campus. My parents helped me haul my trunk and other belongings up the four flights of stairs to my room. Exhausted from our efforts, we decided to rest for a few minutes before setting out to find a quick lunch. As my parents sat down on the very saggy bed and I sank into the tired-looking armchair the previous tenant of this room had left behind, clouds of dust rose from the bed and chair. I had a hard time imagining this room as "home" for the coming year. After the move-in process, my parents and I walked over to Walker Memorial, the dining hall that served the residents of East Campus. The dining hall was almost as dreary as the East Campus dorms, and the food was not much more appealing than the hall in which we sat.

After lunch, my parents left for a couple of hours to check into their hotel and get settled there. I was left to my own devices in East Campus and went up and down the hall meeting quite a few other recently arrived freshmen. Some of them seemed both nice and smart, but there was a disturbingly large number who seemed to be completely inept socially and quite obnoxious. I began to have real doubts about living in East Campus. Despite a jolly dinner at Joyce Chen's with my parents and brothers, I couldn't help but mull over my first day's experience at MIT and by the end of dinner I had pretty much decided to try to join a fraternity if at all possible. Meeting more of my new dorm room neighbors that night sealed the deal for me. East Campus was not at all to my taste.

While the next day was spent meeting my academic advisor, registering for classes, paying tuition and the like, that evening marked the start of fraternity rush week. The entire freshman class was invited to Kresge Auditorium to hear a brief presentation on the mechanics of rushing, after which we were released into a frenzy of fraternities trying to locate the promising candidates they had met during the preceding summer and freshmen trying to find the upperclassmen they had met in the hopes of being invited to stay at their fraternity house for the night. I wound up spending that night at Chi Phi, a fraternity whose house was in Boston's Back Bay neighborhood, across the Charles River from campus.

The next several days were spent visiting various fraternities for meals, visits and/or sleepovers, getting turned on by some, turned off by others, and in general seeking bids to join the ones I found most physically and socially comfortable. The first thing I noticed was that the fraternity houses were all a lot nicer than the East Campus dorms. Further they all had their own kitchens and cooks, and produced infinitely better food than Walker Memorial. More important, the fraternities had few if any of the obnoxious and nerdy types who had so turned me off in East Campus. Of all the houses that I visited, I liked Chi Phi the best, the house where I had spent the first night of rush week. They combined studiousness with a taste for good fun. I guess they liked me as well, as I was offered a bid that I accepted immediately, becoming a provisional member. One of the things I found most attractive was that the members were jointly very committed to maintaining their house, a historic structure that had once been the house of John Andrew, the son of the very wealthy governor of Massachusetts during the Civil War (Figures 13-1 and 13-2). The elegance of the house, and the knowledge that we were personally responsible for repairing any damage we might cause, tempered any "animal house" fraternity behavior.

In the coming weeks I grew to really enjoy living in our fraternity house. The guys were great, the place was beautiful, the food was terrific, and it cost no more than room and board in the awful East Campus/Walker Memorial complex. I soon learned that I had really dodged a bullet in getting out of East Campus. Part way through the first term, there were rumors that one of the most obnoxious students I had met the first day was asked to leave because he had urinated on his sleeping roommate in response to one of the usual minor roommate disagreements. Later that term, another freshman was expelled after he set his room on fire. It seems he had so annoyed the others on his corridor that they filled his room to the ceiling with wads of newspaper while he was out; his reaction upon his return was to throw a match into the wadded-up room. In the following term, there was a massive water fight between the residents of the two East Campus dorms that culminated in each side constructing giant slingshots from highly elastic laboratory tubing to hurl water balloons at the other building with enough force to break windows. These actions seemed to embody the worst of the social issues I had sensed among many of the East Campus-ites on my first day and I was glad that none of it was my problem.

After the excitement of rush week, my fellow freshmen and I settled into what would become our weekly activity cycle. All students were required to take a core curriculum of four semesters each of mathematics and physics, two semesters of chemistry, and a rigorous four-semester humanities sequence. All of these courses proceeded at a breakneck pace. The freshman calculus sequence covered in two semesters the equivalent of what was spread over four terms when I later taught at Amherst College. Physics was equally fast-paced with freshman courses in mechanics in the first term, thermodynamics in the second, electricity and magnetism in the third and optics in the fourth. The freshman science and math courses all ran on a three-week cycle, with an exam every Friday morning at nine AM. These exams rotated among the three subjects on a regular schedule. Because I had placed out of the freshman chemistry and math sequences, I jumped immediately into the required sophomore math sequence and had room in my freshman schedule to study economics in place of chemistry. I was particularly drawn to math and physics and wound up having to make a difficult choice between them when I had to declare my major.

The humanities sequence for freshmen included one year of the classical western tradition in which we read Plato, Aristotle, Aeschylus Thucydides, the Bible, Dante, Milton and a smattering of early Christian writers such as St. Augustine. The second year focused on modern European intellectual history, reading prominent authors from the Enlightenment through the nineteenth and twentieth centuries. While many of the students complained about having to read these books, I found the humanities sequence a delight and finally began to feel almost as well-educated as my parents had been when they completed high school in Italy.

This demanding academic schedule meant that we had classes or study time that ran basically from nine AM to after midnight Sunday through Friday, with breaks for lunch and dinner. To accommodate people's differing class schedules, the fraternity served breakfast between seven-thirty and eight-thirty each morning and had two seatings for lunch at noon and at one o'clock. Dinner was always a sit-down meal at six-thirty, where we were expected to wear coats and ties; this little bit of formality made dinner a great break from our otherwise very hectic schedule. Some of the dinner was held back for those with late labs or other late in the day activities. Our cook, Roosevelt, was a retired navy cook who produced great meals in his ground floor kitchen. We also had a waiter, Bob Jean, who served at the table, hauling the food up from the kitchen to the second-floor butler's pantry on a dumbwaiter. The butler's pantry was a small room just off the formal dining room where all the tableware was kept and where Bob also washed the dishes, assisted by a member who was given a discount off his room and board for doing this work.

On Saturdays during the day, the fraternity's freshmen were expected to clean the common rooms, staircases, hallways, bathrooms, butler's pantry and kitchen. Given that the house had seven common rooms, seven bathrooms, two winding staircases—to reach its basement and five above-ground floors—as well as a full commercial kitchen and pantry (after all, we were feeding forty people and their guests six days a week), this work took each of us several hours, generally put in in the morning and early afternoon. In the later afternoon all the members would tidy up their own rooms (most of the rooms were large doubles or triples) in preparation for the evening. On Friday and Saturday nights we entertained a lot of guests at dinner, and Roosevelt would go to extra lengths to serve something special.

The only day in which we had no meal service was Sunday, although Roosevelt usually left a large tray of cinnamon buns (baked on Saturday afternoon) for us to have for Sunday breakfast. We scrounged our lunches from the left-overs of the preceding Saturday night's dinner. For supper, small groups would go out to eat, or someone would make a run up to Elsie's in Harvard Square or to a local pizza joint, allowing us to take a break from our long day of studying.

Some students managed also to fit sports into this schedule, but I never could juggle my time well enough for such diversions. About the only serious exercise I got every day was the one-mile walk or bike ride across the Charles River and back between our house in Boston and our classes on the MIT campus in Cambridge.

The fraternity had several parties and other social events each year. In one spring-time party several of us went out into the country to cut branches of wild apple tree and dogwood blossoms to turn our house into a spring garden. For another spring party, the fraternity all trooped down to Duxbury beach for an early season beach day. While I was off on a walk along the beach with my date, the local constabulary showed up and kicked all of my friends and their dates off the beach for consuming beer in public. When my date and I got back to where everyone had been, we were astonished to find everyone and all of our belongings gone; we had been left behind with no shoes, no money and dressed only in bathing suits. Ever resourceful, the two of us decided to hitchhike back to Boston; that turned out to be very easy because we quickly learned that an attractive young woman in a bikini is an instant draw for rides. We ended up at the fraternity house ahead of many of our friends, even though they had had a head start.

Every year on Patriots' Day we would all troop out to cheer the runners in the Boston Marathon, a race whose finish line was a few blocks up the street from our fraternity house; one year two of my fraternity brothers waded into the marathon crowd with a boom box and a fake microphone, claiming to be TV reporters and interviewing gullible spectators who all thought they had achieved their fifteen seconds of fame.

At one winter party we covered the entire second floor of the fraternity house with straw, turning its elegant dining room and lounges into a barnyard, complete with free range rabbits and chickens. This particular party was the occasion of a fateful blind date—arranged by one of my fraternity brothers—where I became enraptured by a young Wellesley College student, Carol, who would become my future wife.

Every year on Columbus Day, when classes were always cancelled, the fraternity would hire a bus to take all of us and our dates to Mount Monadnock in New Hampshire, which we all climbed; this was the beginning of an annual rite that Carol and still honor, though sometimes we try to avoid Columbus Day because of the massive crowds.

The only exceptions to our rules for dining room dress and decorum came during reading period and final exam week. These were periods of high stress as we all crammed to learn what we had never quite understood during the regular semester in order to pass our final exams on which much of our semester grades depended. To counter this stress we relaxed the dinner dress code of tie and jacket, though I do recall one fellow coming to dinner wearing only that, and sang raunchy songs to blow off steam. At one point another fraternity brother let it be known that he was bringing a date to dinner during reading period, which only challenged the rest of us to be even more outrageously behaved.

In the inter-term between the end of the first semester and the beginning of the second, the fraternity's new members we subjected to a week of moderate hazing by the upperclassmen. This hazing took the form of being handed an overwhelming list of maintenance projects for the fraternity house, which we were expected to complete while being harangued for our general incompetence at performing them. We also endured a number of rather sophomoric pranks, such as carrying raw eggs in our shirt pockets or keeping live goldfish in the toilet of the ladies' bathroom. At the conclusion of this week, we were then welcomed into full membership at an elaborate dinner attended by the entire undergraduate membership and many alums.

In the course of the spring semester, I began to understand how the fraternity was governed. The house itself was owned by the not-for-profit Beta Foundation, which billed each member for room and board, hired the cook and waiter, and was responsible for overall financial management. The undergraduate body elected officers who loosely governed the group, organized rush week, and planned social events. The elected officers also selected three undergraduates for roles that resulted in reduced room and board fees, like the assistant who helped our house waiter, Bob Jean. Another of these roles was the steward, who was responsible for planning our meals and seeing to it that the cook kept reasonably close to the planned food budget. We could always tell when the food budget was getting out of line because the steward would order up unpopular meals such as liver that would cause a significant fraction of the student body to skip dinner, thereby getting the food budget back under control. The other role was that of house manager. This person was responsible for seeing to it that we all kept up with the day to day upkeep of the building and for organizing the list of major renovations that were dropped onto the freshmen during inter-term.

During the summer between my freshman and sophomore years I went to a German language school in Salzburg. My brothers had both studied French in Switzerland after their freshman years, but I already spoke French with considerable facility. I knew that to get a PhD I would need to pass exams in two of the three languages of French, German or Russian. I had studied three years of German in high school but thought that I needed to be fluent in that language to get past such an exam. The summer school was held in Schloss Klessheim, the summer palace of an eighteenth-century prince-bishop of Salzburg in the village of Klessheim just outside the city limits of Salzburg. The dormitories were in a converted stable, and for classrooms, they had remodeled the prince-bishop's carriage house. We were allowed into the palace itself only twice, for opening and closing exercises. On weekends we would take a bus into the city to attend various musical productions that were part of Salzburg's annual Mozart Festival.

While at the Salzburg summer school learning German, I also learned a fascinating practical lesson in the value of knowing several languages.

One of my friends bought a used motorcycle from a local man. A few days after purchase, the engine began to run rough, and then stopped altogether. He wanted to take it to a mechanic to have the problem diagnosed and took me along as I spoke German a bit better than he did, although I certainly did not understand the special argot of motorcycle mechanics. The repairman kept on insisting that the problem was a bad *kerze*. I recognized the word *kerze*, meaning *candle*, but could not for the life of me figure out what that had to do with motorcycles. Then the thought passed through my mind that in Italian the word for candle, *candela* has a second meaning: *sparkplug*. And so it turned out to be in German as well. After my friend spent the equivalent of a couple of dollars for a new sparkplug for his motorcycle, it ran like a champ.

At the end of each summer, two weeks before the start of classes, the returning undergraduates would all come back to the fraternity house. The first week was given over to another week of maintenance and renovation projects, this time executed by the entire undergraduate body, using the skills that we had been force-fed just before becoming full members. The second week was given over to rush week, during which we recruited the annual cohort of new members from among the entering freshman.

As I moved into my sophomore year I began to take upper level mathematics courses, many of which I found utterly fascinating, and simultaneously to lose my appetite for physics despite the great mathematical elegance of the laws of electromagnetism and quantum mechanics. The most interesting of these math courses were mathematical logic and algebra, which ultimately became the core of my professional interest in graduate school and beyond. Because I had placed out of half the freshman year curriculum, by my third year I found myself in classes with graduate students, which ultimately enabled me to speed up my graduate studies in mathematics. I also took several courses in music and history to fulfill the

MIT requirement that every student take eight semesters of humanities or social science during his four-year undergraduacy, including a minimum of a three-course sequence in one field. These two subjects became life-long passions.

I also placed out of the math department's requirement that one prove his competence in French, German or Russian. When I first proposed to my advisor that I should be exempted from taking French or German classes based on my high school record and my summer course in Salzburg, he reached over to his book shelf, pulled out a German math journal and asked me to translate a randomly chosen article. I struggled with this task as the topic was one about which I knew absolutely nothing. He then told me to go take a certain German course to strengthen my facility with that language. Not willing to take "no" for an answer, I then went to the instructor for the designated German course and pitched to him that I should be exempted from the math department's requirement. He pulled out the final exam he had administered the preceding year and asked me to take it on the spot. After I passed the exam with high marks, the German instructor agreed to send a note to the math department certifying me competent in that language.

If I had to point to the main observations about my undergraduate education at MIT, I would single out four items. First, my very strong high school education prepared me much better than many other entering freshmen for the rigors of an MIT education. While students from weaker schools struggled, especially in their freshman year, I found that I was at a significant advantage, having had solid academic training before coming to the Institute. Secondly, the Institute's faculty and my fellow students reinforced my reverence for academic learning, high culture and the need for a well-rounded education that included not only science but also an appreciation for the humanities and social sciences. They also schooled me in the need for hard work and high standards that are so necessary to achieve excellent results. These lessons paid off in spades when I went to graduate school and found myself one to two years ahead of most of the other graduate students in my cohort and much more broadly educated as well. Thirdly, the fraternity taught me that all this hard work could also be tempered by warm relations with great friends enjoying good times together without detriment to achieving the high goals that we all had for our educations and beyond. Most important, it led me to the love of my life, Carol with whom I have had the pleasure of sharing a long and supremely happy life.

Figure 13-1. Chi Phi house with its Marie Antoinette Balcony, 32 Hereford Street, Boston

Figure 13-2. Chi Phi house, main hall; this room and two adjacent,
equally ornate ones became a barnyard the night I met Carol

Figure 13-3. George in MIT's Great Court 1967

Figure 13.4. Carol Robinson, my fiancée
when I graduated from MIT

Chapter 14

Champaign-Urbana: Educations Within the Ivory Tower and Without

The summer after I graduated from MIT, I worked for the R&D (Research and Development) labs of the St. Regis Paper Company in West Nyack, New York. I lived with my parents in Englewood, New Jersey, for the summer as my work was just a half-hour's drive from their house. And Carol, with whom I had been engaged since earlier that year, was about a three-hour drive away in Providence, Rhode Island, where she had a summer job in a Veterans Administration office and lived at home with her parents. We commuted back and forth all summer, spending most weekends either in Providence or New Jersey. At the end of the summer I left for the University of Illinois in Champaign-Urbana (the university straddled the city line separating these two adjacent cities) to begin my graduate studies in mathematics, while Carol returned to Wellesley College for her senior year. Our plan was that she would join me the following year, entering graduate study in philosophy at the same university. It looked like it was going to be a long and lonely academic year for both of us, but the Vietnam War would change that.

Without a thought about the war, I set off in August on the long drive to central Illinois. I slept badly that night in a motel in some western Pennsylvania town outside of Pittsburgh, and planned to sleep a second night near Chicago, leaving me a final half-day's drive to Champaign-Urbana. As I crossed into Ohio, I noticed a sharp change in the countryside. The forested mountains of Pennsylvania gave way to an open gently rolling Ohio countryside with isolated stands of trees scattered among ubiquitous farm fields. As I continued west into Indiana, the stands of trees shrank both in scale and frequency and the hills appeared only occasionally. By the time I reached Illinois, there were almost no trees other than those I saw in the small towns I drove through; the countryside was nothing but corn and soybean fields as far as the eye could see, and the land was flat as the proverbial pancake. I stopped for supper in Kankakee, Illinois, and while eating a light supper, I suddenly realized that it was four states away since I had spoken to anyone other than the waitresses who took my order for sandwiches, salads and other simple meals and then my payment at the meal's end. I suddenly felt very lonely and decided that instead of getting another lousy night's sleep in some God-forsaken motel, I would push on to Champaign-Urbana after dinner.

I arrived around 10:30 PM. By that time of night, there were few people on the street, most businesses were already closed — including gas stations —and I was faced with the problem of how to find my way around a strange town without a mental picture of its layout or a map. At last, I spotted a fellow who was out walking his dog and stopped to ask him for directions to the graduate student dorm where I had rented a room for the semester. His directions were rather vague, but with a bit of trial and error I finally found the place. Most amazingly, when I got there around 11:00, I also found someone who could get me a key to my room. By the time I had moved in, it was too late to call my beloved Carol, so I called her first thing the next morning. I had not spoken with her since heading west. It

190

was a great relief to hear a familiar voice and to converse about a topic other than ordering a sandwich or asking for my bill. The call helped to relieve the acute loneliness that had hit me at supper the night before.

My room turned out to be in a three-bedroom suite with a shared bathroom. My other two suite mates showed up the next day. One was a graduate student in some engineering discipline whom I hardly ever saw, though I would hear him every weekend as he screamed insults at the coaches of whatever football games were being televised. The second fellow was a first-year law student whom I saw only occasionally.

Perhaps the reason I hardly ever saw my suite mates was because my room was so small that it gave me claustrophobia; so, I tended to be there only to sleep. It measured less than nine feet by nine feet. For storage, there was a miniscule closet and a single storage drawer under the bed in lieu of a dresser. There was a back rest permanently mounted on the wall over one side of the bed under which the bed fit to make a couch for day use. At night, I had to roll the bed out from under this backrest; in this pulled-out position only two feet remained between the bed and the small desk on the opposite side of the room. Needing more storage space for my clothes, I wound up buying a 30-inch wide, 18-inch deep dresser that could be squeezed into the space between the desk and the window, which further reduced the floor space.

I had a quarter-time teaching assignment in addition to my fellowship that covered my tuition and paid me a modest stipend, so during my first day in Champaign-Urbana, I went to the math department to get my office and teaching assignments. My office was in the basement of a building across the street from the headquarters of the math department, next door to the typesetting room for the daily campus newspaper; in those days the newspaper was still being typeset in hot lead, and with 20/20 hindsight,

I wonder what ill-effects I have suffered from this daily contact with the fumes from the lead melting operation next door to my office. As I was one of the first of the new crop of graduate students to show up that fall, I was able to grab one of the few enclosed offices, which I shared with another student. As more graduate students arrived over the course of the next several days, the other teaching assistants in my cohort wound up at desks in a large bullpen with perhaps 40 desks in it. We all got to know each other, and soon, I had a new circle of friends with whom I tended to hang out.

Because I had had a very vigorous program at MIT, I was able to place out of most of the usual first year graduate student program at the University of Illinois. I was also able to take the qualifying exams for formal entry into the PhD program during the first term, whereas all the other graduate students needed at least a full year of study to prepare for this exam. It was a grueling four-hour written exam covering the core areas of mathematics: real and complex analysis, modern algebra, and geometry and topology. When I got my grade back from this exam I was devastated to learn that I had scored only 61%. Two hours later, however, I learned that I had gotten the highest score among the thirty or so students who had sat for the exam and had passed with what were consider to be flying colors. And so I was off to the races.

During the fall semester, the federal government decided the implement a lottery to determine which men would be given all-expense-paid trips to the Vietnam War — uniforms, rifles, bullets and body bags included. The old system of student deferments was to be abolished. The lottery was held more or less coincident with my passing the qualifying exam, and I drew a woefully low number, virtually guaranteeing that I would be drafted into either the army or, even worse, the marines. I soon received a notice from my local draft board classifying me as 1-A, ready for service.

Immediately Carol I began to explore our options for what we could do. One of the first things we did was to move up the date of our wedding, which we had planned for June but to April. I consulted a lawyer on the options of emigration to Canada or draft resistance, neither of which seemed very palatable; the former guaranteed that I would never be able to return to the US and the latter promised several years in jail. Carol's father suggested that I join the National Guard, and he introduced me to a friend of his who headed the Rhode Island guard. But the general was not supportive of the idea as I was not a Rhode Island resident, and as a political appointee he wanted to save his favors for people from that state. In the end I decided to appeal my 1-A classification claiming that I was really a second-year graduate student and therefore grandfathered under the old rules. The basis of my argument was that I had passed my qualifying exams a year early because I had taken so many graduate courses at MIT. So I prepared my letter of appeal and mailed it in, not knowing what to expect.

About a month later, I was summoned in meet with my local draft board. On the appointed day, I flew back to New Jersey and met with the board after dinner. As I walked into the room, I discovered that the chairman of the draft board was my old scoutmaster from many years before. Before the proceedings got started, I had a couple of minutes of quick chitchat with him, asking after his family, especially his son Rick who had been a high school classmate of mine. "Oh Rick is fine, he replied, though he really racked up his knee playing college ball," he replied. I immediately concluded that he had gotten his son out of the military draft by claiming that he had a permanent medical disability, but all I said in reply was, "Gee, I hope he's OK." Oh yeah, he gets on OK and he is about to get married." replied my ex-scoutmaster. I think he understood that I had figured out how he had gotten his kid out of the Vietnam War but did not say anything. Instead I replied, "Well, give

Rick my very best wishes on his forthcoming marriage. Actually I am getting married as well in a couple of months."

At that point we sat down with the rest of the draft board to discuss my case. I outlined the argument that I had made in my letter of appeal and the board members asked me a few perfunctory questions about my plans for my studies. After fifteen minutes, they excused me and I thanked them for taking the time to hear my appeal. Upon returning to my parents' house for the night, I had no idea what impression I had made on them. I was, therefore, delighted and relieved to receive a letter from them a month later reinstating my student deferment. I will never know whether they really bought my argument or whether my former scoutmaster had steered them to granting the deferment--either because he wanted to be nice to me (draft boards were notorious for playing favorites) or because he realized that I had the goods on him for getting his own son a perhaps dubious medical exemption from the military draft. In any case, the board gave me back my student deferment and renewed it in each the following two years, enabling me to marry in peace and continue my graduate studies.

Carol and went ahead with our accelerated wedding date and took a quick honeymoon to the Caribbean during our spring breaks. Despite the fact that she still had a final half semester at Wellesley in which she was supposed to complete her senior thesis, she moved out to Champaign-Urbana, where I had rented a small furnished apartment about a mile from campus. This apartment had been carved out of a large 1920s house, on a main street, across the street from a supermarket and a small shopping mall. This location turned out to be pure serendipity, as we had almost no cooking utensils nor a stock of the usual kitchen staples; every time we started to cook dinner we would discover that we were missing a critical cooking implement or ingredient, and would need to make an emergency trip to the supermarket to buy the item we lacked before we could put a meal on the table. The living/dining and bed rooms had been bedrooms in the original house and were comfortable enough. The kitchen had clearly started life off as a walk-in closet and was so cramped as to make food preparation a real challenge. The bathroom was also a converted closet, about half the size of the kitchen; in fact, the bathroom was so small that the landlord had to furnish it with plumbing fixtures recovered from an elementary school, i.e., a sink that was only knee high, a micro-commode, and a half-sized shower. But as newlyweds, these inconveniences merely added to the romance of our new lives together.

There we began our joint lives as married students, with Carol writing her senior thesis and my completing the graduate courses of my first year at the University of Illinois, including a superb course in mathematical logic given by the man who ultimately became my thesis advisor, Professor William W. Boone. I must have made an impression on him, because part way through the semester he suggested that I apply for a grant to attend a conference at Varenna on Lake Como in Italy that was being held late that summer. He would be one of the speakers and Bill thought it a good idea that I begin to develop a network among academic logicians.

At the end of term, an apartment opened up in the married student's complex, which we eagerly took. While the buildings were fairly spartan with their cement block walls, they at least had functional galley kitchens and normal sized bathrooms. Also their furnishings did not have the tired look and feel of those in our first apartment where the furnishings had probably been recouped from a second- (or third-) hand store.

Right after moving, Carol and I returned east to see our parents, my brothers and their families, her sister and, most important, to enable her to turn in her thesis and graduate. We returned to Urbana for most of the summer, with my taking a couple of summer courses to help prepare for the oral exams I would be taking the following winter. While my fellowship ran for twelve months, giving us some income during the summer, Carol opted to work, since she would not be starting graduate school in philosophy until the fall. In the course of interviewing for summer jobs, she ran into some resistance because she was an outsider who had gone to "one of them fancy eastern schools." This was simply the first of many small incidents that made us feel as if we were "foreigners" as soon as we stepped off the university campus—a somewhat cultivated island set in a very provincial Midwestern sea.

In mid-August we flew to Italy for two weeks of a working vacation. Before we left, my father had given me detailed instructions on how to find the most direct routes into Switzerland; the Russians had just invaded Czechoslovakia to put down the Prague Spring rebellion and he feared that they might choose to continue on to capture more territory in Europe, perhaps rolling over Austria and into northern Italy. We spent the first week at my parents' family home before the war, *Val Salice*, which my family still owned even though my grandmother had died several years before, I now introduced Carol to my Italian relatives in a whirlwind of family visits, and then we spent a week at the mathematics conference in the Villa Monastero in Varenna on Lake Como.

At that conference I got to know several of the world's leading mathematical logicians and for the first time began to feel as though my academic career was underway. The conference proceedings ran mostly in the mornings and early afternoons, leaving us free time in the late afternoons, which Carol and I used for exploring. One afternoon, we climbed up a small mountain above the conference center to the ruins of a Lombard fortress dating back to the sixth century. On another afternoon we drove along the eastern shore of Lake Como and up to the Maloja Pass into Switzerland, in part to see the high Alps in eastern Switzerland, but also in part to test out one of the escape routes into that country that my father had suggested we follow if needed. On yet another afternoon we joined with several other conferees (including a Czech delegate who was now stranded without a country) to take a lake steamer across Lake Como to Bellagio (at the crook in the 'Y' of the lake) and then to Menaggio on the western shore. Bellagio had been the location of a villa owned by the Roman historian Pliny the Younger and was now the site of an extremely elaborate conference center at Villa Serbelloni with its spectacular views down all three arms of Lake Como. At the end of the conference, Carol and I headed back to the US and Champaign-Urbana for the start of my second and her first year as graduate students at the University of Illinois.

One of Carol's first steps when we got back was to visit her department (philosophy) to introduce herself to her faculty, sign up for courses, get her teaching assignment (she was also a teaching assistant) and get a desk in her department's graduate student offices. Her teaching assignment was to lead a recitation section and grade student papers in one of the introductory courses given by Professor F. F turned out to be a very peculiar man; he suffered from many strange fears and went out of his way to avoid situations that might bring these fears to the fore. In particular, he had never had to work with a woman before and was mentally paralyzed at the prospect. The first time that they met, Carol wanted to learn what his expectations would be of her, but he was so nervous he was hardly able to talk. After that, their working relationship was all downhill, until he was obviously avoiding having anything to do with her.

Her office mates also turned out to be a rather unusual bunch, which I will illustrate with two examples, herein called H and R respectively. H was an anti-capitalist radical who bragged about his exploits through which he was trying to destroy capitalism by stealing. He had an extra-large raincoat and fitted it with shelves which he would fill with shop-lifted books, groceries and other merchandise. When H and his wife wanted a new washing machine and dryer, he and a friend dressed up as workmen, went into a laundromat, disconnected the desired appliances, loaded them into a rented truck and drove off. In a third incident, H invited a fellow graduate student home to dinner. When H and his wife were driving their car-less guest to their apartment, they stopped at a grocery store to pick up a couple of items for dinner and broke into a big argument in front of their hapless guest over whose turn it was to steal the steak. H was also a drug dealer, which appeared to be his primary occupation.

R was unusual in a different way. He seemed ten years older than the other graduate students and his deadly serious demeanor was very different from them as well. Further, R seemed to know nothing whatsoever about philosophy and had over the preceding three years been a graduate student in three other departments in totally unrelated disciplines, each for one year. The other students in the office soon deduced that R was really a narcotics agent planted for cover in the philosophy department by some law enforcement agency at the state or federal level. Curiously R and H seemed to have been blissfully unaware of each other's "day jobs." In the following year, R moved on to yet another department.

The end of H's graduate student career came about eighteen months later when he drove to Arizona to pick up a load of drugs from two women. The women spent the night with him, took his money and then disappeared while he slept, leaving no goods in exchange. When H went to the local police in Arizona to report that he had been robbed, they simply laughed at his stupidity and arrested him on the spot. As soon as this story got back to the university, H was immediately expelled.

Carol, some of our fellow teaching assistants and I also had a number of odd experiences with our students, typically freshmen taking survey courses to fulfill some distribution requirement or other for graduation. These students generally did not exhibit the sort of work ethic and disciplined study habits that we recalled from our own undergraduate experiences at MIT and Wellesley. In my first couple of years, I generally taught a class called *Finite Math*, which was a mishmash consisting of some probability and statistics combined with a little elementary financial math such as compound interest, a few bits of decision theory, and other topics related to everyday life. After my first lecture, one of my students came in for office hours wearing a fishnet sweater. She looked me in the eye and announced softly that she would do anything for an *A*. She looked decidedly nonplussed when I suggested that perhaps she should try studying, and then asked her to leave unless she had come for help with a specific topic in that morning's lecture. The good news in her case was that studying worked and she passed the course with good marks as well as intact honor.

Carol's teaching was focused on introductory survey courses in philosophy, whose primary object was to teach students how to construct a cogent and well-reasoned argument from clearly stated assumed first principles. When she was grading the first round of student essays, one stood out from the others because it was a statement of religious faith exhibiting no logic, no reasoning and no clear statement of assumptions. Naturally, she failed the student, who then came in for office hours in a state of rage. When Carol explained to the student why she had failed his essay and what sort of essay she expected, he sullenly left the room. When the next round of papers were handed in, Carol was astounded to see that this student had written a brilliantly reasoned paper with clearly stated assumptions, tight logic and cogent arguments. At the end of the paper, the student had drawn a heavy black line, and penned below it, "The above essay was inspired by the Devil. I deny it as my own work." This student had been dragged out of Plato's cave to see the sun and then ran back inside to the shadow world that he preferred.

As we shared our stories with our fellow TAs, we heard equally appalling stories from them. One graduate student in Carol's department reported getting a totally incoherent paper with scarcely any grammatically correct sentences buried in its random babbling. Needless to say the TA failed the student's paper. The student's next assignment came in with perfectly literate English and included several footnotes in Greek and Latin. This was clearly plagiarized, and so again the student's paper received an *F*. This student's third essay came in as a passable paper, perhaps worth a *C*+, which he was given. The next day the TA received an irate phone call from the student's mother, and the following conversation ensued:

Mother: "What was wrong with Johnny's paper that it only got a *C*+?"

TA: "Johnny assumed obviously false premises and then drew false conclusions based on bad logic."

The TA then proceeded to enumerate the specific failings in the paper. At this point the conversation continued as follows:

Mother: "But doesn't the work deserve better than a *C*+?"

TA: "No ma'am. It is much weaker than other papers that got *A*s and *B*s."

Mother: "But that can't be! I worked so hard for a full ten hours to write this paper for Johnny. He's my baby. I just had to keep him from failing."

TA: "Well ma'am, when you get to heaven maybe all your *C* grades will become *A*+s."

The final story in this vein that I will include was one in which a student was taking a class that his sister had taken two years before, though with a different instructor. His sister had turned in an $A+$ final paper in the class, so he decided to retype it and hand it in as his own work. Two days later the instructor called the student in to his office, and accused him of plagiarism. The student, who could not imagine that his instructor had seen his sister's paper, denied the charge. Then the instructor proceeded to pull a book off the shelf above his desk and to open it to the page from which the paper had been copied verbatim. The student had been caught handing in a paper that his sister had plagiarized and she had gotten away with it.

Returning to our own studies, Carol and I spent most of my second year (and her first) at the University of Illinois preparing for major exams. She took heavy duty courses in the major branches of philosophy, which included deep dives into the work of the major Greek and European Enlightenment philosophers. On the side, she began to prepare for her qualifying exams, which she passed with solid marks at the end of her first year.

In parallel, I took an in-depth program that focused on several areas of mathematical logic, the field in which I hoped to specialize. In addition, I took a couple of classes in other branches of mathematics that I would need to understand in depth to pass my orals, which were scheduled for the first week of the spring semester. Passing these oral exams was the gateway to beginning work on a doctoral thesis. They included one exam in a student's area of specialization plus four others designed to ensure that the student had a broad and deep knowledge of all the major areas of mathematics. To be allowed to begin thesis work, the student first had to pass the exam in his area of specialization. In the event that a student failed one of the other four exams, he could begin thesis work, but would need to retake and pass the remaining exam the following semester. At the end of January, I stood (literally, as I had to solve the problems posed to me on the chalk board) for my orals, passing four of the five exams. Thus, during the spring term I began to search for a suitable thesis topic, while at the same time devoting about 20% of my time to prepping to retake the fifth exam at the end of the term. Mercifully I passed this fifth exam on the second taking and was rewarded with a much quieter office, which I shared with two other thesis students.

During this period Carol and I fell into a very regular routine. After an early breakfast we would both bicycle to campus. Our apartment was about a mile and a half from the central quad, where each of us had offices. We would take the free bus only if it was raining or exceptionally cold. Once on campus, our days were spent attending classes, studying, teaching or preparing our lectures for the classes we taught. At midday we shared a sack lunch under the trees in the main quad, weather permitting, or otherwise in the student union. We each got back to our apartment around six in the evening, prepared supper, ate and cleaned up by seven thirty. And then, we studied until midnight or so. The main exception to this schedule came on Saturdays, when we spent the daytime attending to the mundane business of life, such as shopping, cleaning the apartment and doing our laundry, and the evening going out or socializing with friends. This routinized life meant that we could live very comfortably on $110 a month to cover rent. Another $25 per week covered routine expenses for groceries, gasoline, laundry and the like. My impression was that many of our fellow graduate students were much less devoted to their studies than we were, and judging from their constant complaints about money, also much less frugal.

Our time in Champaign-Urbana coincided with the tumultuous campus turbulences associated with violent opposition to the Vietnam War, the increasingly confrontational civil rights movement, and an emerging women's rights and environmental consciousness. These movements independently and in combination resulted in almost daily campus demonstrations that were increasingly nasty, often threatening to turn violent. Once, when we were attending a lunch time anti-war demonstration in front of the student union, I noticed several grey-suited, grey-necktied, grey-faced middle-aged men hanging out of upper story windows taking pictures of the crowd with cameras with extra-long lenses. These guys were clearly FBI agents "taking names". On several occasions, the National Guard was called out, fanning out across the campus in full battle dress with automatic weapons, armored cars and tanks to break up peace and/or civil rights marches.

On one occasion a confrontation occurred between environmentalists and the campus police when students tried to take down the American flag and replace it with an Earth Day banner. The crowd of students was nose to nose with a line of police who were champing at the bit for an opportunity to break a few heads. Fortunate cooler heads prevailed and the flag pole was soon sporting both banners.

Another time, as an anti-war demonstration passed a McDonald's shop, the students threatened to set fire to it unless the owner took down the American flag. The owner panicked because a requirement of his franchise agreement was that he fly an oversized American flag at all times; if he took down the flag he could lose his business, and if he did not, his shop might be burnt to the ground. He put in a frantic call to the McDonald's head office in Chicago asking for advice. The response from the senior vice-president with whom he spoke showed Solomon-like wisdom. The SVP suggested that shop owner hold off the students for half an hour to give the SVP time to dispatch a truckload of hamburger buns that the shop owner should make sure would back into the flagpole, knocking it down. Then the students would be satisfied because the flag was down and the shop owner could tell corporate headquarters the flag was down only because of an unfortunate accident.

Sometimes the different political movements threatened to go to war with each other. At one point a crowd of several thousand students staging an anti-war march came near another equal-sized march of members of the local black community protesting the police killing of an unarmed black teenager near campus. There was a lot of name-calling and more than a little pushing and shoving between the two groups as each accused the other of insensitivity to what it believed was the more important issue.

I will never forget the time I had gone to the bursar's office to cash a check. I noticed that the campus policeman standing guard was wearing a large can of pepper spray on his belt. When the policeman observed my interest in the new weapon that he was carrying, he grabbed his billy club and nastily snarled, "Whaddya staring at?" I meekly replied "Sir, isn't that can on your belt a new weapon for you guys?" To which he snarled even more nastily "That's a bug bomb to get rid of stinkin' vermin like you!" At that point he threatened me with his billy club, and I dashed out of the building, ducking into the cafeteria crowd in the nearby Student Union.

My office at this time was located on the second floor of a building whose ground floor housed the campus police department. I became paranoid that the students would burn down the building and with it all my thesis notes and partial results. I took to xeroxing my work at the end of every day and keeping a second copy at home, where it was presumably safer than above the campus police office.

Most of the Champaign-Urbana locals were much more conservative politically than the university community. This different slant often became visible at community events. One Fourth of July Carol and I decided to attend the annual fireworks that were staged in the university's football stadium. Before the fireworks, a local dignitary, a colonel at the Air Force base just outside of town got up to give a speech. In his speech he started by denouncing the war protesters and civil rights demonstrators, questioning their patriotism and their right to live in America. Immediately, the students began to boo him and make catcalls, trying to drown him out. Then the townsfolk began to scream at the students, making threats and trying to drown them out. The ugly scene threatened to turn violent, when some bright soul had the idea to start the fireworks show a bit earlier than planned to divert everyone from what felt like an incipient riot. We never went to another fireworks show during our tenure as graduate students.

Despite living in Champaign-Urbana for several years, Carol and I never felt at home there. Any time we wandered off campus, we felt the extreme provincialism of the place. The town's location in downstate Illinois was firmly in the Bible Belt. I once calculated that there was a church for every hundred or so people, and most of these were of the extreme evangelical fringe of the Protestant majority. On more than one occasion we heard anti-Catholic comments directed our way, because people assumed that with an Italian surname we must be Catholics. There was also an 800-line that one could ring up to hear anti-Semitic messages, mostly directed at the state's Jewish governor, Samuel Shapiro.

At one point, a professor in the math department, Hiram Paley, was running for mayor of Urbana. The hot issue of the day was whether or not restaurants should serve liquor by the drink on Sunday. Whenever the town council held hearings a Bible toting crowd would appear to argue that the town should not encourage sinful behavior. Paley favored the proposal because he recognized that the town needed the tax revenue to support its basic services such as police, fire and schools. One evening, he received a phone call at home that ran as follows:

> Caller: "How can you support liquor by the drink on Sunday? The men are all out carousing the other six days, and they shouldn't be allowed to do it on the Lord's day. No proper Christian folk could support such a measure!"

> Paley: "As far as I know, it's not against Catholic doctrine to have a drink on Sunday."

> Caller: "Well, we all know they're not Christians!"

Paley was careful not to tell the caller that he was Jewish. Amazingly, he was elected despite the prevalence of such attitudes among the voters; there were enough academic families in Urbana to tip the balance in the election.

Despite all the turmoil caused by fractious politics in favor of or against the Vietnam War, civil rights for blacks, and equality for women — as well as the raw town/gown friction — Carol and I managed to make good progress on our studies. By the end of my second and her first year at the University of Illinois, I had passed my orals and Carol and passed her qualifying exams. During the spring semester of my second year I developed a warm relationship with Professor Boone – *Bill* to me now – as I began my thesis research on a complex of logical problems in combinatorial group theory. As brilliant as Bill was at mathematics, he was the classic absent-minded professor. Once when he and I went out to lunch in a local diner, he ordered a tuna fish sandwich; when the waitress brought it out, he insisted that he had ordered chicken salad. Clearly he had mixed up the chicken of the sea with the chicken of the land. On several occasions, when he was travelling in Europe, he would get his time zones backwards and call me up in the middle of the night to ask some question or another about my thesis work. Perhaps the most characteristic story about his absent-mindedness happened one day when his secretary of several years' standing waddled, very pregnant, into his office to tell him that she was going to stop working for a while. "Oh, Mrs. Stevenson," Bill said addressing her very formally as he always did, "Are you getting married?" Bill was totally oblivious of the facts that (1) she already was married and (2) she was eight and a half months pregnant.

After my second year, Bill organized a three-week conference at the University of California at Irvine for the time between the end of the summer session at the University of Illinois and the start of the fall semester. I was invited along as part of my doctoral training. Carol and I opted to drive to Irvine, making stops at several national parks on the way out and back. These stops were our first introduction to the wild beauty of the western national parks, and convinced us to visit many more of these parks over the following many years.

Bill's Irvine conference was very productive but also peculiar in some respects. UC Irvine had only recently been founded, and the campus had only a few buildings in the middle of what was still the Irvine Ranch with its rolling pasture land and thousands of head of beef cattle. The only people on campus at the time other than Bill's mathematical colleagues were the San Diego Chargers — the football team was doing its summer training camp there. Unsurprisingly, it was not hard to tell who belonged to which group, even from quite a distance.

Bill's early life had been very difficult and from that life he had learned the value of hard work and dogged determination. His father had died when he was a teenager in the midst of the Great Depression, six weeks before

the passage of the Social Security Act with its benefits for widows and or-
phans. Bill had to drop out of high school to work in a machine shop in
Cincinnati in order to support his family. It was hard, dirty work, but somehow he managed to earn a high school diploma while working full time,
and then go on to college with a combination of scholarships and part-time
work, ultimately getting into Princeton's graduate mathematics program.
There he wrote a thesis under the guidance of the great Alonzo Church,
whose seminal work in logic and computability theory laid the groundwork
in both the foundations of mathematics and what is now called computer
science. Church's theorem proved that there could be no mechanical system
for deciding the provability or non-provability of a given logical statement
in a mathematical system strong enough to enable arithmetic. Church had
earlier directed the thesis work of Alan Turing in which Turing develop a
theoretical model of primitive computing machines (since known as Turing
machines), and showed that the question of whether or not a given machine
would ever stop was equivalent to Church's theorem. Bill's doctoral thesis
demonstrated that the word problem for finitely presented groups was logi-
cally unsolvable. His argument was a very complex combinatorial proof in
which he doggedly demonstrated by brute force that every Turing machine
could be simulated by a finitely presented group whose word problem was
equivalent to the halting problem for the corresponding Turing machine.
Then he concluded that since the halting problem for Turing machines was
unsolvable, so also must the word problem for finitely presented groups be
unsolvable. Bill's example reinforced in me my lesson at MIT on the importance of dogged hard work to achieve success.

Towards the end of my second year as a graduate student ominous signs
began to show up that the academic job market for PhD mathematicians
was beginning to dry up. Historically the better mathematics graduate
students from the University of Illinois had found jobs at the better state
universities around the country. That year, only one or two students got

such a job, and a number of strong students had been forced to take jobs at bush league institutions in the middle of nowhere. The body of doctoral students was sufficiently upset that the department head called us all together to assure us that this must have been an aberrant year and that all would be back to normal the following year. Bill's other student, who had finished that year, had done well, winning a fellowship to Oxford, so I was not too worried. I figured that Bill was highly respected and had connections in many important universities. Somehow, all would work out. The following year, my third as a graduate student, the job seeking results of the department's doctoral students were noticeably worse, and this time the department head had to acknowledge that the times were changing. Nonetheless, he assured us that we would all find jobs somewhere, even if not at the most prestigious universities. Bill's student who had gone for a post-doc at Oxford had won a second post-doc at the Institute for Advanced Study and was being actively recruited for a junior faculty post at Princeton. I figured that things would work out OK for me as well.

The following fall I began to gear up a job search as I expected to receive my degree at the end of my fourth year at the university. Carol was about to take her orals and begin work on a thesis. Our theory was that she could complete her thesis remotely using the facilities of whatever university I ended up at. Bill urged me to apply for several prestigious post-docs on the theory that they would enable me to build up a body of research and publications. This work would stand me in good stead in applying for a permanent academic position at a serious university one or two years down the road.

Around Thanksgiving I was awarded a NATO fellowship, allowing me to spend a year at Oxford's Mathematical Institute. Carol and I were thrilled at the opportunity and looked forward to spending a year there.

Such a prospect would benefit the academic careers of both of us, as Oxford was also the center of a renowned school of academic philosophers. It looked like we were both on our way to satisfying academic careers.

Two days after receiving my post-doc, I suddenly heard from my military draft board. The local board sent me a letter revoking my student deferment and classifying me 1-A, ready for service. With that short note they put in jeopardy the careers that both Carol and I had been so looking forward to. A two-year hiatus in my academic work at this juncture would put an end to any hopes of landing a position at a major university.

About a month after the initial letter revoking my deferment, the draft board sent me a second letter summoning me for a pre-induction physical exam. These guys seemed to be really serious about sending me to Vietnam. They wanted to verify that I was of sound enough mind and body to be trained to kill. The board's letter directed me to report to some place in New Jersey. I wrote back that I now lived in Illinois and it would be a hardship to show up in New Jersey for a physical exam. I also sent them a long letter asking that they reinstate my student deferment for six months until I completed my doctoral studies, reminding them of all the reasons that I had cited in my discussions with them three years previously. About a month later, I received another letter commanding me to appear for a pre-induction physical at an examination center in Chicago.

On the appointed day for the physical exam, I (along with about twenty-five other unfortunates) showed up at the Champaign bus station at the appointed hour of five AM, two hours before dawn in the dead of winter, to board the Army's bus which was supposed to pick us up and take us to Chicago. In the long-standing military tradition of hurry up and wait, we were left standing outside in the freezing cold for more than an hour until the bus showed up. We then all shuffled onto the bus for the three-hour ride to Chicago. Hardly anyone spoke during the entire time on the bus.

When the bus got to Chicago, we were driven to a massive four-story warehouse on the city's rough south side. Some gruff sergeant then ordered us off the bus and into the building, where we met hundreds of other men all there for the same purpose. As we entered, we each were issued an ID card on a lanyard which we were supposed to wear all day.

This was my first introduction to mass production medicine in which we recruits were the raw materials for this vast factory. The process worked like this:

1. The recruits were divided into batches of forty for processing.

2. Each successive batch was then called up and sent into a locker room, where we were commanded to strip down to our undershorts and lock the rest of clothes in an empty locker. We then spent the rest of the day being sent around this frigid building wearing nothing but undershorts and the lanyards with our ID tags.

3. After the locker room strip-down, a batch would be routed to the first production station, where each member in the batch would be weighed and measured. In a pattern repeated at most of the work stations, there were two soldiers working this phase of production. The first, a military doctor or nurse would take the measurements and call out the readings to the second, a scribe, who would write them down. The batch was then moved into an empty room and told to wait until the next work station was ready to receive it.

4. At the second work station, a nurse verified that we were all alive by checking that we were breathing and had hearts and pulses, facts that she called out to the scribe who was following her taking notes. (This was a very important test; after all, if we were dead, we could not fight very effectively.) Upon completion of this phase of production, the batch then had to wait for the next workstation to be ready to receive it.

5. Each batch was then ushered on to each successive work station where it was examined to make sure that each member had the requisite numbers of arms, legs, hands, feet, fingers, and toes, could see and hear (so we would be able find the enemy?), had a sufficient number of teeth (To bite the enemy?), was able to urinate (Were we supposed to pee on the enemy?), and so on. And after each production station, the batch had to wait for the next work station to be ready to receive it.

6. The last production station was organized slightly differently from the others. Unlike the more conventional stations, in this one the doctor had two assistants. The first flunky carried the usual clip board to write down the doctor's findings, and the other bore a box full of rubber gloves and a large plastic trash bag. The recruits in the batch were then ordered to line up, drop their shorts and bend over. (Were we supposed to frighten the enemy troops by mooning at them?) The doctor then went down the line, successively taking a rubber glove from the flunky to his left, administering a rectal exam to the hapless recruit, then dropping the used glove into the trash bag, and calling out his findings to the flunky to his right. He would then move on to the next recruit in line, repeating the same sequence of steps forty times. The inventor of the assembly line, Henry Ford, would have been proud of the design of this process.

7. After the last work station, the entire batch was pronounced fit for military service and sent back to the locker room to get dressed. From the locker room the batch was dismissed to return to the buses to take the various individuals back to where they had come from. This had taken all day, and I did not get back to the Champaign bus terminal until about eight PM.

After experiencing this snippet of military life, I was all the more determined to avoid the draft at all cost. About a month after my pre-induction physical I received two letters from my draft board. The first certified that I was physically fit to serve. The second letter rejected my request to reinstate my student deferment and indicated that I had thirty days in which to appeal the board's decision.

It was now the end of February and I had just over six months to my twenty-sixth birthday when I would be past the age at which I could be drafted. Stretching the appeals process out that long was a long shot but I had to try. It would take every bit of cleverness to slow the bureaucratic processes of the military draft system to a crawl. Precisely on the thirtieth day I mailed a registered letter to the appeals board asking it to reinstate my student deferment. It took the appeal's board about two months to send me a letter rejecting my appeal. It was now the end of May. I had to hold out for another one hundred three days. I then filed a new letter with my draft board indicating that I has morally opposed to killing people. The legal rules required them to suspend the process of drafting me until they had taken the time to consider this new objection to my being drafted into the army. In parallel with this process, I held back my thesis so that instead of graduating in June, I would graduate at the end of August, in the hopes that this delay might buy me some time with the draft board.

At this point luck entered into the picture. The law governing the military draft was due to expire on June thirtieth. Congress was busily working on an updated version of this law with the intent to have the new law in place before the old one expired. However, the press of other business before Congress caused delays in the passage of the new law. The old draft law expired at the end of June, forcing the suspension of all activities of the military draft system before my local board had considered my new request to avoid military service. All through the month of July, Carol and I tensely waited as the new draft bill moved through the process of being enacted into law. For whatever reason, these steps happened very slowly and the law had still not passed when Congress recessed for a six-week summer vacation on the last day in July. There would be no draft law in place until after my twenty-sixth birthday.

On the first of August I handed in my thesis, we bought plane tickets for England, and Carol and I began to pack up our books and clothes for shipment overseas. On the second of August, we went to the infirmary to get the certificates of good health which UK government required of all prospective long-term residents. While she was filling out the forms, the nurse who had probably never been outside the confines of Champaign County gave us important health advice for living in England, "Whatever you do, don't drink the water over there." In response, I asked, "What are we supposed to do, drink beer all day for an entire year?" In any case, we were getting out of provincial Champaign-Urbana and my academic career was back on track with no side visits to Vietnam.

Chapter 15

An Education about the Socialist Paradise

My student days coincided with the upheavals of the Vietnam War, with its attendant student-led demonstrations opposing American involvement. My politics in those days were well-left-of center, fueled by a combination of my opposition to the war and the general appeal of socialist promises of a fairer shake for the downtrodden. Socialists promised the less fortunate more freedom and a greater degree of social and economic equality with the rest of society. Shortly after Carol and I arrived in Oxford for my post-doc at the Mathematical Institute, we travelled to the other side of the Iron Curtain to Bucharest, Romania, to attend an academic conference on mathematical logic and the philosophy of science. Now we would have an opportunity to see for ourselves how well the socialist countries were delivering on these promises.

We flew from London to Vienna to begin our trip, and transferred directly to the Orient Express for our Iron Curtain adventure. On the way out of Austria, we shared a train compartment with a very elegantly dressed and coifed Viennese woman who I guessed was in her fifties. I struck up a conversation with her in German and learned that she was on her way to Budapest to get a new set of false teeth, "where they do much better work at half the price that I would have to pay in Vienna." This story struck both of us as very dubious. When *Frau Dentures*, as I subsequently named her, stepped out to go to the toilet, Carol and I began to speculate that perhaps she was going one way with plastic teeth and the other with gold, or maybe she was a spy bringing western secrets to the KGB agents in Budapest, or perhaps she was planning to smuggle Hungarian or Russian secrets back out to the CIA in Vienna. We never did decide what her game was, but it surely was not dental work.

When the train got to the Hungarian border, it stopped briefly on the Austrian side, where the border officials checked everyone's passports and waved us on. Then the train moved through the gate making the border and stopped again for the Hungarians to do their bit. The border guards came through the train, suspiciously quizzed every passenger on his residency, profession, and reason for his entry into Hungary, meticulously inspected everyone's luggage, and took away all our passports and travel documents. Then they made us all get out and stand on the platform for more than an hour, leaving our luggage on the train while they disassembled all the seats, looked inside every storage closet, opened every utility panel and unscrewed every lightbulb (really!) to look for smuggled goods and/or subversive documents. Presumably they also rifled through everyone's luggage a second time while we were outside. Eventually, they let us re-board the train, returned all of our documents and let the train proceed on its way.

When the train stopped in Budapest around supper time, Frau Dentures got off and her place was taken by a well-dressed Romanian gentleman carrying a large tote bag full of small packages in addition to his suitcase. As the train pulled out of the station, Carol and I started up a conversation with him. Like most educated Romanians of the time, he spoke excellent French. He turned out to be the secretary-general of the Romanian National Volleyball Federation. While the job sounded pretty minor league to us, it allowed him to travel freely to the West to arrange what were deemed to be politically important volley ball matches between the Romanian national team and the national teams of various countries in Western Europe. His travel privileges also allowed him to buy western luxury goods to bring home. We soon learned that his tote bag was filled with such items as French wines, cognac, Scotch whiskey, tinned pâté de foie, fine cheeses, and Paris fashions for his wife. We had brought along some bread, cheese and fruit for our supper that we wound up sharing with *M. Volley-Ball* (as I subsequently dubbed him) while he contributed a bottle of wine and a tin of pâté to our shared dinner.

Late that night, after we had fallen asleep, the train arrived at the Romanian border, where we were subjected twice to the drill that we had experienced upon our entry into Hungary. First the Hungarian border guards inspected everyone and everything, and then the whole process was repeated by the Romanians on the suspicion that someone might be trying to smuggle subversive materials or decadent capitalist commodities such as decent wine or brandy from Communist Hungary to Communist Romania—unlikely as that was. During the night the train made stops at several Romanian towns. I was struck by the size of the crowds on the station platforms, even at the wee hours of the morning. When we arrived in Bucharest at about ten AM, we alit from the train with M. Volley-Ball, who introduced us briefly to his wife as she had come to the station to meet him; she was very fashionably dressed in the latest Paris couture, which contrasted sharply with the generally drab attire of everyone else in the station crowd. Clearly his political rank brought important privileges—so much for socialist equality! We then bid each other adieu and went our separate ways.

At the station, we found a table set up to greet the conference attendees. The people at the table gathered up about a dozen of us, and then loaded us and a "guide" from the Ministry of Tourism into a special bus to take us to our hotels. At each hotel several people would get off, while the bus waited to make sure that they had checked in before moving on. When we got to our hotel, Carol and I went in to register, only to discover that there had been a bureaucratic screw-up; the Ministry of Tourism had not authorized the hotel to put us up. The "guide" then explained that we would need to go to the Ministry to sort things out. He instructed the bus driver to take us and another conference attendee with the same problem, a Scottish graduate student in philosophy of science named Duncan.

During the bus ride to the Ministry I madly paged through the Romanian language phrase book we had taken with us, hoping to find the appropriate words to explain our problem to the government functionaries at the Ministry of Tourism. I discovered to my horror that the book mostly contained dialogs for dealing with assorted disasters, such as how to say to the dentist "You have pulled the wrong tooth!" or to the hairdresser "Help! You dyed my hair the wrong color!" or to the dry cleaner "You have ruined my favorite suit!" Unfortunately, the book did not offer any phrases to address bureaucratic blunders.

When we arrived at the Ministry, we were ushered into large room where numerous clerks sat at desks dealing with other tourists who had found themselves in various difficulties. After waiting for what seemed like a couple of hours, we were called up to one of the desks where we patiently explained our problem to the clerk in a mixture of English and French; he seemed to understand neither language particularly well, but that was better than trying to communicate in Romanian, which we did not understand at all. After we explained our problem, he disappeared into a back room, reappearing about fifteen minutes later with an inch-thick file—about us!

He proceeded to peruse our file for about another fifteen minutes. We could not imagine what was in that file and suspected that it was mostly filled with blank paper and that its primary purpose was to intimidate us. Ultimately the functionary explained that the conference attendees had filled all of available hotel rooms in the city and that we would need to stay with a family that was renting out a couple of rooms in its apartment to foreign visitors. He then made a big show of arranging the stay and handed us some official looking papers for us to give to our hosts, authorizing them to put us up. Our "guide" then ushered us back outside, where our bus was still waiting for us, and we were taken to the apartment building where we were to be put up. Interestingly, Duncan was ordered to stay in the other rental room in the same apartment.

The building where we were being put up looked quite shabby, as did most of central Bucharest. It probably had not gotten much maintenance work since before the war. It was built around a central courtyard which we noted was now being used to raise chickens. After passing the porter's lodge (and no doubt having our visit noted and reported to the police), the three of us climbed the two flights of stairs to our designated apartment. We were let in by a middle-aged woman, evidently the householder, and shown to our rooms. When Duncan asked about the bath, we were informed in halting French that hot water was available only for two hours in the morning because of the limited supply of firewood for the central boiler. She informed us that we could bathe only on alternate mornings as her family needed to bathe as well as wash dishes and clothes on the other days. So much for the socialist workers' paradise.

It being lunch time, we suggested to Duncan that the three of us go to the center of town to find a restaurant. We walked some distance before coming to what our guidebook had described as the principal thoroughfare of the best part of town. There we found a restaurant that the book recommended as "superior". A tuxedoed major domo showed us to a table, where we then sat for ages while trying without success to get the attention of a waiter. When at last a waiter came by with menus, we asked for glasses of water which he produced after another interminable wait. Two of the three glasses had clear smudges of lipstick on them from previous patrons, an obvious symptom of the lack of fuel for heating the dishwashing water. The waiter seemed quite put out with us, when we asked that he replace the glasses with clean ones. We next started to order only to learn that most of the items on the menu were not available. We suspected that this was a symptom of food shortages, which would also explain the chickens in the courtyard of our apartment building. About an hour after we arrived at the restaurant, we ordered our lunches and a round of beer in the hopes that the alcohol in the beer would disinfect the glasses in which it was served and the food with which it would mix in our stomachs. Shortly after the food arrived, a plate of tough non-descript meat and some boiled potatoes and green beans, a man approached our table with a mop and a bucket of filthy, foul smelling water to wash the floor beneath our feet. It seemed that the foul smell came from some disinfectant that had been added to the water in the bucket to improve its rather dubious cleaning ability, but its primary effect was to so nauseate us that we could hardly eat our meals. It would have been nice to chalk up this misadventure to a single badly managed restaurant, but our experience during the rest of the conference confirmed that this restaurant was no worse than the several others that our guidebook recommended. Such was the promised socialist utopia.

After lunch, the three of us walked to the conference center to present our credentials and pick up our programs and ID badges. Carol and I were amused to see a huge silver bowl filled with Israeli oranges on the table in the entry hall. The oranges were for sale but were priced at several dollars apiece to guarantee that no one would buy them. At the time Romania was trying to prove its independence from the USSR to curry favor with the US by following a "deviant" foreign policy. This deviance was manifested by their slightly cozying up to Israel at time when the Soviet Russians were conducting an anti-Semitic campaign and vilifying Israel to win favor with Israel's Arab enemies, notably Syria and Egypt. The bowl of Israeli oranges was meant to be a symbolic stick in the eye to the Soviet delegation to the conference. The high price on the oranges was to make sure that none were sold, so that they would remain on view for the entire conference.

When Carol and I registered at the conference we were given tickets to the opening reception to be held that evening. The highlight of this reception from the point of view of the conference organizers was that we would all have an opportunity to shake hands with Nicolae Ceauşescu, the Communist dictator of Romania. That evening, all the delegates came to a heroic-scaled, though rather tastelessly designed, building whose interior was more gaudy than fancy, for the grand reception. At the entrance was a group of burly guards with lists of the invitees, checking each off as they entered. One couple was turned away because they had brought a baby in a backpack, and the baby had not been invited. As Carol and I were checked in I noticed that next to each guest's name was the price of his hotel room; based on this price the guest would then be escorted to a section of the hall with fancier or less fancy refreshments. Because Carol and I were staying with a family, our hotel bill was minimal, and we were put in a corner that only served crudités and bits of tasteless cheese. When I tried to sneak over to the caviar table, I was quickly apprehended by a "hostess" and escorted back to my corner. At the appropriate time, the group in our corner was lined up to shake hands with Ceauşescu; that was the only time in our lives that Carol and I knowingly shook hands with a murderer. Such was the socialist equality of Romania.

The conference itself was quite dull. Many of the sessions consisted of dogmatic political diatribes on the Marxist-Leninist approach to the philosophy of science. The mathematical sessions were only slightly less boring. One afternoon, Carol and I decided to play hooky and go see the sights of Bucharest such as they were. Our first stop was the national cathedral, a smallish but attractive Byzantine style church. Inside we attached ourselves to a tour group led by an Italian-speaking guide. In addition to pointing out various artistic and architectural features of the church, the guide explained to the tourists from Rome some of the ritual differences between the Eastern Orthodox and Roman Catholic churches. One such explanation went as follows:

Tourist Woman: "Where are the confessional booths?"

Romanian Guide: "Unlike in the Roman Church where you tell your sins to the priest in private, in our church, you stand up in front of the whole congregation to confess your sins."

Tourist Woman: "[Gasp] All your sins? In front of everyone?"

Romanian Guide: "Just like in your church, there are the sins you tell the priest and the ones you don't."

After the cathedral, we decided to go to the National Museum. Unfortunately, the only map we had was a minute sketch in our guidebook that was only slightly better than useless. I had tried to buy a proper street map of the city, but there were none to be found. I suspect that the Romanian government had followed the Russian model of turning street maps, telephone directories, and other simple reference works into state secrets. At one point we turned down what our guidebook's map suggested was the shortest route to our destination. Suddenly two soldiers popped out of a doorway, pressing their AK-47s to our bellies and gesticulating to make it clear that we were in a place where we were not supposed to go. We beat a hasty retreat and then turned down another street, getting ourselves hopelessly lost. Carol and I tried to stop various passersby to ask for help, first in French, which up to that time had worked at least with better educated Romanians, and then in German which had worked once or twice before. But we struck out six times in a row. On the seventh try, I stopped two men in their late twenties, trying first French, and then German, and getting nothing but shrugged shoulders indicating that they did not understand a word of what I had asked. Out of desperation, I tried Italian; immediately the face of one of the men brightened up. It turned out that he was an opera fan and had taught himself Italian to understand his favorite operas. He and his friend then looked at our map, but they could not make out how its diagram related to the city's street plan. Instead they agreed to walk us to our intended destination. This warm friendliness totally changed our mood from the frustration that we felt with the dreary surroundings and negative experiences of the preceding several days.

The next day was our final day in Bucharest. We boarded the train that evening and went to our reserved seats. Our plan was to get off in Budapest and squeeze as much sightseeing as we could into our allowed forty-eight hours of stopover time, and then to proceed on to Vienna for a few days' vacation before returning to England.

As the train pulled out of the station, a soldier stepped into our compartment and gesticulated that he wanted my seat. I pointed to my ticket and stayed put. The soldier stepped out again and then returned with the conductor. The conductor explained to me in French that the soldier was entitled to my seat. I argued back that I had a reserved seat and was certainly not going to leave my wife to spend the night on her own in the otherwise full compartment. The conductor argued back even more vehemently and then so did I. Meanwhile, all the Romanians all stared studiously at their feet, no doubt hoping that the soldier would not notice them and decide to take their seats instead. After about fifteen minutes of arguing back and forth in French, the conductor said he would see what he could do and he disappeared with the soldier.

As the night wore on, people got out at various stops along the way. At about two AM, Carol and I were the last passengers in our compartment when the conductor suddenly came in. He shook me awake and then led me to an empty compartment. In this empty compartment he announced in French that I could now give him a gift for the favor he had done for me in protecting me from the demands of the soldier. (My father had warned me about the Turkish legacy of *baksheesh* that infected officialdom in most of the Balkan countries.) At that point I pretended to suddenly lose all understanding of French and spoke only in English with a fake Texas accent since Europeans tend to view Texans as the epitome of ignorant Americans. The conductor insisted that I needed to give him a gift, and I continued to pretend not to understand a word he said. In frustration, the conductor let me return to Carol without extracting a bribe from me. The next stop was Timisoara the capital of Romanian Transylvania. At that stop the train changed crew, and we were rid of the bribe-seeking conductor.

At this stop a woman with characteristically Hungarian (Magyar) features got on the train. (Most Hungarians are descended from the Magyars, a tribe that migrated from Central Asia to Central Europe in the ninth century). She joined us in our compartment, carrying a large mesh tote bag full of small parcels in addition to her suitcase. I struck up a conversation with her in German and learned that she was on a trip to Budapest to visit relatives who had ended up on the other side of the border in the waning days of World War II. Pointing to the mesh bag, she indicated that it was full of presents for her relatives. She got very excited when we told her that we were making a brief stopover in Budapest and she began to list sights we should be sure to see and foods we should be sure to sample. At about six AM we got to the Hungarian border, where we went through the usual drill of getting our luggage inspected and our documents taken away while we stood on the platform as the border guards semi-dismantled the train's interior looking for contraband. This time, however, there was a difference. When the Romanian border guard looked at the Hungarian woman's tote bag, he pointed to a bottle of Romanian brandy that was at the top of the bag; this bottle of cheap booze was to be his bribe for letting her through. Then on the Hungarian side of the border, the same little game was played, with the Hungarian border guard taking some other item from the top of her bag as his bribe for letting her into Hungary. Both of the crooked border guards had been totally shameless in their demands and made no effort to conceal what was going on from us. After the train got underway again, the Hungarian woman's mood was much more subdued and she turned to me and said in German, "Those were no gentlemen."

At about ten in the morning we arrived in Budapest on a brilliantly sunny day. We quickly got ourselves a hotel room. While we did not speak a word of Hungarian and could make no sense of even the simplest signs because Hungarian is a language from Central Asia unrelated to any of the Indo-European languages that we spoke, we soon discovered that older, educated Hungarians often were fluent in German as a holdover from Hungary's historical links to Austria as part of the Austro-Hungarian Empire. We quickly acquired a map of the city and set about seeing the sights.

While Hungary's Communist government strictly toed the Soviet line in foreign policy, they had allowed a modest level capitalism to operate internally. The rules were that individuals were allowed to own small businesses but could only hire family members to work in them. The result was that the streets were filled with bustling small shops and restaurants. While the buildings looked somewhat down at the heels and still bore the bullet holes from the abortive Hungarian revolt in 1956—in which the unarmed Hungarians tried to drive out the Russian troops that had occupied the country since the end of World War II—the people on the street were noticeably more prosperous than those we had encountered in Romania. They were relatively well-dressed and coifed, surely as a result of the many tailoring and hair-styling boutiques we saw, and there were many shoppers visiting the well-stocked shops along the main boulevards.

That evening Carol and I had dinner in a little hole-in-the-wall restaurant in the Fischer-Bastei district that epitomized for us Hungary's approach to family capitalism. The father was the head waiter, assisted by his son. His wife was the cook, his daughter the dishwasher, and his brother-in-law was the fiddler who serenaded us with Gypsy music. Unlike the situation in Romania, the place was spotless and the food delicious.

Unfortunately, the only misadventure of our Hungarian sojourn was at that same restaurant. Half-way through the meal I began to have stomach cramps, which were no doubt the results of the several days of eating unsanitary food in Romania. I asked the owner which way to the toilets, and he pointed to a small corridor next to the kitchen. When I got to the end of the hall, I was faced with two doors, one labelled *Ferfi* and the other *Noi*. Obviously these words meant Men and Women, but I hadn't a clue as to which was which. I was feeling more and more desperate, when suddenly the *Noi* door opened and a woman stepped out. I quickly jumped into the *Ferfi* room, barely avoiding a most embarrassing accident.

We enjoyed our brief visit to Budapest and would have willingly extended our stay. However, we feared being arrested if we overstayed our visa, and so we reluctantly left for Austria on the last train that would get us out within the allowed forty-eight hours. As we left the station, I noted to Carol that the contrast between the misery of rigidly socialist Romania and the prosperity of slightly capitalist Hungary taught us much about the hollowness of socialism's utopian promises.

During our train ride back to Vienna, Carol and I were both hit with additional urgent bouts of indigestion as reminders of our restaurant meals in Bucharest. Between episodes I looked through my English/German dictionary to learn how to describe our symptoms in German. As soon as we alit from the train, I went to the nearest pharmacy and explained our issues to the man behind the counter as best I could without being too graphic. The pharmacist produced a bottle of large dark-gray tablets which we were supposed to dissolve on our tongues once every four hours. In addition, he advised us to limit our food intake to tea without milk and dry toast. This was a bit of a let-down as we had both been looking forward to visiting some of Vienna's famous cafés with their fabulous pastries, not to mention some of the city's well-known restaurants and beer halls. Nonetheless, the cure gradually took hold and by the end of our second day in Vienna, and we almost felt normal again.

After the visit to the pharmacy, Carol and I went to the tourist office in the station and booked ourselves into a *pension* (inn) on the *Ringstrasse* – considered one of the most beautiful boulevards in the world and encircling the old historic city of Vienna. The *pension* was formed out of several formerly separate apartments on the third floor of a handsome five story building. Our room had a lovely balcony overlooking the *Ringstrasse*. After we checked in, dropped our bags, and went yet-again to the bathroom, we were able to visit some of the major museums and other tourist sites of the central city. When we went to St. Stephen's Cathedral, I suggested that we climb the bell tower for its marvelous view. Little did I know that

227

the top part of the climb entailed going outside on a rickety iron stair-case that made a full turn around the exterior of the tower before letting us back into the belfry. When I was about half way around the exposed staircase, I made the mistake of looking at the roof of the church with its dizzying array of colored tiles. I became completely disoriented and my fear of heights overwhelmed me, leaving me unable to move up or down the stairs. I stayed motionless where I was for a good half hour, before I summoned the courage to creep back down to the bottom of the exposed part of the staircase. At tea time that afternoon we went to the café at the Hotel Sacher (home of the famous *Sachertorte*). While we did stick to part of our diet, by ordering tea without milk, we allowed ourselves the indulgence of slices of *Sachertorte* and *Dobosztorte*; about an hour later we paid for our sins with urgent runs to the bathroom. Supper that night was limited to the prescribed tea and toast.

The next morning we had a tea and toast breakfast on our room's balcony. On the tea tray was a pot of jam, which bees soon found, setting up a steady stream of bees that would raid the jam pot and then return to their hives with this rich "nectar." I decided I wanted to have a bit of jam to enliven my dry toast, and soon learned how to time taking a spoonful of jam between the bee arrivals. After breakfast Carol and I took the trolley out to *Schönbrünn*, the fabulous royal palace for the Austro-Hungarian emperors. After touring the palace we had a lunch of tea and toast and spent the afternoon wandering through the palace's beautiful and very extensive gardens.

Late in the afternoon we returned to the city. We decided that we felt well enough to be able to sit through a theatrical production, so I booked tick-ets to see Strauss's very amusing opera, *Ariadne auf Naxos*. At the opera we shared a box with a 70-ish gentleman, his much younger wife and their young son. During intermission we struck up a conversation with them, first in German and then in English, as he turned out to be a Canadian of Viennese extraction. We learned that they too had been at *Schönbrünn* that afternoon. The father had taken his eleven-year-old son to the spot in the palace gardens where he had been patted on the head by the emperor Franz Josef in 1910, when he had been eleven. After the opera, Carol and I went to an underground beer hall for a light supper, beer (of course!) and a dose of the brass band *oompah* music known in Austria as *schrammelmusik*. And we had no ill effects from this supper; we had now recovered from the cursed digestive effects of Romania's socialist paradise.

The following day we rented a car to drive up the Danube valley from Vienna to Dürnstein Castle and the abbey at Melk. When I called Hertz to reserve the car, I Germanized the pronunciation of our surname because I was well aware of the continuing bad blood that many Austrians feel towards Italians over the transfer of a province in the Dolomites from Austria to Italy at the end of World War I. The man at the other end of the line refused to reserve a car for me, because he thought I had said that my name was *Sachertorte* and that I was a teenager playing a prank. When I understood his misapprehension, I was able to clear up the issue, get a car and set off with Carol for the Danube Valley.

Our first stop was Dürnstein, where Richard the Lionheart had been held for ransom on his way back to England from the fighting in the Crusades; it sits on a high hill overlooking the Danube and is sternly imposing. Our next stop was Melk Abbey, which was very much its antithesis. Melk is a beautiful baroque abbey near the river, though parts of the structure date back to the early middle ages. Its cloister has a wonderfully peaceful atmosphere. That evening we unwound from our day's drive with a light supper at an outdoor café in the Vienna Woods accompanied by the local Grinzinger wine.

And then it was time to return Oxford and work. And with this return, we brought with us our lessons about the vacuity of socialist promises and a sheaf of great stories about our misadventures. These stories were surely more interesting than any we might have had from a trip that had proceeded without mishap.

Figure 15-1. Armed soldier guarding
a public building, Bucharest, 1971

Figure 15-2. Bucharest Cathedral, 1971

Figure 15-3. Parliament, Budapest, 1971

Figure 15-4. Fischerbastei, Budapest, 1971

Figure 15-5.
Melk Abbey 1971

Figure 15-6.
Dürnstein Castle,
1971

Figure 15-7.
Schönbrunn Palace,
Vienna 1971

Chapter 16

Travel as Education

There is an old joke that goes something like this:

What is the difference between Heaven and Hell?

In Heaven, the French are the cooks, the Brits are the policemen, the Germans are the engineers, the Swiss are the organizers and the Italians are the lovers.

In Hell, the Brits are the cooks, the Germans are the policemen, the French are the engineers, the Italians are the organizers and the Swiss are the lovers.

When I first told this joke to my wife, she asked, "What's wrong with the Swiss as lovers?" to which I replied, "Imagine a country in which bank fraud is considered a crime of passion, and life is so orderly that cows do not leave poops in their pastures."

While I do not subscribe to the theory of national characters, there are strong differences in cultural norms among countries which need to be understood and respected. Without a deep understanding of these norms it is difficult to do business in these countries or to understand their politics, literature or art. Widespread ignorance of these variations in social norms is a large part of what underlies the common overseas image of us as a nation of Ugly Americans.

I believe that international travel is a key to acquiring a deep feel for these variations in cultural norms. When I say *travel*, I specifically exclude packaged tours in which you touch the local culture only slightly, and in which the tour guide presents you with a sanitized, Disney-fied version of life in that place; tour operators tend to focus on showing you the great monuments without teaching you about the historical context and culture that drove the creation of these things. Likewise, I exclude staying in some resort hotel populated only with people like yourself and that carefully insulates you from local life. Rather, I plan the trip on my own, learning in advance about the local history and culture, and mastering the basics of how to navigate our way through local society. My knowledge of several foreign languages helps, though with phrase books, I usual am able to pick up enough to deal with the basics of finding my way around, dining in restaurants, and dealing with hotels and transport services.

In the course of my life I have visited nearly two dozen countries for work or pleasure. My wife and I have made it a point to take our children on many of these trips to expose them to cultures different from their own. We wanted them to learn to operate outside their comfort zone by immersing them in foreign cultures and also to know our foreign relatives on their home turf so that they too would experience our cultural heritage directly and not merely view it as some distant historical fact to read about in books. Along the way, the boys absorbed a great deal about what cultural and behavioral norms apply in different countries and even in different parts of the US.

On our first trip to Italy when our children were four and seven years old respectively, we went out for lunch with my cousin Emanuele Levi-Montalcini in a country restaurant up the hill from our former villa, in *Val Salice*. I asked my cousin what he suggested I order for the kids; he proposed *fritto misto*—a platter of mixed fried seafood—on the theory that they could pick and choose what to eat. When the boys' platter arrived it contained an assortment of fried fish and shellfish arrayed around a whole fried frog. While the kids did not complain about the frog, I noticed that they left it untouched as they ate the remaining items. They had learned two lessons: (i) some people eat frogs and, more important, (ii) you should not make a fuss if there is something put before you that you would prefer not to eat. The latter lesson is one that too many Americans have not yet learned.

Another culinary lesson occurred one day in the French countryside. I took the boys into a butcher shop to buy some dry sausage for a picnic. When I looked into the glass cases, I realized I had a golden opportunity to teach them the words for various parts of the (animal) body and also show them how different the French attitudes were from ours about what is fit to eat. In addition to the more or less conventional cuts of meat, the glass cases held *museaux de porc* (pig snouts) and *les pieds de porc* (pig trotters), *queues de boeuf* (oxtails), *foie de veau* (calves' liver), *rognons* (kidneys), *cerveaux* (brains) and *tripe* (intestines).

The boys also learned how to deal with minor crises while travelling. We had a car accident in Italy, a fishhook injury in Scotland, and a reservation mix-up on Air France; in the latter case, we got caught in a finger pointing game between the French and Italian employees of the airline that had messed up our reservations. The gate agents in Italy and France preferred to blame the problem on each other than to take the initiative to sort out the mess and it was left to us, the poor passengers, to get them to focus on getting us to our destination instead of complaining about the incompetence of their fellow employees in another country.

These lessons paid off several times along the way. When Michael's youth orchestra went on tour to England, he got lost one night in London and managed to get help to find his way back to his hotel from an evening with friends of ours who live just outside the city in Essex. On another occasion, when Michael was a medical student, he and several fellow students were faced with a woman about to deliver a baby who spoke only Spanish at a time when the hospital's Spanish translator was off-duty. The good news was that this was the woman's fourth child, so she knew much better what to do than did a group of third year medical students. The other good news was that Michael subsequently asked me to arrange for him to go to visit our Argentine cousins in order to take a crash course in medical Spanish, a course that served him well a couple of years later when he was a surgical resident in San Diego, on the Mexican border.

When David first moved to California, he took a month's vacation to bicycle up the coast from San Jose to the Oregon border, and then down through the Cascades and northern Sierras on the way back, in order to learn about the "real" California. He has since had the pleasure of introducing some of his new friends and coworkers, and later, his wife and children to beautiful parts of that large state that are most unlike Silicon Valley, where they all live and work. I think our children have put our lessons to good use.

Over the years my work has also benefitted from my travels early in life, in school, and in adulthood with my wife and children. My multicultural background has enabled me to work cross-culturally by focusing me on the cultural differences that can make or break a business initiative. This became one of my stock services for clients over the course of my career. I am continually astounded at how culturally ignorant supposedly well-educated people are about the likely behavior of potential customers in foreign markets. Being able to play "foreigner" for them has brought enormous value to these clients. Let me illustrate with a few examples.

I was once working with an Italian publisher on translating their traditional print products into new media formats; he was expecting that such products would have universal appeal. This publisher's first such product was a beautiful, richly illustrated interactive course in art history which it had developed based on the text book that it sold to all Italian high school students for their required course in art history. After the editor showed me his new product, he turned to me and the following conversation ensured:

Editor: "We showed the first edition of this interactive course to the President of Italy and he was very impressed. Surely there is a big market for this product in the United States."

Me: "99% of Americans have no knowledge of and less interest in art history. If you showed this product to Ronald Reagan, he would be yawning within five minutes."

Editor: Disappointed silence.

Me: "In the US, this product needs to be targeted at a specialized niche market, and here is one idea for how you might reach it. Perhaps you could repackage the interactive course as a TV series for the Public Broadcasting System. The American PBS audience is relatively dense with people interested in high culture. Then you could sell DVDs of the shows to those who watch the TV series. But you will need to make sure that the narrator for the show has a British accent."

Editor: "Why British? They know nothing about art."

Me: "Americans think of the British as very cultured. A narrator with a British accent will reinforce their appreciation of your product."

Based on this simple conversation, the editor realized that he and his team totally lacked the basic market understanding necessary for success in the American market. His company then refocused its development of e-products on the Italian market, one whose behavior they understood deeply.

At another time, my colleagues and I were working with a major West Coast company with global operations. The company had developed a new interactive advertising service, which they decided should be initially rolled out and refined in France before being introduced in the US. Their idea was to release the product trial in May, monitor market performance over the summer in France, refine the product and then to release it in the US in September. My team's role was to develop the plan for the market trial in France, and then to capture immediate customer feedback in France for two rounds of quick-reaction product releases in preparation for the autumnal American release. One of our first findings was that the American development team had not listened to feedback from their French colleagues: the product needed special features required for compliance with French law governing advertising, and the Americans had cut these out in the rush to get an early release of the product. As it happened, our client's product development schedule had slipped and it would not be ready for release until mid-July. When my colleagues and I suggested that we would need to postpone the French trial until the fall because most French offices close for vacation for the entire month of August, the American product manager was furious with us. "Surely you can find some companies to try our new service." I pushed back, noting that the consumers, whose reactions to the ads were of prime interest to the advertisers, would also be on vacation. The product manager reluctantly agreed to postpone the French roll-out until September. He did not truly believe our concerns about the French vacation culture until he moved to Paris in mid-August to monitor the roll-out and discovered that he could not find a plumber to fix a leaking toilet in his apartment in the month of August. Ultimately our work in France helped our client improve the product and develop appropriate national marketing and sales approaches that led to success on a global scale.

A third example involved cross-cultural issues for Arthur D. Little, Inc. (ADL), America's first management consulting firm and my employer at the time. ADL was working with an American client with a Canadian corporate parent. They were already doing a significant business in both North America and Western Europe and they now wished to expand their business into Asia. We were engaged to gauge the receptivity for our client's services in Korea, Japan, Taiwan and Hong Kong. Our direct client was an American; his head of international services was a Belgian who claimed to know everything about doing business overseas, though our client had doubts about the Belgian's understanding of Asian markets. I assigned the field work for this project to a Korean member of my staff who was a native speaker of Korean and fully fluent in Japanese and also had a solid speaking ability in Chinese. She and I also reached out to the head of ADL's Tokyo office to help us with introductions to key companies in that country that might be sales prospects for our client's business. When she arrived in Tokyo she discovered that the junior staffer in our Tokyo office who had been assigned to assist her would not work under the direction of a female colleague, let alone with one who was Korean. She called me in desperation, and I had to pull together a three-way call with her and the head of the Tokyo office to get him to order his staffer to cooperate. Ultimately the solution was to have her work with her Japanese colleague in English so as not to have to adopt the subservient manner of speaking that Japanese women traditionally use when speaking with men. Once the Japanese staffer was on board, she proceeded to have very fruitful meetings with a number of Japanese companies, also conducted in English for the same reason (with occasional reversions to Japanese to clarify items not immediately understood in English) and then completed the rest of her work in the other three countries. When she presented her findings to our client and his team, our results turned out to strongly contradict the dubious advice that he had received from his Belgian head of international sales. This was a prime example of how real facts can drive out ill-informed opinions; acquiring those facts required getting past two sets of cultural barriers, those of ADL and also of ADL's client.

These episodes happened to us repeatedly with American and foreign clients who depended on us to translate and adjust their business models cross-culturally. They also illustrate some important personal learning that I derived from travel and why Carol and I sought to add significant doses of both foreign and domestic travel to our sons' upbringing. While such travel is costly, we viewed it as an investment in our own education and that of our children. In the course of these travels we have come to know many people, understand their history and culture, and experience some very memorable adventures (and misadventures!) that have made life truly engaging.

PART 5 ON WORK

Chapter 17

My First Jobs

Digging Out

The first work I did for pay was shoveling snow when I was in my early teens. While this may seem quaint, I include it because modern teens seem to be too precious to take on such work. Whenever we had a snow day that resulted in school being closed, my friends and I would grab our snow shovels and range up and down the nearby streets, offering our services to clear sidewalks and driveways. Of course, the first snow shoveling job was always for my parents, but that did not count, since I was expected to do this and other chores for free as my contribution to the overall household economy. As soon as the home job was done, I would team up with friend to earn some pocket money. Our approach was to ring the doorbell of any house that had not yet been shoveled out and ask whoever answered whether or not they needed us boys to clear their snow. We had a strong ally in a town ordinance that required householders to clear their sidewalks of any snow fall within twenty-four hours. Snow storms that were big enough to cause school to be cancelled were also likely to have dumped enough snow that it would be unlikely to melt within the time required by law.

Usually we let our employers set the price, which ranged from $5 to $10 (about $25-$50 in modern money) for the job, depending on how long the driveway was and two of us could complete a job in anywhere from thirty minutes to one hour. Occasionally a particularly generous house-holder would give us $15 or $20, but those were very rare. One critical lesson we had to learn was to check out the size of the job and agree upon a walk-away minimum price before ringing the doorbell. Our teacher for this lesson was an elderly widow who hired us for only two dollars; her driveway, which we had not checked out in advance, was extraordinarily long and took us nearly an hour and a half to clear. She didn't even have the good graces to offer us cookies or hot chocolate for our pains! The only redeeming element of that job was that she was old and infirm and we had done a good deed, but that did not prove to be much satisfaction for the measly pay that we earned for all that work.

Campus or Camp

In the spring of my senior year in high school, just before I had commit-ted to going to MIT, I went up there for a day to take one last look at the place before signing on the dotted line. At that time I was already eager to take my independence from home and wanted a pre-taste of the new life I would be leading starting the following fall. While I was there, I decided to look for a summer job on campus. I asked around and soon found the campus office in which faculty looking for students to work for the summer would list open opportunities. I followed up on several listings and within a couple of hours I had landed a job writing software for a professor in the department of mechanical engineering who was developing the earliest prototypes of artificial hips. I was on cloud nine. While the pay was modest, it was enough to live on for the summer and would enable me to salt away sufficient spending money for the academic year. This job was my ticket for getting out of the house, a most important goal.

When I got home that evening and announced my success, my mother went ballistic. I was the last of her children and she was not yet ready for me to leave home. She insisted that I had to stay home for the summer and I had to write a very awkward letter to the man who had hired me turning down the job offer that I had so eagerly accepted just a few hours before. The odd part of this episode was that my mother had encouraged me very strongly when I had shown an interest in computers the two preceding summers, and now she was blocking me from earning a living in the same field. In any case, I did not get to do this job.

I was then at a loss for what to do for the summer. At about the time when school let out for the summer, I noticed that a local day camp was advertising for counsellors. I figured that since I had been a camper, how hard could being a counsellor be? I drove out to the camp, met the owner, was hired and started the new job ten days later. My assignment was to lead a troop of a dozen or so seven-year-old boys with the assistance of a junior counsellor. As a free benefit, the owner offered that I could get to and from work by riding on the same camp bus as the campers. The element that bothered me the most about the job was that the pay was really lousy, about a third of what I would have earned as a programmer at MIT.

I quickly learned that I had been had by the owner. There was only one other counsellor on the bus, a rather timid junior counsellor. She and I

244

were expected to keep an unruly bunch of kids quiet and in their seats while the kids wanted anything but. In addition, the junior counsellor who was assigned to me as my assistant with my group turned out to be useless. He was supposed to spend half the day giving tennis lessons to the older children and half the day helping me with our seven-year-olds. Instead, he would sneak back to the tennis courts with attractive female counsellors for games of tennis, and who knows what else, leaving me to wrangle the kids on my own. After two weeks he was fired. With 20/20 hindsight I should have demanded a pay raise, given that my duties had been expanded, but I didn't.

As for the children ten of the twelve were pleasant kids. The other two, however, were another story. One was a whiner who would constantly come crying to me over the most idiotically trivial of issues. The other was a seven-year-old bully who quickly took to shaking down the other kids for their candy money; he especially delighted in picking on the whiner, making a bad situation even worse. For the first couple of weeks I tried to get the whiner to take some initiative in sorting out simple issues on his own, and attempted the reform the bully. The bully's response whenever I spoke to him about his behavior was to start kicking me in the shins. Finally, I had had enough of him and took the only other disciplinary action I could take: I sent him to the camp director. The camp director tried to talk with the boy, but the child's response was not only to start kicking the director but also to throw stones at him.

Ten days later, the camp had Parents' Day. I was pleased to see that the bully's mother came and resolved to find a time to have a discreet private discussion with her. She was a pleasant woman, well-spoken and with refined manners. Around lunch time, I took her aside to talk about the issues we were having with her son, enumerating his bullying, extortion, shin kicking, rock throwing, and other inappropriate behaviors. Her reaction was the classic, "What? My little Johnny? Couldn't be! At home he is such a perfect angel." Clearly I was not going to get any help from the home front.

At the four-week mark, about half the children in my group were scheduled to drop out and be replaced by new kids. I was hoping that the whiner and the bully would be among the leavers, but I had no such luck. About the only good things I can say about my experience as a camp counsellor were (1) that the season only lasted a short eight weeks and (2) that I had learned about an occupation that I should not follow.

The Laboratory

During my second year at MIT I wavered between majoring in mathematics and physics. Although I would ultimately choose math, while I was deciding (and to help me resolve the question) I opted to work for a summer in the MIT physics lab of Professor Martin Deutsch. I had had him for my first semester freshman physics course and greatly appreciated his professorial style. He was the son of Viennese psychiatrists (his mother was Freud's last student). They had immigrated to the US during the 1930s when Nazi ascendency had made life increasingly difficult for Jewish intellectuals in Vienna. He was nominated for (but did not win) a Nobel prize in 1956 for his discovery of positronium, an evanescent exotic atom (i.e., atoms that include unusual, often unstable, particles), that is similar to hydrogen. Positronium consists of an electron and a positron orbiting each other, making it the simplest combination of matter and anti-matter. Its discovery amounted to a breakthrough in understanding how anti-matter functions in the universe. In his lab, I worked as a programmer, designing and building software to automate the analysis of photographs of the tracks of subatomic particles, thereby making it possible to identify very rare physical events that would otherwise be lost in the masses of data generated by the typical high energy physics experiment.

Deutsch was a remarkable polymath who seemed to know almost everything about almost everything. I remember that at one point he was very frustrated with the limitations of our PDP-1 computer. Because our programs were too big to fit into memory, he identified several frequently repeated instruction sequences in our programs and then wired new primitive instructions into the computer's circuit boards that would execute these sequences as single instructions. With the new hard-wired instructions, we could just fit our software into the system. His remarkable breadth and depth of knowledge gave him an uncanny ability to synthesize new approaches and new ideas by pulling together disparate pieces of seeming unrelated information. In my life I have sought to emulate him and seek to vacuum up knowledge in many fields and on rare occasions have been able to emulate his remarkable synthesis ability.

The following summer I again worked in Professor Deutsch's laboratory, but this time the work was focused on building equipment for a major experiment he was planning to run that fall at the Cambridge Electron Accelerator (CEA), a lab at Harvard behind the major scientific buildings along Oxford Street. The month of June was spent assembling an array of particle detectors, some of which were meant to detect showers of particles that might represent the decay patterns of the particular subatomic particles he was seeking, while other detectors were designed to rule our spurious events that might result from such random events as the passage of cosmic rays through our equipment. Around the end of June, we began to move our equipment to CEA and to stage it for final assembly when it would be time to run the experiment.

One night there was a terrible explosion and fire at CEA caused by liquid hydrogen leaking from a bubble chamber that was part of an experiment being run at the time by another team of physicists. In this explosion one person was killed and another eight were seriously injured by falling debris and the ensuing fire. Also the building's roof and its supporting beams collapsed crushing all the devices that Deutsch's team had been assembling in anticipation of running an experiment at the end of the summer.

The next day the local Cambridge newspaper ran a horribly distorted front-page article under the headline CAMBRIDGE ATOM PLANT BLAST. The reporter made it seem as if someone had set off a nuclear weapon on the Harvard campus. It did not help that CEA was funded by the Atomic Energy Commission, the forerunner of today's Nuclear Regulatory Commission. The reporter clearly had no idea what he was talking about, but he succeeded in tripping off a panic among the local populace. The resulting public relations disaster in the Cambridge community was the first of several that I would experience in my lifetime. As I look back on this incident, it reminds me yet again of how disastrous it can be when ignorant leadership that pretends to have expertise (in this case the newspaper and its reporter, and in my Hebrew School days, the Hebrew teachers) leads an uninformed public astray.

This explosion also had an additional very personal effect. I concluded that I was not cut out to be a physicist. It took too much effort to plan and execute experiments, the desired results often did not appear, and there were too many ways in which one could suffer multi-year setbacks for totally extraneous reasons.

A Taste of Corporate Life

My first corporate job was near my family home in New Jersey in the Research and Development (R&D) labs of the St. Regis Paper Company, a company that was subsequently acquired by what is now called the International Paper Company. I worked there as a stopgap the summer between my undergraduate years at MIT and graduate school at the University of Illinois, commuting as much as possible to Providence, Rhode Island, where Carol lived with her family between her junior and senior year at Wellesley and had her own summer job. Stopgap though it was, I learned important lessons about work while at the paper company. I was put to the task of solving a seemingly basic problem at the very heart of the work of the R&D department. In simple terms, the R&D lab was charged with developing ways to improve the physical properties of the various types of paper the company produced. One of the most important properties of paper is its resistance to tearing when it is dry or, even more important, when it is wet.

The problem was that the way the lab prepared samples of paper to test differed in a critical way from how paper was produced in a mill. In the lab, paper samples were produced taking a metal cylinder with a wire mesh at the bottom and pouring a watery slurry of wood pulp in through it. The mesh would trap the fibers and let the water pass through, creating a disk of wet paper which could then be dried and tested for its physical properties. In a paper mill, the pulp slurry would be sprayed onto a fast-moving mesh, creating a long continuous sheet that would pass over hot rollers to dry it and then be rolled up at the end of the line into a massive roll of paper weighing several tons. In the lab samples, the wood fibers that made up the paper would be randomly aligned, giving it the same tensile strength in any direction. In a paper mill, the act of spraying the slurry onto a moving mesh had the effect of biasing the direction of the wood fibers in the direction of the motion of the mesh onto which the slurry was sprayed, giving different resistance to tearing, depending on whether the force is applied with the grain or across it. Thus the physical properties of the lab-produced samples offered only limited information about what the properties would be if the paper were to be produced under factory conditions.

My boss in the R&D lab had developed a specialized test instrument to overcome this problem. His instrument had four jaws to grip the edges of disk of paper along the x- and y-axes and apply different forces along the two axes. By calibrating the relative pulling forces in the two dimensions to reflect the difference in tensile strength of manufactured paper along the grain and across it, he hoped to be able to be able to simulate the properties of the manufactured product in the central portion of lab-produced samples. My job for the summer was to develop a mathematical model for how the stresses would be distributed around the disks of lab-produced paper in order to determine how closely the central part of the disk would behave like manufactured paper.

Creating such a model entailed developing numerical solutions to the complex differential equations that governed the distribution of stresses. Unfortunately, I knew little about differential equations and even less about numerical analysis. I quickly acquired a couple of books in each subject and spent a week studying them intensely. After about a month I had developed and refined a proposed approach that seemed to satisfy my boss. He then authorized me to spend a modest amount of mainframe computer time (in those days computer time cost thousands of dollars per hour and was carefully rationed) running my models to develop tables that he could use to calibrate his test instrument to deliver results that could use lab-produced paper samples to closely simulate how manufactured paper would behave.

250

I then set about programming my approach. At the time, programming entailed submitting a deck of punched cards to a central computer and then waiting until the next morning to see if the program had run correctly. Invariably there would be bugs in the software, so that the entire day would be spent hunting down bugs and then resubmitting the corrected deck for another overnight run. The slowness of this primitive process meant that it took me more than three weeks of these overnight cycles to get a functioning program, but ultimately I prevailed against the demons inside the computer and was able to deliver a finished set of tables to my boss the week before the end of my summer job. From this experience I learned never to shy away from things about which I knew nothing. With a bit of hard work one can learn enough about almost any subject and apply primitive tools to get creditable results.

I also learned another important lesson from my summer work at St. Regis Paper. The summer internship program was the pet project of the divisional head of human resources. Towards the end of the summer the senior vice president for R&D invited the twenty-odd interns and their immediate bosses down to his super-deluxe house in Princeton, New Jersey, for a pool party and barbecue. The SVP and the HR head were to be our hosts. The party was quite tame for the first couple of hours, but then it changed complexion when two of the interns, one from Duke and the other from the University of Virginia, who had been drinking rather more beer than they should have, began tossing the other interns into the pool. Having soaked all the interns, those two then turned their attention to bigger game. I will never forget the look on the HR man's face as he was being heaved into the pool while fully dressed. Half of his face was laughing, to go along with the gag, while the other had a look of terror on it as he looked at the SVP to try to determine whether or not he was going to get fired for these two interns' drunken shenanigans. Ever since that time I have never had more than one drink at any public gathering;

my long-term reputation and good name is worth a lot more to me than the momentary fun that might go with partying it up.

* * * * *

Although I wound up not following any of these lines of work professionally, I did learn a lot about adapting to very different work environments. In snow shoveling and camp counselling, I came to understand the need to stick up for myself in negotiating work terms. In the work with Professor Deutsch and his staff I gained a deep appreciation for the value of a broad education and a base of experience in multiple fields. I also had the pleasure of working with a close-knit team towards a complex common goal, and I came to recognize that sometimes the outcome of the team's efforts can be totally out of its control. And in the work for St. Regis Paper I learned not to shy away from tasks that I might not have the background to tackle, and to remember that my relationships with colleagues could be irreparably harmed by a few stupid actions.

Chapter 18

My Academic Career

Oxford

Carol and I spent our first post-Urbana year at Oxford University in England. I had a NATO fellowship which afforded us a very comfortable living even though it paid less than $6000 (admittedly tax-free) for the year. Upon our arrival in England, we had a very rude shock. During the night in which we had flown from New York to London, President Nixon had suspended convertibility of the dollar into gold, thereby scuttling the Bretton Woods Agreement that had fixed exchange rates around the world since World War II. Apparently a decade of undisciplined spending by the US government to finance the Vietnam War and Lyndon Johnson's Great Society was coming home to roost, and several foreign governments had begun a run on the dollar, demanding that the Americans deliver gold in exchange for the dollars held by their central banks.

When we arrived in London, we discovered that no one would accept the dollar-denominated travelers' checks that we had brought with us to tide us over until my first salary check would arrive from NATO. Fortunately, some establishments accepted my American Express card because their banks would accept the chits and pay the merchants in pounds sterling. (American Express promised to absorb the exchange rate risk from the banks, keeping them whole.) With the Amex card, we were able to buy train tickets from London's Heathrow Airport to Oxford, take a taxi from the train station to the Old Parsonage Hotel across the street from the Mathematical Institute at Oxford, and cover a week's worth of room and board at the hotel.

That afternoon I called on Professor Graham Higman, a very distinguished group theorist and head of the Maths Institute (Figure 18-1) to introduce myself. During our conversation, I mentioned I our financial problem, and he immediately offered to have the Institute advance me a modest sum in pounds to tide us over until the dust settled in the international financial markets. He also wrote me a letter of introduction to the manager of a nearby branch of Barclay's Bank; at that time in England, one could not open a bank account without a letter of introduction from someone known personally to the local branch manager. In the meanwhile, I placed an urgent call to my father asking for a short-term loan of some usable money, which he was able to wire to my new Barclay's account from Switzerland (where he had some residual funds dating back to the days when he and my mother had smuggled money out of Italy just prior to their departure in 1939). Fortunately my father's money arrived in time for us to make our previously planned trip to Romania that was to take place a week later.

In the subsequent several days I made the rounds of the handful of other faculty whom I had met at various conferences to reintroduce myself and learn about their current research interests. Typically these meetings would happen over the morning coffee and afternoon tea sessions held daily in the Institute's common room at eleven AM and four PM respectively. Occasionally we would meet for a lunch or dinner at their respective colleges' High

Tables—the faculty dining tables were at the front of the dining hall on a platform raised above the floor of the rest of the room. These initial meetings in turn resulted in introductions to others, and I soon knew a reasonable cross section of the Oxford Maths faculty. During the days I introduced myself to my new colleagues, Carol made similar visits to several members of the philosophy faculty, although she was at a disadvantage because she did not know anyone who could introduce her around. The secretary of the Maths Institute at the university had found us an apartment which was the upstairs half of a detached house with a lovely garden in Summertown, a district of Oxford about one mile north of campus. Our landlord, Doctor Burn, a retired professor of pharmacology, was a very refined and scholarly man, whose acquaintance added to the pleasure of our living in his house.

As foreign nationals resident in the UK we were required to register with the local police station. When we went in to do so, a kindly sergeant thought he should warn us about some of the dangers we faced in the UK. In particular, he cautioned us to always lock our bicycles—as well as any car we might buy—as the Oxford police had at least one complaint a week of a stolen bicycle.

After we had been in Oxford for a couple of weeks we decided to buy a used car so that we would be able to tour outside of town. In town we had little need for one since the bicycles we had acquired sufficed for going to the university or shopping for groceries. If we wished to go a bit further, the city had a fine network of city and interurban buses as well as excellent train service to London. However, these modes of transport had their limitations.

At first I tried to buy a car privately by answering an advert in the local newspaper. The seller brought his car around to our house and suggested that I take it out for a short drive to try it out. This was my first experience driving on the left side of the road. Within a few blocks I found myself having to negotiate a roundabout in which traffic circulates in the opposite direction and from which the exits were all to the left instead of the right. I became thoroughly confused and went around two full turns before I could get out of the roundabout. The car seller was sure that I would crack up his car. But we did get out and managed to find our way back to our house without having to revisit the terror of the roundabout. I rather liked the car, and conditioned a purchase on its passing a mechanical review by the Royal Automobile Club (RAC). The inspection revealed potential mechanical issues that killed the sale.

Carol and I then went to an auto dealer a few blocks from our house to look at used cars. We were assigned to a sales rep named Colley who turned out to be the stereotypical used car salesman. He constantly wore an obviously fake smile, which was surmounted by a ratty little moustache. He reminded me of the crooked salesman in the Roald Dahl story, *Matilda*. Colley must have thought we were total rubes because he tried every sales trick in the book such as pricing up the cars and then offering us false discounts, and touting dubious advantages of the various cars he had for sale. The only time Colley dropped his fake smile is when I caught him in a flat out lie. Nonetheless we found a car we liked and it passed the RAC mechanical review. We bought it and it gave us fine service for the entire year. At the end of the year we sold it back to the same dealer, and this time there were no tricks. I guess Colley had learned that we were not as dumb as he had hoped.

When Professor Higman had had the Maths Institute building built, he had insisted that all surfaces in the common room such as walls and tables should be made of erasable whiteboard, and he saw to it that there was always a ready supply if dry-erase markers. The morning coffee and afternoon tea times turned into hotbeds of research as various members would meet and share ideas on their current research, sketching them out on the tables and walls. After coffee and tea, the Institute's custodian, would simply dust off these scribblings with a damp cloth. It was an environment that just made you want to do mathematics and was surely the most stimulating academic environment I have ever enjoyed. In my year there I produced several of my best journal articles.

But the environment at Oxford was not all work. Carol and I would take a day off for excursions almost every weekend. We particularly enjoyed long rambles in the countryside along public footpaths that traversed farms and fields that had been in production probably since Roman times. Perhaps our favorite walk was through Port Meadow, a common pasturage documented in William the Conqueror's Domesday Book (1085)—the great land survey that established taxes after the Norman Conquest. Port Meadow ended at such favorite riverside pubs as the Trout (with its flock of peafowl), the Perch (with its thatch-roof) or the antique White Hart (with its roaring fire). But it was equally wonderful to wander among the back alleys of Oxford, peering into the gardens and visiting the public rooms of the older colleges, some of which date back to the Middle Ages. At other times we would drive up into the Cotswolds and visit one or another Downton-Abbey-esque country estate. When we were in the mood for a day of sightseeing and culture, we would head down to London.

While we were in Oxford, I was made a visiting fellow at Wolfson College, a then newly formed college endowed principally by Sir Isaac Wolfson, who had made his fortune in retailing. At the time, the college did not yet have its own buildings and operated out of a couple of Victorian houses on Banbury Road, a few blocks from the Maths Institute. The college's first master, Sir Isaiah Berlin, the noted historian of ideas, had previously been a fellow at All Souls College, one of the oldest and most traditional colleges at Oxford. In some sense Sir Isaiah was a natural choice to lead Wolfson, as the college shared with All Souls a mission as a research institution with no undergraduates. However, Sir Isaiah created within Wolfson an egalitarian ethos which was much the opposite of that of the traditional Oxford colleges. For example, at Wolfson, graduate students and fellows dined together and shared a single common room, whereas at the traditional colleges, the fellows ate sumptuous meals at High Table while the students were rushed through institutional meals at tables on the floor of the dining hall. Similarly, the fellows at the traditional colleges had plush common rooms where they drank port and brandy, smoked cigars and took snuff, while the undergraduates had more utilitarian common rooms in which the potables were limited to beer. In one notable case, Sir Isaiah instituted a Wolfson tradition that parodied the High Table traditions of the old colleges. At the old colleges, the fellows would dine on High Table, but take their sweets in the common room along with port (that always had to move clockwise around the table!) in a process that was imbued with a great deal of traditional English stuffiness; there was a rule at these post-prandial gatherings that one was not to sit with the same people as those with whom one had dined. At Wolfson, where dessert would be served at the same table as the main meal, Sir Isaiah would rise before the serving of the sweets to announce that every alternate person should rise and shift four seats to his left, thus achieving the same mixing with considerable laughter and confused commotion and without the traditional stuffiness.

One unexpected benefit of having a college affiliation came during the winter, when the National Union of Mineworkers went on strike and set up picket lines at the mostly coal-fired power plants, reducing electricity production by half as many electricity workers refused to cross the miners' picket lines. In response, the government imposed rotating power cuts to conserve electricity, with different parts of town having their electricity cut off for alternating four-hour stretches. Fortunately, our apartment and Wolfson College were in different parts of the electricity grid, so that on nights when we had no power with which to cook our supper, the college would have power and we could dine in college.

While we lived in Oxford, Carol and I also came face to face with the ugly side of English racism. Once, when we were standing in queue at Palm's delicatessen in Oxford's Covered Market, Carol noticed several bins containing a variety of different types of yams and sweet potatoes. She asked me if I knew the differences among them to which I replied that I did not. Overhearing us, the elegantly dressed Jamaican woman behind us very kindly proceeded to explain the uses and methods of preparing each. Carol decided to try some based on this lady's recommendations. A few minutes later (this particular queue was both long and slow) I noticed a display of very large tins of Indian curry on a shelf behind the counter, and pointed out to Carol this reflection of England's large population of immigrants from India and Pakistan. Overhearing us, a lower middle class woman standing ahead of us butted into our private conversation and announced in a loud tone of voice, "Those are curries for the coarse 'colored' taste!" I am sure that the Jamaican woman behind us was the target of this mean-spirited comment, and I felt as though I was about to fall through the floor with embarrassment at the loud woman's gross behavior. Unfortunately, this was not an isolated incident. We regularly saw graffiti with nasty references to *Wogs* (an English racial slur aimed at dark skinned people of African or South Asian descent) and *Pakkies* (a slur aimed specifically at South Asians from Pakistan, Bangladesh, Sri Lanka and India). On one occasion, we even found ourselves discriminated against because we were Americans. When Carol and I were on holiday in Wales, we stopped at a B&B to enquire if they had a room we could rent for a few days. The landlady responded with what seemed an odd question, "Will you be taking a lot of baths?" I replied, "After a tramp up and down the mountains, I generally like to wash before dinner." She then asked, "You're Americans aren't you?" to which I answered in the affirmative. She then continued, "No rooms for you. Americans take too many baths." and then she decisively slammed the door in my face.

Notwithstanding these experiences, we generally found life at Oxford most congenial. At one point I applied for a teaching position there, a fellowship at Magdalen College. Magdalen was Graham Higman's college, so I thought I might have a shot at it with his backing. A few weeks later I learned that I was on the short list and was invited to interview. The interview process was quite unlike that in the US. My interview consisted of being invited to dine on High Table. During the cocktail hour before dinner, I spoke with a number of other college fellows representing diverse academic disciplines. At dinner, I was seated between a mathematician and a physicist with whom I conversed on all manner of subjects, though virtually no time was spent discussing our research or teaching interests. When we retired to the fellows' common room for port and sweets, I was seated next to the college chaplain who was totally drunk. The chaplain decided that it was his duty to teach me how to take snuff, which he did between stories about his misadventures as a religious advisor, first to the staff at Harrod's department store in London and then at Magdalen. It seemed that they were more concerned about my social profile than about my academic credentials. During the course of the evening, I learned that one of the others on the short list was another logician, Angus McIntyre. I knew Angus quite well from several academic conferences and from his having invited me a couple of months earlier to give a lecture at his university in Aberdeen in the far north of Scotland. He was a first-rate mathematician, and I knew I had some tough competition for this job. In the end neither Angus nor I was awarded the fellowship; instead it went to another Oxonian who presumably fit the desired profile better than an American or a Scotsman could.

During that winter, while I was interviewing for the Magdalen fellowship, my thesis adviser at the University of Illinois, Bill Boone, urged me to apply for a research fellowship at the Institute for Advanced Study in Princeton, New Jersey. Bill reasoned that from there I would surely be able to move to a major US university for permanent employment. So apply I did, and about a month later was invited to spend a year there, with an option for a second year if I wanted. With that invitation in my pocket, I doubled down on my research work at Oxford and wrapped up what was surely the most satisfying academic experience that I would ever have. At the end of the summer of 1972, Carol and I packed up our things and prepared to move to Princeton.

The Institute for Advanced Study

The Institute for Advanced Study (Figure 18-2) had been organized in the 1930s to provide an academic home for the great European mathematicians and physicists who were being driven out of their universities by the Nazis for the sins of being Jewish, socialist, and/or gay. Among its early faculty were Albert Einstein, John von Neumann, and Kurt Gödel. Before my time, the Institute had expanded its areas of study to also include historical studies, and was in the midst of developing a School of Social Sciences. The institution had a small permanent faculty of perhaps a dozen and a half pre-eminent scholars, and about 200 members who were there for periods ranging from one semester to two years. The members were a mix of well-established faculty from other universities, who were on sabbatical leave, and junior researchers like myself, who were out to make a name for themselves and win a permanent faculty appointment at a significant university.

On my first day at the Institute, my secretary asked me whether I was a historian or a mathematician, a question I found very odd. I responded that I was a mathematician and then asked her why she had asked. It seems that I had violated an unwritten dress code. Having just come from England, I went to work in light-weight woolen slacks, necktie and

261

a tweed jacket. My secretary informed me that such was the uniform of the historians; mathematicians were supposed to wear jeans and sandals. I continued to wear tweeds and was astonished one evening when I accidentally walked in on a black-tie reception given by the historians.

On my second day I went to pay a call on Kurt Gödel, whose assistant I nominally was. I had been warned in advance by my Illinois thesis advisor that Gödel was very eccentric and lived a hermetic life, keeping company almost exclusively with his wife. Despite the warning, I was not prepared for this visit. I entered his office on a blazing hot day in August and found a gaunt, almost skeletal old man seated at his desk wearing a dark winter-weight suit, heavy overcoat, scarf and hat. We spoke briefly and exchanged pleasantries, but before I could turn our conversation to mathematics, he bid me good day. When I later shared this experience with Bill, he told me that Gödel was so aware of his influence that he was reluctant to discuss mathematics with anyone for fear of sending their research efforts down some blind alley. Bill indicated that Gödel was also germophobic and had paranoid fears of being poisoned. In any case, I never saw Gödel again during my two-year tenure at the Institute.

The mathematicians at the Institute had a very idiosyncratic social structure. The topologists and the number theorists battled for the top of the pecking order. The rest of us were decidedly second-class citizens. The topologists were such a cohesive group that they all ate together in the cafeteria at what was derisively called the topologists training table; non-topologists were not welcome. The leader of the number theorists was a faculty member named Andre Weil, a haughty Frenchman who—it was said—divided all mankind into two categories: those beneath contempt … and those worthy of contempt. The only person other than himself who was exempt from this put-down was Kurt Gödel, whose work he admired above all except his own.

While we were at the Institute, the director, Carl Kaysen, started a School of Social Science and appointed its first permanent faculty member, Clifford Geertz, likely the most influential cultural anthropologist of the day. However, when Kaysen attempted to appoint the sociologist Robert Bellah (whose book *Beyond Belief* examined religion across cultures), a war broke out among the rest of the faculty. The opponents were led by Andre Weil, who proceeded to write public letters denouncing Kaysen and Bellah in the cruelest, nastiest, and most personal terms. In one of these letters he described Bellah as "the worst appointment since Caligula's horse." The controversy exploded onto the pages of the *New York Times*, where the physicist Freeman Dyson described the differences as "a question of taste especially when you're dealing with a subject like religion." At one point there was so much bad blood that members of the faculty were refusing to speak to one another and were communicating only by means of handwritten letters. Ultimately Bellah withdrew his name from consideration and to this day the School of Social Science has only one permanent faculty slot, the one which Geertz had initially held.

The atmosphere among the Institute's younger members was very tense during the whole time we were there. First of all, there was the intense competition among us for the increasingly scarce tenure-track positions at universities, and most of those openings were at secondary or tertiary institutions. This pressure-cooker atmosphere was exacerbated by the fact that we all lived together in Institute housing so that we were bumping into each other 24/7. The members' apartments were in two groups, of which the older group was in small four-apartment units that offered a bit of separation. The newer apartments were organized around an open grassy area with floor to ceiling windows all facing each other across the open green. These newer apartments' total lack of privacy resulted in many social pathologies including a remarkably high divorce rate.

During this time I was madly writing mathematics papers and trying to come up with a reasonable and permanent academic home. At one point I was invited to interview at a university in Tennessee. While this university's math department had one or two distinguished faculty, I found it very uncomfortable to be in an institution where the principal cultural outlets were football and the Grand Ole Opry. I turned down their job offer. At another point I interviewed for a job at New York's City College. This institution had traditionally been the university of choice for brilliant but impecunious New Yorkers and had produced a prodigious list of important scholars and prominent men and women of letters. In the late 1960s, the school had gone to open enrollment and dropped all requirements for admission other than a high school diploma. As a result, the math faculty was reduced to teaching elementary school arithmetic to totally innumerate young men and women. This clearly would not do. Finally, I interviewed for a job at Amherst College. While the math faculty was nothing to write home about, the student body was very bright and its location in rural New England was both beautiful and culturally congenial. Also, two junior faculty members in the math department had been graduate students with me at the University of Illinois, though one was leaving as he saw no possibility of getting tenure there. I should have taken his leaving as a warning, but I trusted the dean of the faculty and the senior math department staff. They all assured me that this position would lead to tenure and, as proof of their good intentions, offered me three years' credit towards tenure for the years I had spent in Oxford and Princeton. I took this job, wrapped up my final year at the Institute, and Carol and I moved to Amherst.

Amherst College

The core of the Amherst College campus occupies the top a small hill with a breathtaking view of the Holyoke Range, a chain of hills that ran east to west separating the southern part of the town of Amherst from South Hadley, the home of Mt. Holyoke College. The valley between the college and the hills is mostly beautiful open farmland with a few scattered houses and the small campus of Hampshire College in the far distance. Climbing up the hill each morning from our college-supplied apartment at its eastern base was an absolute delight.

Amherst College had a strong reputation for its English and history faculties. The college had been founded in the early 1800s by some of the last remnants of the Boston area Puritans as a refuge for pious young men to keep them safe from the liberal theology that had taken root at Harvard. Over the years, it had evolved into a "prep school" for law and medical schools, a job that it performed extremely well. Indeed, the college faculty had two committees whose job it was to screen and sort the annual crops of applicants to those professional schools and see to it that each student was directed towards the law or medical school that the committee deemed "appropriate" for that student. Those committees also coached the applicants so that their applications would be well-received by these law and medical school admissions committees. During my years at Amherst, it also developed a strong reputation as a feeder school into Wall Street internships for students who would ultimately apply to business school.

The math department was housed in Williston Hall, a small three-story building on the main quad that dated to the mid-1800s. It contained two classrooms on each of the two lower two floors; the top floor was given over to faculty offices and the math department library. The mathematics faculty was made up of three full professors of whom one was a former Oxford don, one associate professor, and three assistant professors. The faculty was almost exclusively focused on teaching; as best I could tell, none of the faculty other than myself had done any original mathematics since completing their doctorates. Half the math department's teaching load was first semester calculus as that subject was a prerequisite for the science subjects

265

for pre-med students and also for many economics courses for the students who were aiming for Wall Street. All this made for an easy life for the math faculty. Each term each of them would teach a class in first semester calculus, which they had already taught for many years, and another in an area of their own choosing. Unlike the situation in major universities, they felt no need or obligation to engage in mathematical research. These duties could easily be fulfilled in less than twenty hours per week during term time and summers were theirs to enjoy in whatever way they wanted.

In the meanwhile, I continued to do research in addition to my teaching duties. Within a couple of months, I organized a weekly logic seminar that included several faculty from the math and computer science departments at UMass (also in Amherst, about a mile from the Amherst College campus) and one other individual from Hampshire College. I also commuted to the biweekly logic colloquium at MIT. The drive to MIT was a grueling one and a half hours from Amherst, but I judged it worthwhile because it enabled me to stay near the cutting edge of research. In addition I applied for and won a research grant from the National Science Foundation.

I soon began to sense a bit of resentment towards me from my departmental colleagues on account of my research. They clearly felt that it somehow made them look bad because they had done little to none of it. The first complaints were that I was taking up too much of the department secretary's time typing up my research papers for publication. At other times there were mild digs about my working too hard or that I was spending too much time at UMass or MIT.

On the other hand, I found the majority of our students to be bright and highly motivated. For the most part they combined studiousness, gregariousness and social polish in a most pleasing way. I would regularly invite my classes to our apartment for informal get-togethers. I soon developed an easy rapport with my students. I got in the habit of giving untimed exams in the evenings. The exams would begin after supper; the students could work as long as they needed, provided that they did not confer among themselves. When they were done they would slip their papers under my office door for me to grade the next morning. One morning I was surprised to find greasy smudges on their exam papers. When I asked about the source of the smudges, I learned that they had bribed the janitor to bring them all a late night round of pizza, and they had made a party out of their exam session. Another time, when I handed out the exam questions, one student stood up and declared that they were too hard. Immediately all the others did the same as they moved toward the door, all laughing; clearly they had conspired in this prank on me. I responded by pulling out my grade book, and announcing with a twinkle in my eye and a grin that I could have the last laugh. They immediately returned to their seats and began to work on the exam.

One day while I was sitting at lunch with several colleagues from assorted departments, the conversation turned to a recently published and rather controversial book. The conversation quickly turned as hot and heavy as one could imagine among a group of academics. However, something seemed to be missing from the conversation; it lacked specificity and the same one or two items seemed to be cited over and over. Finally, I asked for a show of hands of who had read the book. It turned out that no one had read it and the entire discussion had been based on a short review of the book that had been published that morning in the *New York Times*. This intellectual superficiality seemed to epitomize much of the college faculty for me. It bothered me that the faculty seemed to contain many who liked to think of themselves as learned professors, even though most of their learning was at best a few inches deep.

One fall I had the idea that my department should teach a course or two in computer science to better prepare our students for a world in which information technology was playing an ever-increasing role. As I began to ask my math department colleagues, I got the same response from all of them. Computer science was seen as vocational education and was therefore unfit to be taught at Amherst College. I then had the brilliant idea to offer a course in mathematical economics. Every two weeks, I would assign a project to build a computer-based model of whatever economic theory I had been teaching during that time. Thus I got to teach basic software design and development in a way that avoided the deadly label of *vocational education*. This course had the further advantage of drawing in students from the college's most popular major, economics, to take additional courses in the math department, a factor that could figure into the dean's annual allocation of incremental faculty slots.

During my second year, the dean cut the math department's library budget by $500, and suggested that we eliminate a subscription to a leading Japanese math journal. While the department had been subscribing to that journal since the end of World War II, the thick layer of dust on the top of the bound volumes suggested that it was little read. Nonetheless my colleagues were incensed at the idea of dropping this subscription and called a departmental meeting to discuss how to respond to the dean's request. We spent more than two hours word-smithing a letter of protest to the dean, though the final resolution was that I offered to cover half the $500 from my research grant's book budget if the dean would match it from the large overhead charges that he took from my grant, since the dean's office got to claim an overhead slice out of my grant amounting to two-thirds of the money allowed for my summer salary and research expenses. This whole episode, in which seven grown men spent two hours arguing over how to claw back a measly $500 from the dean, left a rather bitter taste in my mouth; clearly this was a group of people who did not value their time because they did not have much else to do with it.

During my second year at Amherst, I began to hear new ominous comments from some of my math department colleagues. One fellow told me the story of someone who had been denied tenure some years back and was now teaching in a boarding school in New Hampshire. Two other colleagues suggested that I should let them out of the promise they had made to bring me up for tenure after four years and wait out the customary seven years in the hopes that someone in the department might retire or resign to go elsewhere. I then went to the library and paged through about forty years' worth of college catalogs, only to discover that the math department had always had at least two untenured faculty members. At that point the department had seven members of whom five were tenured, and none was older than fifty-five—meaning that there was no slot for me to be tenured into, and there was essentially zero likelihood of one opening up. In short, the hiring promise that I was on a tenure track had been a complete lie.

Given that the employment situation in academic mathematics had continued to deteriorate ever since I had been a graduate student, I recognized that my academic career was in pretty serious trouble. I certainly had no desire to end up teaching in a boarding school. At that time computer science was a rapidly growing field, so I decided to spiff up my software skills and shift my research more in that direction, figuring that I would then have an option to go into academic computer science of else into industry. To improve my software skills I wrote a BASIC interpreter for an early desktop computer whose native language was APL. I also began to do some research work in theoretical computer science in collaboration with Richard Tenney at UMass. Richard and I developed an early proof that the vector reachability problem was algorithmically solvable. On the strength of that result I applied for a semester of sabbatical leave for the fall of my third year at Amherst. I took this sabbatical in MIT's computer science department. Unfortunately, another researcher found a flaw in our proof just as I got to MIT, so that semester was largely spent trying unsuccessfully to patch the proof. About six months later another professor at Johns Hopkins built on our initial work and completed the proof that had eluded us. That decided me on leaving academic life altogether.

What little spare time I had during that semester at MIT and the following spring semester when I was back at Amherst, I spent looking for a job in industry. A number of my interviews were for what turned out to be deadly jobs in big bureaucratic companies. I recall interviewing at Bell Labs, at the time the premier industrial research lab in the country. Each of the five people with whom I spoke began the discussion with a ten-minute explanation of AT&T's seven-digit employee numbering system in which the first digit defined the broad division in which one worked, the next the relevant subdivision, the third the sub-sub-division, and so on until the last digit specified the individual within that seven-level hierarchy. After the third round of hearing that explanation, I was ready to run out the door screaming. The job on offer at another company, Computer Sciences, would last only as long as their government contract with NASA, at which point everyone working on it would be laid off. IBM wanted to hire me to do some narrowly specialized work optimizing firmware, giving me skills that would have zero portability into more interesting work elsewhere within the company, and even less to jobs in other companies if this one did not work out.

One company that had intrigued me from the literature that I had read in the MIT Career Services Office was Arthur D. Little, Inc. (ADL), a Boston-based management consulting firm. I sent in a cold letter to Dr. Frank Allen, the head of their group doing consulting on planning and managing corporate IT departments. Having heard nothing back, I called his office to set up an appointment. His assistant told me that she would review my request with him when he returned from vacation and get back to me. Again I heard nothing further, so I called his assistant again, and again she promised that I would hear from someone shortly. After about two weeks I got a call from a certain Darrow Lebovici inviting me to lunch. Much later I learned that Frank Allen had dismissed my resume as that of a useless academic and had detailed someone to take me to lunch to tell me to get lost. That person in turn had also thought I was useless and had bucked the job of taking me to lunch to Darrow. In any case, on the appointed day, I put on my best navy-blue suit and hugged my wife and infant son for good luck before leaving for the drive from Amherst to Cambridge. Unfortunately, my son hugged me back with a fistful of well-mashed bananas, and I had to hurriedly change my suit, losing precious time. I then hopped in my car and drove to ADL as fast as I dared for my lunch with Darrow.

The lunch turned out to be a most interesting experience for both Darrow and me. He discovered that I was not an ordinary academic but instead one who also read the *Wall Street Journal* on a daily basis and had more than passing familiarity with the world of corporate America. I discovered that the work of ADL consultants was remarkably varied and totally fascinating. Of particular interest was the fact that I would not be pigeon-holed into some narrow specialty as would be required in most large, bureaucratic or-ganization. In addition, the work of ADL consultants was "close to the cash register" in the sense that there was an obvious and direct link between their work and how the company generated revenue and profit. Further as Dar-row began to describe his colleagues, I learned that about one third of them had PhDs in the hard sciences, and another third had MBAs from major business schools, with the remainder having had rather varied backgrounds relating to the IT industry; in short the company was full of people like me.

By the end of lunch Darrow decided that he should not tell me to get lost notwithstanding his boss's orders. Instead, he took the initiative of bringing me across the street to the department's offices and lining up a series of im-promptu interviews with those who happened to be there that day instead of on site with clients. By the end of the day I was invited back to meet Frank

Allen and the other senior members of his team the following week. Two weeks later I was offered a job that paid about twice my academic salary, and the rest, as they say, is history. I then took an unpaid leave from Amherst for my fourth year there as a hedge against this job not working out and launched my consulting career.

Figure 18-1. The Oxford Maths Institute, 1971

Figure 18-2. The Institute for Advanced Study, Princeton NJ 1972

Figure 18.3. In 1974, Amherst College's
Williston Hall housed its Math Department

Figure 18-4. View of the Holyoke Range from
Amherst College's War Memorial

Figure 18-5. Sudbury House, Amherst College's housing for its most
junior faculty, where Carol and I lived for our first two years at Amherst

Figure 18.6. In 1976, we had sufficient seniority to move into a six-room apartment on the ground floor in the college-owned building at 233 South Pleasant Street

Figure 18.7. Carol and I joined Amherst's miniscule 5-year-old Jewish community around the time that it acquired its first home, the then-disused Second Congregational Church.The community pledged to preserve the building's neoclassical architecture, including the acorn-topped spire.

Chapter 19

I Go Commercial

During my last semester at Amherst, while I was trying to decide whether or not to accept the offer from Arthur D. Little, Inc., I read a detailed description of the company in a book entitled *Think Tanks* that covered a number of consulting organizations. From this book I learned about some of ADL's core operational elements. First and foremost was its fluid structure, in which teams would form for each specific client case and then dissolve at the completion of the project. The company's core metric, billability, tracked how much time each employee spent on revenue generating projects. In essence, employees volunteered for projects and if a person developed a reputation for substandard work, that person soon found case leaders unwilling to take him or her on; conversely, case leaders who were difficult to work with found few volunteers for their projects. This approach created an interesting balance that resulted in case team members going the extra mile to please their case leaders, and case leaders going the extra mile to ensure that their teams had satisfying experiences on their projects. Success ensured profitable employment and the successful delivery of quality client work, without which a person would be asked to leave the company.

In addition to reading about ADL's work, I asked my prospective boss to send me a representative set of case reports so that I might learn more about information systems and the work of the IT management group. A couple of weeks later, a heavy box was delivered to my door in Amherst containing about twenty case reports on various projects for major US companies. At the time, case reports were long text documents in which the case team would define the objective of the work, describe its findings, include copious data to back up these findings, and then give recommendation for overcoming the shortcomings found in the client's current situation. I immediately dove into these reports, and the more I read, the more excited I became about working for ADL. The first thing I noticed was that the reports were very well written and generally buttressed with significant data, so that anyone totally unfamiliar with the client's business could immediately understand what was at issue, why it was important, and how to resolve it. I also noticed that these reports were addressed to senior executives at major American companies. That fact suggested that through my work at ADL I would develop a set of senior level relationships outside the company that might ultimately lead to further career opportunities.

When the spring term at Amherst College was done, Carol and I took a quick vacation to Nantucket and then moved to a house we had rented in Cambridge. On the appointed day I reported for work at ADL. After a couple of hours of formalities, filling out forms and the like, I was taken over to my new office. The first thing that I noticed was that more than half the offices were dark; people were working at client sites, keeping their billability up. I stopped in to see Frank Allen, the group's head; after the usual pleasantries, Frank provided me with a list of my colleagues and a several page weekly report of all the new client projects that had just been commissioned across the entire company together with the names of those who were going to lead those projects. The unvoiced implication was that I had to get to know my colleagues, especially those who had new projects in need of staffing.

I quickly learned that ADL was a very different kind of company from any of the others at which I had interviewed. About a week after I joined ADL, Frank's entire group was called into the auditorium where the then corporate head of facilities, Dr. Dick Heitman, explained that the company had outgrown its Acorn Park headquarters, and several groups including ours would be moved to a suburban office park some ten miles away. Dick then described some of the "features" of this new office, including its bullpen (in place of enclosed offices) and its vending machines (in place of the subsidized cafeteria in Acorn Park). During the presentation, Frank stood up repeatedly to challenge Dick, even though Dick substantially outranked him. Frank first rejected the open plan bullpen as incompatible with the confidentiality that we promised our clients. Then he pointed out that vending machines would drive the staff out of the building for lunch, thereby hindering the formation of the informal networks among the staff that the central cafeteria in Acorn Park nurtured, and which were the basis on which many projects were staffed with the appropriate skills. As I watched Dick being forced to back down on his schemes (which no doubt were rooted in efforts to save money), I realized that I had joined a company whose internal style was very much to my liking.

I came to greatly admire Frank Allen's management style. He hired the best he could find, encouraged them to exert their personal initiative to expand the group's capabilities and grow the business, and otherwise kept out of the way. Frank best trait as a manager was that he was deeply supportive of his staff, sometimes to a fault in that he could be slow to deal with non-performers. In particular, Frank's standing up to Dick Heitman over ideas that ran counter to   how Frank felt staff should be treated was a model I took deeply to heart.

During my initial meeting with Frank he asked me to take on an internal project, developing a white paper on how best to manage large software development projects. He explained to me he had noticed that in the preceding couple of years a number of clients had called on ADL to recommend improvements to how they managed their IT departments after large, expensive software projects had gone seriously awry. This was a subject about which I knew absolutely nothing, but I said I would see what I could do. I guess Frank decided that since I was an academic who had written some software in his life I must be able to shed some light on what was becoming a very contentious issue in the IT world. In any case, he explained that these sorts of white papers were a way to establish ADL's credentials as experts in various areas and were used as part of a regular direct mail campaign to keep the company's name in front of prospective clients. I saw this internal project as a mechanism to become better known among my new colleagues. As Frank and I wrapped up our meeting, he took me to my new office and introduced me to the assistant that I would share with two other colleagues.

That afternoon I organized two efforts. The first was to call the administrative assistants of each of my thirty or so colleagues in Frank's group to set up times to meet their bosses for lunch or coffee to introduce myself and to learn about their specific areas of work. My hope was that these meetings would get me staffed on client projects fairly quickly. Because of my colleagues' travel schedules it took me more than two months to see most of them. I could not organize meetings with a couple of them who were on long-term assignments overseas and would not be returning to the office for several months. I also went to the company library to see what I could learn about managing software development projects from books and journal articles on the subject.

After I returned from the library with a stack of books and journal articles, I quickly learned that the state of the art in managing software development projects was a real mess. Large numbers of projects were deemed failures and there were dozens of warring camps, each claiming that using some methodology they had developed was the key to success—and that everyone else's ideas were useless.

As I read further during the ensuing several days I discovered that the software development approaches being touted by the warring camps were of three general types.

1. *Project planning tools.* These were to enable software development teams to break down their projects into a series of tasks. Then, taking into account that some of these tasks had to be accomplished before others could be started, teams would be able to guess at the time and effort required for each task and create a schedule and budget for what was needed to build the desired system.

2. *Project control tools.* These were supposed to track how much money and effort was being spent on the project and use this information to estimate how much more time and effort was needed.

3. *Software development methodologies.* These methodologies were to accomplish three things: (1) specify a standard set of tasks required to complete each element of the project, (2) produce a flow of work that would result in projects being completed on time and on budget and (3) meet the needs of the business departments requesting them.

I was struck by the total lack of data supporting the strong claims made by the various approaches and decided I needed a statistical sample of projects that had been built using the proposed approaches to determine which one was the best. So I returned to Frank to report on what I had learned and proposed that I conduct a survey among corporate heads of IT to learn what their teams had done, how they had gone about organizing their work, and what outcomes were achieved. I had never done a survey before, but what could be so hard about running a survey?

I spent a couple of weeks telephoning corporate heads of IT at Fortune 500 companies. I deliberately avoided calling recent ADL clients so respondents wouldn't feel compelled to color their answers to reflect their company's relationship with ours. This turned out to be a difficult exercise as many potential respondents refused to participate. However, by end of two weeks, I had responses covering seventy-nine projects at thirty-seven companies, all of which were given for nothing more than a promise to share the findings when the study was completed. I had discovered that people love to talk about their jobs to anyone who will listen, and that was the real benefit that I was offering in exchange for their cooperation. This discovery served me very well in much of the rest of career.

Initially, I asked each respondent some general questions about what constituted success or failure for software development projects. Then I asked to identify two or three recently finished projects in their organization, describe their objectives in general terms, talk about the time and effort that went into them and, finally, to talk about their approach to project management.

What I learned from my survey was that software projects had a very sorry but remediable history of failure, defined as either (1) substantially not meeting functional requirements, or (2) requiring at least 50% more time or money to complete than had been budgeted. When I say *remediable* I mean that if a project used none of the tool types previously mentioned (planning, control, or development technologies) it had a 46% probability of failure. If it used just one of those tool types, its probability of failure fell to 23%. If it used any two of these tool types, its probability of failure fell to 11%. Finally, if the project used all three tool types, the probability of failure fell to 4%. Moreover, the data showed that in fact it mattered little which specific tool was used, so endless debates over the best individual tools were pointless. This project showed me the power of even a modest amount of well-analyzed hard data to end a lot of heated internal arguments supported by little more than personal opinions. This observation then became a hallmark of all of my client work. We had to have real data and we had to analyze it so that would tell a compelling story that pointed towards actionable conclusions.

As I was working on this project I began to be staffed on a number of client assignments. These fell into three broad categories: management audits of IT departments; development of new IT services; and business strategies for those in information services.

Management audits of corporate IT departments—the first project type—focused on problems with the IT department and its management team. The clients for these projects were usually the boss to whom the IT manager reported. The work on these projects generally consisted of reviewing the several parts of the IT function that were not serving well the operating side of the business. I soon developed a mental checklist of the main things that could be done wrong and then checked off which items applied at a given company. Based on this analysis we would recommend a wholesale shakeup in the department's governance and management processes to remedy the situation. As one colleague of mine observed, there was little sport in these projects because IT management was mostly made up of technical specialists who had never had to make, sell, or account for anything and therefore only marginally understood the real drivers of the business their departments were supposed to serve. Moreover, in senior management's view, IT was just another overhead function that got in the way of doing the real business. Management's interest in these projects was simply that we make the "IT headache" go away so they could focus on the producing and selling products and services at a solid profit.

The second project type was to work with an IT department to help it plan and develop new services. In this case, the parent company was looking to achieve substantially greater revenues and/or internal productivity through more effective use of information and information technology. These projects were a lot more interesting in that they required our project teams to quickly understand the fundamental drivers of the client's P&L and then identify ways in which the technology could be used to either add value to what was delivered to the client's customers or improve the productivity of the client's operations. This work with its positive value addition was much more to my taste than the usually adversarial management audits. In addition, these projects got the full attention of senior management because they directly affected their bottom line. In short, they were close to the client's cash register and therefore seen as very important at the most senior levels of the client company.

The third project type consisted of business strategy cases for companies in the information industry, including companies that sold hardware, software, content, and network services. These companies were selling information technology products and services to corporate IT departments. At the time most such technology was sold on the basis of technical product features because that was the only language understood by the corporate IT managers. Our work for our strategy clients consisted primarily in helping them understand the business problems facing the IT managers' internal customers, developing products and

284

services that addressed those problems, and selling them based on the value of those solutions to the ultimate user. I found this work the most interesting. It had us working with line executives to bring immediate P&L value rather than with IT managers several levels removed from how a business really generated its profits. Also these projects were much more profitable because these types of projects were of highly tangible and near-term value to our clients. This is where I made the bulk of my consulting career.

There were many real pleasures of working at ADL. First, the projects themselves were fascinating and generally very complex, forcing my colleagues and me to be at the top of our game and to innovate constantly as we developed solutions. Second, I had wonderful colleagues, many of whom became life-long friends. Third, the ADL management system afforded a lot of autonomy, and this gave project teams a day to day stake in the contribution their work created for the overall profitability of the business. Last, the company's core value of always doing the right thing by clients imbued the staff with a highly service-oriented ethic. This ethic supported ADL's expectation that fees would follow service and did indeed result in much repeat business.

Part of what made ADL so much fun was the irreverent attitude that the staff took towards the small internal bureaucracy. When I had first joined ADL, all thirty-odd business units and the dozen or so remote offices all reported to a single individual, the Chief Professional Officer. When the fellow who had been in that role for some twenty-plus years retired, the CEO split that job among seven individuals who constituted the Management Committee. ADLers, being a group who were generally unawed by hierarchy, soon dubbed the group *The Seven Dwarfs*. Then an e-mail which originated in the San Francisco office spread around the company setting up a name-the-dwarf contest. We quickly reached consensus on who were Grumpy, Dopey, Happy and Doc, though we had a harder time settling on who might be Sleepy or Sneezy and surely none of them was Bashful. This event and many others like it show that ADL *really* was a different kind of company from any other I had ever encountered.

These first few years at ADL taught me many lessons about how to achieve business success, lessons that I would put to good use in the future. As I look back on it, these lessons included the following:

- A business managed using real data and solid analytics that tell a compelling story is much more likely to be successful than one in which political power determines strategy without reference to the facts.
- The power of mobilizing initiative of individuals and small groups of staff to generate and execute business ideas is very important for business success; the central planning business model never works as well. Management needs to act as Frank Allen did to foster this approach and keep the corporate bureaucracy from stifling it.
- It is important not to take oneself or the imperial "Pooh-Bahs" too seriously, having good fun should be part of the game. Business should not be a continual "death march."
- Finally, at a personal level, activities that were "close to the cash register" were the ones I was most comfortable with; I was not cut out for back-office anonymity.

Chapter 20

Applying My initial Business Lessons

Connexions

When I was in my third year at Arthur D. Little, Inc., I had been doing more and more work on business strategy for companies in the information industry and less and less on management audits and planning for corporate IT functions. At that time the Internet with its browsers and search engines had not yet been invented, but much of the componentry was already underway. Packet switched networks had been developed initially for the military-sponsored ARPAnet, and a number of companies were offering commercial versions of them with dial-up access. Hayes had just introduced first cheap modems (up to that time, dial-up modems were large, costly devices), and Apple had just started selling the first mass market personal computer.

At this time, the first consumer-oriented services also popped up, such as The Source, CompuServe, and also a service called Trilogy, an unlikely joint venture of Sears Roebuck, CBS, and IBM; these services were growing like topsy, particularly CompuServe, which ultimately absorbed both Trilogy and The Source, before it was swallowed in turn by AOL, a later arrival with a very aggressive marketing model. Business oriented on-line services grew up on these networks such as stock quote services, on-line legal research tools, and technical document retrieval systems. France Telecom launched a national on-line service called Minitel with very inexpensive proprietary terminals and soon had millions of users. The first e-mail systems also appeared, but they were all closed systems with incompatible protocols meaning you could communicate with others in a given system but could not exchange messages with anyone on another system.

One afternoon, I was discussing all these developments with one of my ADL colleagues, Bob Kvaal, and we began to speculate about how we could profit from them. Somewhere among all these developments there had to be a great business opportunity. We observed that businesses were willing to pay a great deal more than consumers for these services so we focused our speculation on services that might serve either market but that could depend on businesses to pay for most or all of the cost. Furthermore, we recognized that those with easy access to these networks and computer terminals were engineers at technology companies, notably the burgeoning computer industry and technology companies serving the Defense Department. On-line product catalogs were one idea we considered and discarded because at that time the bandwidth and graphics could not replicate the functionality of richly illustrated print catalogs. But we kept on thinking about analogous services that could benefit from simplified and more directed on-line communication. We were most excited about products that would appeal to clients likely to have network access and personal computers but that did not require large amounts of information to be transferred back and forth.

A few weeks after that initial discussion, I happened to buy the Sunday edition of the *Boston Globe*, a paper I almost never buy. An entire thirty-page section of the paper was devoted to classified advertising, mostly for real estate, automobiles and jobs. While real estate and auto ads were mostly aimed at a general audience, the job ads were overwhelmingly for technology companies seeking to hire engineers. Moreover, these ads were almost all text-only and fairly brief. This was perfect content for the data communications technology of the time where a 1200 baud (bits per second) modem was the most common network interface device. I dug into the economics of these classified ads, and soon discovered that *Globe*'s near monopoly on Boston's classified ad market for professional jobs meant that they could charge an arm and a leg for advertising these positions. Upon further research, I discovered that the national market for help-wanted advertising was a multi-billion dollar market, and a large fraction of that market was devoted to reaching engineers and other technical professionals on behalf of the computer, telecom and defense industries. This was starting look interesting.

Bob and I were excited by this analysis of the technical help-wanted advertising market and decided to kick in a couple thousand dollars apiece to determine whether engineers and other tech professionals would use an on-line ad system to look for jobs. Our market trial entailed buying some time and network capacity from a timesharing service (an early version of what is now referred to as cloud computing) and conduct a small direct marketing campaign to our target audience to see if they would use the system. Working nights and weekends, I mocked up and tested a prototype system with a bunch of dummy help-wanted ads for engineering jobs, all the while also doing my day job as a management consultant. In parallel, Bob and my wife Carol developed a mailing piece and identified possible suppliers of mailing lists dense in engineers. As part of my day job, I was doing research on behalf of one of the commercial data network providers on what sorts of companies might be interested in putting on-line services on their networks. In the course of this work, I had to call on several companies in Atlanta to gauge their interest. At the end of the day in Atlanta, I stopped in to see the CEO of Hayes to interest him in our market trial and came away with a mailing list of several thousand modem owners. We were good to go.

We did one final round of testing on the prototype software and then dropped several thousand letters in the mail on a Wednesday morning. Our thinking was that people would receive them on Friday or Saturday and give our prototype a trial over the weekend. That was what happened. By Sunday afternoon, I began to be concerned that the response rate was so high that we were going to blow our trial budget. On Monday we had a massive spike of activity, peaking at lunch time, with a secondary spike in the late afternoon as the work day wound down. By that evening we had blown our budget, and we decided to leave the prototype up for just another two days. Out total response rate in less than a week was over 20%, an unheard-of response to a direct marketing campaign, where a 2% response rate is generally judged to be a home run. The instrumentation we had built into the software prototype indicated that people were engaged with the ads, staying on the system for a long while, and a significant number of them applied for jobs. In short, we had learned that large numbers of dogs would eat the dog food.

Bob and I then visited a number of high-tech hiring managers and HR staff to understand what issues they had with the current help-wanted adverting model. Overwhelmingly they told us that it was too expensive and turned up too many totally unqualified candidates. Based on what we learned from these interviews, we formulated a business model in which we would:

1. Tailor each week's direct marketing to job seekers (to interest them in using our system) to the mix of new ads on the system to ensure maximal flow of qualified candidates.

2. Endow the system with sorting tools to enable hiring managers to quickly sort through the incoming resumes to identify the best candidates from the pool of applicants.

3. Price the advertising on our system at a significant discount to newspaper help-wanted ads.

4. Quickly expand the business geographically among the major centers of the high technology industry to capitalize on the fact that most hiring was local, and whatever inter-regional hiring was done was from one major center to another.

Armed with this data and business model, Bob and I set out to raise money for a business we named *Connexions*. One of the first people we approached was Jerry Rubin, the founder of the extraordinarily successful Lexis on-line legal research system. Jerry agreed to invest and also to serve as board chairman of the company we were organizing. We then raised enough additional funding from what have since come to be called *angel investors*. Now we were able to quit our day-jobs.

In the following six months, we rented offices, hired a small team to specify and build the needed systems, and began a search for a head of sales and marketing. It was a whirlwind of writing software, meeting prospective advertisers, and locating appropriate mailing lists. We also had to raise the A-round of venture capital to fund the product launch in the Boston and Silicon Valley markets. This meant an endless series of meetings with venture capitalists (VCs), often with VC fund managers who were used to backing manufacturing businesses and did not understand the value of intangible assets such as software, audience share, and services. After many frustrating meetings, we finally got our A-round funding from a consortium of three funds: first from one of the early funders of software companies; second from a part of the pension fund of what was then America's largest retailer and catalog merchant; and third from a wealthy family that had previously invested alongside these two groups. These investors understood immediately the value of our advertising-funded and direct-marketing enabled on-line business model.

As we rolled out the application and the direct marketing model for build readership, both worked like champs. I had designed the application to be very modular with tightly defined interfaces between the modules, using principals which later became known as *object-oriented programming*; this architecture enabled us to roll out new versions of the software weekly, a then-revolutionary approach. We continued to get very high response rates, and when people got on our system they were well engaged with it.

We began to see very interesting cross-country traffic on our systems, with job applicants actively pursuing opportunities in our core markets. As I tracked the traffic on our network, I quickly observed what later came to be known as *Metcalf's law*: The traffic on our network was proportional to the product of the number of ads on the system and the number of active job applicants.

But sales to HR professionals were slower than we expected. In part, the issue was HR departments' innate conservatism which was driven by the fact that HR managers had many more opportunities to fail than to succeed. But a bigger problem was Gerry, our head of sales—he talked a good game but never seemed to deliver real results. My first inkling that he was going to be a problem came shortly after he was hired, when I started receiving telephone calls from Jerry's creditors. This guy apparently made a great show of living in style, but his lifestyle was built on a mountain of debt. It appeared he owed money all across the country.

A couple of months later, when I was chatting with Gerry after work, he began to tell me stories of his supposed sexual conquests, though it was clear to me that these were all flights of fancy. This event immediately brought to mind Jimmy, the bragging, lying bully from Les Roches, my boarding school in Switzerland. The next morning I telephoned my partner Bob who had gone to the west coast to open our Silicon Valley sales office. About halfway through the call, I said, "By the way, Bob, I think we have a problem with Gerry." "What sort of a problem?" Bob asked back. "Last night he tried to pass off his sex fantasies as fact," I replied. "I wonder what else he has been lying about?" Over the next few weeks I went on several sales calls with Gerry to understand why his sales results were so far behind plan. It turned out that many of the hot leads he had assured us would "close any day now" were in fact pretty cold. In frustration, we fired him and hired two new salesmen in the Boston office. Without a job, Gerry's financial house of cards came crashing down around him. It turned out that he had bought a very fancy house on a sliver of equity and was carrying a huge mortgage. The mortgage holder foreclosed on the house after he missed several payments; it sold for less than the value of the mortgage, and Gerry lost just about all he owned.

In the middle of all this drama, it became clear that we would need a lot more money than we had originally expected to get the business off the ground and drive it toward profitability. One of our venture capital investors got cold feet about the business, and refused to go along with a new round of financing; in the process, this firm infected our other two VCs with doubts that we could solve the sales problem. When we thought we had a new syndicate put together for a B round, we went back to our original VCs to ask if they would join in. They offered us only a small bridge loan to the closing date on the new round, provided that my partner and I also put in bridge funding, to which we readily assented. With this half-hearted support from the A-round VCs, the new funders turned cautious, and at the last minute, we could not close a deal with them, and the business was forced to close its doors.

Closing down the business was an interesting exercise in its own right. Our ad agency immediately got a court order seizing our bank account, leaving us with no cash with which to do an orderly wind-down of the business. Our intent had been to share our remaining cash among the several creditors of the company on an equitable basis. For lack of funds, could not even hire a lawyer to force the ad agency to disgorge the funds they had seized. This experience left a very bitter taste on our mouths and in the mouths of the other organizations that had supplied services to us.

The failure of Connexions was an unhappy experience, and we marked our final day of operations with a staff party which might be better described as a meal of condolence. The atmosphere was positively funereal. The dozen or so staffers who had worked so hard to get things going had one last get together before all going on the unemployment rolls.

However, as I looked back on the experience, I realized what an amazing learning opportunity it had been. In no other environment could I have learned so much about marketing, sales, software development, customer service and corporate finance—and honed the knack for translating strategic and tactical business initiatives into the language of finance, the lingua franca of what has come to be called the *C-suite*, the group of top-level executives who lead major corporations. In short, these lessons gave me the view point of a CEO and enabled me to step up the range of consulting services I could offer and to offer them to much higher level clients than I had worked with before.

After my partner and I wrapped up Connexions, he and I discussed returning to ADL. Ultimately he opted to set up as an advisor to VC firms with troubled investments. Over time his new line of work morphed into buying VCs' failed investments for a song, and then trying to wring out some terminal value from them by selling a key overlooked intangible asset such as a patent, a piece of software, or a base of customers. A mutual friend of ours characterized this business as "robbing the graves of grave robbers." Notwithstanding our friend's teasing, my partner made quite a good living. I instead opted to return to ADL, where my new skills quickly caused my career to soar.

ADL, Part 2

After I returned to ADL I focused exclusively on the needs of senior executives in the information industry, utilizing the broad set of skills I had developed during my first stint at ADL and at Connexions. These same capabilities also became part of my day to day approach in looking at internal issues within ADL. About one year after my return, I was at an offsite meeting with Frank, his fifteen to twenty more senior staff members, and Frank's then boss, Dick Heitman, a member of ADL's Management Committee. At lunch I was seated with Dick and five or six other people and the conversation turned to our respective recent client cases of involving business turn-arounds. In the course of that discussion, I outlined a holistic approach addressing all elements of both the revenue and cost sides of the ledger that I had recently used with one of my clients.

I thought little about that luncheon conversation until about a month later, when, out of the blue, Dick summoned me to his office. It seemed that another of Dick's groups, one focused on operations research, was floundering after many years of business success. Its founding leader had retired a few years previously and his successor, a consummate consultant, seemed to lack the leadership skills to sustain the business. Dick began to ask my advice on what he could do to help the current leader to turn the business around. I guess the holistic approach to business turnarounds that I had outlined during that luncheon had made quite an impression on Dick. After another couple of weeks, I was called back to Dick's office and offered the job of fixing that business. I was now Frank Allen's peer.

The turn-around was a remarkably simple one. When I first took over this group, its staff was a rather dispirited group of people who had been left behind in a corporate reorganization that had seen many of their immediate colleagues, a logistics team, transferred to a group covering the discrete manufacturing industries. I quickly realized that the people who now worked for me were highly talented but most of whom lacked a focus on business development. The core issue was that the group defined itself around on a narrow set of technical capabilities collectively known as Operations Research rather than on well-defined sets of clients. As a result it was unclear to them where they should focus their client development attention for both the external client and the internal ADL case leader markets. After a quick review of the group's list of clients for the preceding several years, it struck me that almost all of its work was for various service industries such as retailers, insurance companies, and law firms. This dovetailed nicely with my own interest with information service companies. Armed with this observation, I assigned various senior staff members to promote our capabilities in these vertical markets, both internally at ADL and with external clients. With this simple change, the business began to take off, with a growing stream of new client assignments and rising staff billability, our revenues began to grow at about 10% per year, and profits grew at twice that rate as we were able to sell a larger percentage of the staff's time.

Early in my tenure, I led a client project in which we helped our client identify his most profitable customers and then refocus his sales force on finding additional customers with the same profile. One afternoon, while I was discussing this project with one of my vice-presidents, Debbie Adamian, she asked if we could do a similar analysis for our own business. After we batted the idea around for a few minutes, we decided to see if we could figure out which clients give us the most business for the least business development cost. Digging through various accounting data that I received monthly, we developed a taxonomy of the individual buyers (i.e., not IBM, But Mr. X or Ms. Y who was head of marketing for the enterprise division of IBM) our group's services as follows:

- *A* clients were ones had retained our group's services multiple times and knew the range of our capabilities.

- *B* clients were individuals who had retained us at least once.

- *C* clients were individuals who were familiar with our work for their colleagues but had never retained us themselves.

- *D* clients were individuals who did not know us at all, or as Deb described them, those whose first question upon meeting us would be to ask "Arthur D. Who?"

We quickly discovered that winning an incremental $100,000 from A's cost us an average of $2500. For B's the number was a $5500. For C's it was $10,500. And for D's it was $93,000. In short, we had quantified the value of client relationships and thereby discovered the value of relationship-based business development.

Deb and I quickly shared these findings with our colleagues at one of my quarterly meetings with the entire staff in order to focus everyone on seeking follow-on business with A, B and C clients, and to stop all efforts at chasing business with Ds. The core method for expanding the account base of organizations with whom we worked was to follow up with As and Bs who had new or enlarged responsibilities in their current companies or who had joined new companies.

That year I set an aggressive revenue target for our group. As I was walking thorough the proposed budget with my team at another quarterly staff meeting, I explained that we were going to grow our revenues by 20%. To add a challenge to the message, I placed a magnum of champagne on the podium which we would drink at the end of each quarter if met that target. To reinforce the message, I also put up a box of dry dog food which we would eat if we missed this target by five or more percentage points. Finally, to make this a sporting challenge, I offered to serve champagne to the staff and also eat the dog biscuits at the final quarterly staff meeting if we beat the 20% target by five or more percentage points. I wound up eating the dog biscuits every quarter, washed down with champagne (which made the biscuits rather more palatable) at each of my quarterly staff meetings.

In the course of running this business I learned to be very flexible with how I managed the staff along the lines that Frank Allen had followed and also when to be firm. At one point three people came into my office proposing to build a business selling corporate strategy work to post offices around the globe. I thought this was a truly dumb idea, and in the course of a half-hour's discussion the trio in question came around to my point of view, or so I thought. Instead they kept below the radar scope with their efforts, and three months later they presented me with a signed engagement letter from the US Postal Service for $1 million dollars' worth of strategy work. In short order they then grew the business with the USPS and expanded it several fold with work for its counterparts in Canada and several European countries via referrals from their very satisfied USPS clients. I had to eat a bit of crow for my earlier efforts to discourage them, but gladly did so publicly to encourage others to follow their entrepreneurial instincts.

In a different situation, after ADL's struggling banking group had been merged into my team, we received an unsolicited request for proposals to develop a new strategy for the National Bank of Uganda. I met with the team that wanted to pursue it, and we jointly agreed that (1) it was a D client, and therefore unlikely to be profitable work, and (2) the job would be impossible to staff because no one would want to sign up for six months in a hell hole which was just beginning to recover from two decades of terrible misrule by the recently deposed cruel and sadistic dictator, Idi Amin. Two weeks later I received an expense report from the then leader of the banking group for a trip to the capital of Uganda to meet with the bank officials. I was furious, and wanted to fire him on the spot, especially after I learned from his colleagues that the real purpose of his trip had been to visit with a relative of his who was a missionary in that country. I called the offender in and chewed him out firmly over this nonsense. I let him know that the next time he pulled such a stunt, I would refuse to cover his expenses, but I also decided not to fire him because this was his first offense. The good news was that he chose to retire a few months later, ensuring that there would be no repeat of this problem from him.

As head of the service industries P&L, I reported to a member of ADL's Management Committee, though which member seemed to change every couple of years as retirements, deaths and reorganizations seemed to cause constant change at that level. My first boss from that committee was Dick Heitman, better known as Grumpy from the 'name-the-dwarf' contest; his other direct reports were Frank Allen (who was about to retire) the head of the group that served the telecom industry, and two internal groups, the corporate IT department and the head of facilities, buildings and grounds. About three weeks into my new role, Dick invited all of his direct reports to a dinner meeting. During the meeting Dick raked the fellow in charge of the telecom group over the coals for the poor financial results he had been turning in for the preceding twelve months. The rest of us sat there silently staring down at our dishes, fearing that we might be next. When the meeting came to a mercifully early end, I pulled aside the head of IT, who had reported to Dick for several years already, to ask if all of Dick's meetings were like this to which he nodded "Yes". I then asked how one could avoid being the victim, to which he replied, "Don't be Dick's biggest problem."

I soon learned how to stay on Dick's good side. I kept on turning in solid, profitable business growth. I discovered that Dick would pore through everyone's monthly P&L statements and then needle them about line items that seemed off. This was particularly a problem in that the company had an old home-brew accounting system with no edit checks on inputs. Mistakes made in the corporate accounting department routinely found their way into the financial reports. I made it a habit to collect my P&L statements directly from the IT department the evening that they ran the monthly reports; I would then spend that entire evening examining my figures, rooting out the mistakes, and producing a corrected statement which I made sure would be on Dick's desk when he got in the next morning.

Dick was obsessed with cost control. At one point, the CEO detailed him to acquire a corporate limousine to be used to transport senior client executives who might be visiting in our offices. Dick's response was to buy a pearl grey Checker taxicab, for which he was much derided behind his back. Two years later, when the CEO of Ford came for a visit, he was not amused to be met with the Checker instead of with a Lincoln.

After I had been in my new role for a few months, I noticed that my group's sole PC was in constant use as my staff did the elaborate quantitative studies as part of its work for our clients. The lack of adequate computing resources was constraining our ability to get our work done efficiently. I sent Dick a requisition for a PC for each of the forty-plus members of the consulting staff. He called me, quite disturbed by this proposed expense and could not see how we would cover its cost. He suggested that we should buy one more machine and establish a sign-up sheet as a means of allocating this scarce resource among the staff. I responded that it made no sense to queue up employees being paid six figure salaries in order to maximize the utilization machines costing less than $2000. He agreed when I suggested that we simply raise the billing rates of the staff by a few dollars an hour to cover the cost of the equipment. The one catch was that my group had to "lease" the machines at inflated rates from the facilities department (which also reported to Dick), so he could report an increased "profit"—a small price to pay for the improvements in the speed and quality of my group's work that these machines would enable.

Another sore point at this stage in my career was that my pay and that of all but one of my senior staff were woefully below market rates. Remembering the resentment that I had felt as an underpaid camp counsellor, I feared that we would soon have a series of departures, with myself in the lead. I went to Dick with a proposal that we do a systematic upgrading of salary levels which he rejected out of hand, complaining that it would increase my costs with no evidence that we would achieve any increase in revenues. I was very confident that we could increase our hourly billing rates with little to no loss in business because we were selling our services very cheaply but needed a way to hedge my bets to satisfy Dick. So I returned to Dick a couple of weeks later to propose a bonus system for my senior staff tied to their own performance and the group's overall profitability. He allowed me to go ahead, and we phased the new system in the following year, raising billing rates and then accruing bonus reserves monthly as the increased revenue and profits flowed in. At some point the HR department found out about our non-standard compensation system. They were furious that we had not consulted them. They demanded that we stop the program at the end of its first year, but also agreed that to put in a massive salary adjustment for the following year, bringing my staff and me closer to market rates of pay. In retrospect theirs was a really dumb idea because salaries were close to a fixed cost, and, unlike the bonus system I had developed, could not be cut if the business flow weakened. But I was overruled by the HR people who, speaking frankly, did not have the least inkling of how the company made money; they just wanted us to be like everyone else.

After about two years, Dick retired and I was assigned to work for one of his Management Committee colleagues Ashok Kalelkar. Ashok had a reputation as a very political animal, but I managed to work reasonably well with him. His other groups were engineering-oriented technical practices and I believe he had only a limited understanding of what our people did for clients, which meant that he did little to meddle in our business. So long as we turned in decent numbers he pretty much left us alone. One concern I had going in was that, earlier in his career, he had fired a fellow who was the domestic partner of one of my senior staff, Louise F. This man had been an internal rival of Ashok's and Ashok had found a pretext to get him out of the way. Louise was concerned that he might go after her as well since she knew about all the ugly details of that episode. I suggested to Ashok that we grant Louise a well-deserved promotion to vice-president to reassure and make peace with her and he readily agreed.

After about eighteen months, the Management Committee was reorganized again, and I was assigned to work for Elliott Wilbur, a fellow whose previous role had been to head the company's practice with the chemicals industry. Elliott was an affable man whom I had gotten to know moderately well before he was promoted to the Management Committee, though I soon learned that he was not to be trusted. At that time he had four groups reporting to him, mine, the two groups focused on discrete manufacturing companies and process industries, and ADL's San Francisco office. Mine and Process Industries were solidly profitable, Discrete Manufacturing was moderately profitable, and the San Francisco office was losing money by the bucket and rapidly collapsing. At one point Elliott pushed me to take over the San Francisco office, with all sorts of vague promises about how much of a hero I would be if I turned it around. When I looked under the covers of that office's business, I discovered that most of its senior staff who held the main client relationships had already decamped to other firms; turning it around would have entailed a brutal and costly, many-year rebuilding effort. I knew ADL's CEO would not have the patience to wait that long, so I turned the job down.

At about that time, Elliot promised those of us running his other groups that we would not be held to account for the collapse of the San Francisco office. By the time the year ended, we learned that the losses in that office had wiped out the profits generated by the other three of Elliot's groups, whose heads would not only be denied annual bonuses, but we would be forced to return 10% of our base salaries to make up for the shortfall. Having just finished a year in which my group's profits had grown by 41%, I was not pleased. When I reminded Elliot of his promise, he denied that

303

he had ever given such assurances. I nearly quit on the spot but then held back, knowing that we would retire in another year. I figured that with his retirement I would get someone more to my liking, and get a shot to succeed him on the Management Committee.

Shortly after the collapse of the San Francisco office, another member of the Management Committee resigned because he was dying of cancer. His groups were assigned to various other members of the Management Committee. Elliott picked up a group focused on the pharmaceuticals industry, headed by a Ms. X, a woman with a reputation among the staff for fancy talk of what she was going to do, followed by weak follow through and mediocre results. Because her previous boss had quite a bad reputation as an office Romeo, rumor had it that she had used unorthodox tactics to become head of her group. I personally saw her as a false front covering an empty interior and was greatly offended by her political posturing. It soon became clear to me that she was my main rival to succeed Elliot, and that rivalry began to go badly for me quite quickly. Somehow she got the ear of the CEO even though I thought I had very solid relations with him. She was soon being invited to senior level meetings from which I was excluded. By the time Elliot retired in June of that year, she had won the prize and succeeded him.

As she assumed her new role she lost no time putting her stamp on the business in highly visible ways. She had an oversized ego and an even larger posterior and required all of us to stroke the former and kiss the latter. She established weekly staff meetings whose primary purpose appeared to be the enable her to show off to the rest of us and to get us to nod yes to whatever ideas she put forward. It soon became clear that she considered herself to be much more important than our clients. At one point, I was summoned to meet with the board chairman of one of our clients at a time that conflicted with Ms. X's weekly staff meeting. I mentioned this to her several days in advance and she indicated that she had no issue with my skipping her meeting to see a high-level client. However, the day following her meeting, she severely chastised me in public for missing her weekly meeting.

She immediately appropriated the business development budgets from the groups that worked for her and used those funds to build a personal staff to further her private agendas. Some of those funds went to hire a team of personal publicists to promote her both within and outside the company. Another person she hired onto her personal staff was an expensive HR professional not under the control of the corporate HR department. I strongly suspected that his charter was to identify exploitable weaknesses among her direct reports; he kept on pushing us to take various psychological and personality tests that did not appear to have any other purpose. Increasingly she exerted more and more central control over a business that was highly dependent in individual initiative; this approach was the beginning of issues that eventually led to the failure of her business, and ultimately of ADL as a whole.

One of her early moves was to force all of her direct reports including her HR fellow to go as a group on an Outward Bound trip, supposedly to build teamwork. Actually the trip did not work quite as she had planned. When she presented the idea at one of her weekly staff meetings she described it as a sailing trip in the Florida Keys. For four days, we would sail about during the day and, in the evenings, pull up to a beach, have a cocktail, and grill a few steaks for supper. She had her publicists promote her idea for this trip to the rest of ADL.

The realities of this trip did not sink in to her until we arrived at the Outward Bound's base on a small island in the Florida Keys. We were going to be confined to a 30-foot open boat for the duration. While the boat had a small sail, it sailed very poorly to windward, and we would have to spend most of the trip as galley slaves, rowing this heavy, clumsy boat from place to place. The accommodations were so crowded that to sleep we would need to lay the oars across the seats and lie down on top of them across the boat, with each person's head wedged between the feet of those afore and abaft of him. The boat had no toilet. Instead we had to use a bucket on the boat's small foredeck.

As the reality began to sink in to Ms. X's, her mood turned blacker and blacker. I think she hit her low point on the trip the first evening when she had to bed down on the hard oars in the middle of the group of us, and her mood stayed that way until the trip ended. Of course, when we returned to Cambridge she lied in her typical fashion, telling all who would listen what a wonderful bonding experience this had been. My personal observation was that all this enforced togetherness among a group of people who did not particularly like each other did little to increase their camaraderie.

Towards year-end, it came time for the annual budget-setting process. Because I sensed that the markets my group served were softening I proposed a budget with a modest increase in revenue. She turned that proposal down flat. In its place she unilaterally imposed a revenue budget which was an enormous jump over up from current results. Given that she had already taken away our budget for business development, I knew that her goals for me were absolutely unachievable, but she would not budge from her demands. I was clearly being set up for failure so that she could fire me.

As the new year unfolded I became increasingly upset working for this madwoman. My wife soon noticed that I was coming home from work more and more agitated, often needing to unburden myself at home after yet another day's frustrations. Carol became concerned that I would begin to have health problems if I continued at ADL, and encouraged me to begin to look for work elsewhere.

The end of my ADL career occurred later that year. Ms. X suddenly relieved me of all management responsibilities and split up my group among her other direct reports. Fortunately, I had kept a hand in the consulting side of the business, unlike most of my peers who had become pure managers. As a result, I was able to quickly line up about $2.5 million worth of new business spread over three clients, making me virtually fire-proof; I was not going to be jobless. In parallel to delivering all this new work with several trusted colleagues, I also launched an effort to find a new corporate home. I resigned from ADL eight months later.

About one year later, Ms. X was fired as the impact of her wrong-headed leadership and management style drove the businesses that reported to her into a downward spiral. The CEO then appointed a succession of replacements who were unable to right the ship, and staff left the company in droves.

In retrospect, the promotion of this woman was a symptom of a disease that was beginning to infect all of ADL. Over time, the company's CEO, who took his new job around the time of my promotion, was also pushing ever more in the direction of exerting tight control over the partners who ran the various business units. He started requiring us each to invest hundreds of thousands of dollars in the business through the company's several stock ownership vehicles so that he would have a hand in all of our pockets. He also made organizational demands on us that caused the company's entire management team to focus more on internal issues rather than on the core capability of delivering high quality professional services to important external clients. Ultimately, as the company floundered, the

Board, which up to that time had been complacent about the problems festering within the company, fired the CEO. He was replaced by someone who was even worse, and after another three years, the company could no longer service its debt. It fell into bankruptcy in 2000 and was dismembered with the various remnants sold at auction. Thus ended the world's oldest management consultancy, a company organized in 1886.

After I had left the company these issues became much more apparent to me. Fortunately, I had the brilliant foresight to turn fifty, the minimum age at which one could withdraw his funds from the firm, one month before they closed the stock redemption windows for the company's Employee Stock Ownership Plan, its Investment Plan, and the Memorial Drive Trust, the employees' pension plan. By that time ADL was no longer generating enough cash to be able to honor its promise to buy back its stock from those who were approaching retirement age. Those who had remained at ADL to the bitter end lost the bulk of their life savings which were about 70% invested in ADL stock. I was grateful to have left when I did. One poor idiot who had borrowed hundreds of thousands of dollars to buy all the stock that the CEO was forcing down our throats was left financially crippled.

Listening to the Market

After I left ADL, I went to Mercer Management Consulting, since renamed Oliver Wyman. Their growth strategy was to hire senior partners from other firms with books of clients. Mercer's parent company, Marsh & McLennan, heavily incented Mercer's senior management to grow the business quickly and at a low cost. During my four years there, they learned that the existing strategy was costly and they could not acquire enough new business through it fast enough to earn the desired cash and stock bonuses. Then senior management discovered that they could acquire independent companies and MarshMac, the corporate parent, would not charge Mercer the cost of capital required. Hiring of individual senior partners was out and there was a mad dash to acquire whole businesses, each with at least $50 M in revenues. In this turmoil, I and all of the other recently hired senior partners were phased out, conveniently just a few months short of the five-year vesting period for the company's pension plan and most of our stock options.

As I began to take stock of what to do next, I thought I would like to cross over to the client side and take on a senior management role with one of my clients. My second son was about to enter university and I was faced with having to cover two college tuitions, so a steady job without the ups and downs of the gig-economy was very appealing. My thinking about the client side was that an awful lot of senior executives were not all that sharp and I could quickly make my mark in such an organization. A couple of my friends warned me that what senior guys in large organizations lacked in smarts was more than made up for by their instinct for organizational politics, an area in which I was much less skilled. Nonetheless, I continued working this angle for some time, and reached out to many past clients looking for an appropriate situation.

However, in my discussions with my past clients, they kept offering me substantial consulting assignments instead of jobs, so I decided the market was speaking to me and I had better listen. It seemed I was the brand the market sought, and I had the good sense to take advantage of the situation. I quickly changed direction and set up a private consulting practice. Luckily for me, I had negotiated a deal when I initially went to Mercer in which my personal clients would be exempted from the very onerous and rigidly enforced non-compete agreements that Mercer imposed on all new hires. Mercer had no success trying to take my clients away from me, and I soon had a to-die-for client list of a dozen Fortune 500 accounts in the information industry, including Cisco Systems, Microsoft, AT&T, ADP, Northrop Grumman, and Time Warner. Moreover, a number of my projects involved some very exciting international work for the European subsidiaries of major US and Canadian companies. After just three months, I was making more money than I ever did working for others and in the second year the business grew by another 50%. At any given time I had several substantial six-figure projects running with up to a dozen subcontractors supporting the work.

At one point I considered the idea of building the business to the level of its being a salable asset, with perhaps five to seven million dollars in revenue, a property that could be sold for ten to fifteen million dollars. But I was very concerned about the amount of working capital that such an enterprise would require and whether I wanted to invest that big a share of our total family capital on the chance of making a lucky sale. I also considered taking on a partner with whom to share the financial risk. As I thought further about potential partners I developed strict criteria that such a partner would need to meet. This person would need to be of unimpeachable integrity and honesty, have a strong track record of delivering excellent client work on time and on budget, and adhere to the old ADL principle of "always do the right thing," In addition any person I might consider would need to have demonstrated have strong client development skills and have the financial wherewithal to enable us to grow the business to a substantial scale.

My thinking soon focused on a woman with whom I had worked off and on for many years as the ideal business partner. Unfortunately just as my ideas began to gel, she suddenly encountered a terrible reversal in her personal life. Her husband of many years, to whom she was very devoted, ran off with a much younger woman. A very unpleasant divorce fight ensued. I had seen other friends and colleagues become so consumed by various legal problems that they could not focus on their other business and family obligations, so I was concerned that her legal battle would be a major distraction. My judgment turned out to have been prescient; the divorce fight became very nasty and lasted more than four years; it would have seriously impeded development of a solid business partnership. Ultimately, I abandoned the idea of expanding my business beyond what I could develop on my own.

One of the cleverest ideas I had during those years was to set up a defined benefit pension plan for myself. At age fifty-five, I promised myself that at age sixty-five I would receive the maximum pension allowed by law. To fund the pension, I was required by the Department of Labor rules to sock away six-figure sums annually. These contributions were considered business expenses, so Uncle Sam and the governor of Massachusetts were paying 43% of the cost of funding the pension. When the stock market crash occurred during the Great Recession of 2008-2009, Department of Labor required additional monies to be deposited to make up for the decline in the value of the plan's securities portfolio. During the subsequent market recovery, this pension plan quickly grew to a substantial sum. When I turned sixty-five, Department of Labor rules required me to take taxable payments from the pension plan, so I rolled over the pension plan's assets into a personal IRA, which allowed the funds to continue to grow on a tax deferred basis until at age seventy and a half. Finally, when President Obama proposed and subsequently passed a massive tax increase, I rolled the IRA over to a Roth IRA, paying the taxes from other funds, guaranteeing that this retirement money could grow completely tax free until both my wife and I are dead or the government changes the rules.

In any case, I kept this business running full blast until the death of my brother Peter in the summer of 2011 when I began to taper down my work. But I so enjoyed working with clients and colleagues that I did not give it up and fully retire until age seventy-and-a-half in 2016. By that time, I had accumulated more than enough money to seriously consider retirement. The after-tax returns on the taxable portion of our investment portfolio (taxed at around 27%) were so much larger than the results from working (taxed at around 65%) that it would have been foolish to keep at it. In short, the government had made it uneconomic to work, and thus ended my second entrepreneurial gig and my working life. It was now time to enjoy the rewards of a career well learned and executed.

PART 5 ON MY ALPINE- AND RIVIERA- INSPIRED LOVE OF THE MOUNTAINS AND THE SEA

Chapter 21

The Alps

Torino, the large Italian city in the northwestern corner of that country and the city where my parents grew up, is very close to where the Alps separate Italy from Switzerland to the north and France to the west. The highest peaks in the Alps are visible from Torino on clear days. The Italian royal family, the House of Savoy, had its roots in those mountains dating back to the year 1000. The Savoys reigned from Torino from the Middle Ages until 1864, when the national capital was moved first to Florence and later to Rome as part of the Italian unification process.

During my parents' youth, the Italian crown prince, Umberto II—who was one year older than my father—resided in Torino. He lived mainly in the Castle of Moncalieri and the Palace of Stupinigi, studying with his tutors. Umberto was much taken with mountain sports such as climbing, hiking, skiing and hunting. He hunted *cinghiali* [wild boar], *camosci* [chamois] and *stambecchi* [ibex] at the royal hunting preserve in the Valle d'Aosta, an hour's drive north of Torino. In this dimension, he followed the interests of his grandmother, Queen Margherita of Savoy who had a summer palace at Gressoney in the Valle d'Aosta and who was an avid mountain climber. Consequently, mountain sports were the height of fashion among proper Torinesi, my parents' families included. My father and mother both learned to hike and ski as children and their families vacationed in the mountains most summers.

The Alps represented an escape from the pressures of daily life. Their stark crags and glaciers were softened by high Alpine meadows with their profusion of wildflowers. During the summers, the mountain folk pastured their innumerable cows on those meadows and produced fontina cheese from the cows' milk. The rich grazing of the high Alps is said to give the cheese its distinct flavor and aroma, and today fontina has PDO (protected designation of origin) status. During the winters these Alpine herders and their cows retreated to the picturesque villages in the valleys that have since become resorts for the rich and famous.

When Mussolini's government decreed the Fascist Racial Laws in 1938 that took away most civil rights from Italy's Hebrew community, the mountains became an important safe haven. My parents and many of their friends skied across them to France and Switzerland to spirit assets out of the country in preparation for their eventual emigration. Later, when the German Nazis occupied northern Italy, these same mountains became important bases for the Italian Resistance as well as escape routes to Switzerland for many Hebrews, including my Uncle Ruggiero and some of my Levi and Montalcini cousins. The independent-minded mountain folk also harbored countless Hebrews and other anti-Fascists who were unable to escape across the border.

This history of the Alps as refuge and center of stubborn independence from central authority is an ancient one in those parts. For example, several valleys in the Piemontese Alps (due west of Torino and south of the Valle d'Aosta) became home and hiding place for an ancient Protestant population, the Waldenses. They took their name from a rich merchant, Peter Waldo of Lyon in the Middle Ages, who gave away his fortune and began to preach against many of the excesses and high living of the papal court and numerous doctrinal elements of the Roman Catholic Dogma. At some point the pope declared them to be heretics and they became a persecuted minority. They were subjected to the Inquisition in the 1400s, and yet they persisted in their approach to religion despite the best efforts of the Dominicans and Franciscans to force them to submit to the authority of the popes. In 1679, when Louis XIV decided to suppress the French Protestant movements by military force, he induced his niece, the dowager duchess of Savoy and regent for her minor son, Duke Vittorio Amadeo II, to attack the Piemontese Waldensians. At one point the ducal army surrounded the entire population, several thousand strong, on an Alpine mountain top, with the intent to annihilate it the next day. That night, under cover of darkness, the entire Waldensian community slipped past the sleeping ducal soldiers, and crossed into Protestant Switzerland, where they remained for several years, until Vittorio Amadeo II agreed to end the military campaign against them.

Perhaps as a consequence of their being both fashionable and a source of refuge, the Alps, particularly the Valle d'Aosta, came to have an almost mystical quality in our family's life, and this value has continued to my generation and my children's. When I was a child, we took numerous vacations to various side valleys of the Valle d'Aosta including Courmayeur, at the foot of the Monte Bianco (Mont Blanc), Cervinia, just below the Cervino (Matterhorn) and Gressoney, a village below the Monte Rosa, and these vacations are some of my fondest childhood memories. These vacations consisted of spending long days hiking, generally with a picnic lunch followed by a hearty peasant-style dinner of perhaps, bread, the local fontina cheese, and a dense vegetable soup or polenta topped with a rich game stew. On one of our vacations there, my brother Albert went on a climbing expedition with some of our Treves cousins, topping the twin peaks, Castor and Pollux.

When I was a child during the 1950s, the Valle d'Aosta was a very poor region. Indeed, the area was so poor that the local residents received government subsidies for essentials such as fuel, bread, and salt, and also for such less-essential goods as chocolate and brandy. The locals eked out meager livings farming minute terraced fields by hand in the lower valleys and dairying in the uplands. In winter they kept their cows in the villages, often in buildings that consisted of a stone barn on the ground floor, surmounted by a wooden upper story where the family lived. In summer they would drive their cows up into the Alpine meadows to pasture, with the cowherds taking up summer residence in small wooden cottages called *baite*. During this season, the cows would give copious quantities of milk richly flavored from their diet of mountain flowers. The cowherds would turn this milk into butter and cheese which they would store in cool caves dug out of the mountain sides until the end of the season. The proceeds from the sale of these dairy products would be their cash income for the year. In the fall, these small-time farmers would hunt *cinghiali, camosci*, and other game to gather a winter meat supply. They would preserve these meats by smoking or drying them. Their vegetables would come from kitchen gardens tended by their wives, and every household kept a few chickens to supply eggs for the table. The chickens themselves were rarely eaten as they were considered a luxury food. Likewise, the eating of beef, pork or veal was very rare.

These hardy, independent mountain folk had been living in this way at least since Roman times. Aosta, the regional capital, had been a Roman garrison town and still retains its Roman walls, rectilinear street plan, and theater. A number of the side valleys have stone bridges that were built 2000 years ago and are still serviceable and in daily use today. During the Middle Ages, the area was divided into dozens of independent fiefdoms, each dominated by a massive castle, many of which are still standing and some of which are still inhabited. The House of Savoy, who came to rule all of Italy, originated from this region as lords of one of these feudal holdings.

In the 1980s, Carol and I began to take our sons on vacations to the Alps, particularly to the Valle d'Aosta. In successive trips, we witnessed the decline and eventual replacement of the old way of life by a new much more prosperous economy based on tourism. Our first trip, in 1984, was to Courmayeur, perhaps the most accessible resort because of its lower altitude. In preparation for our visit, I teased my younger son that the local farmers had bred a special type of cow with legs longer on one side than the other. The purpose of this supposed adaptation was to make it easier for them to graze on steep mountainsides.

Once there, we lost no time embracing the traditional Alpine experience, hiking into France via the Val Veny up to the Col de Checrouit (Figures 21-1 21-2, and 21-3). By late morning, just as we were passing the tree line, it began to snow (in July no less!). Now quite wet and thoroughly chilled, we sought refuge in a *baita*—the traditional summer residence for a cowherd. Enlarged to serve as a climber's hostel, this *baita* opened into a large warm room set up as a rustic restaurant, where we immediately sat down to a hearty luncheon of polenta with *camoscio* stew. By the time we finished eating, the snow had stopped and we resumed our hike. Soon I noticed my son carefully examining the legs of a large herd of cows to see which side was shorter—evidently he had taken my teasing seriously. After about fifteen minutes' study, he ran up to me and asked again, "Are you sure about the cows having shorter legs on one side?" At that point I confessed my prank and he learned to be skeptical of dubious stories, even when they came from his omniscient parents. Climbing ever higher on our hike, we passed the hulk of a military fort. Built before World War II, the fort had been subsequently decommissioned in compliance with the peace treaty ending the war. Finally, we reached the summit of the pass. On the Italian side of the border was a sign warmly welcoming visitors. On the French side was a stern message advising one to comply with French law.

On another day we experienced a much more modern aspect of Alpine life. We took the cable car up the Italian side of the Monte Bianco and across the Mer de Glace on the French side, planning to end our journey at Chamonix. The cable car on the Italian side was a sturdy system whose towers were anchored in solid rock. The cars held a couple dozen passengers each and were solid enough that passengers felt confident about their safety. On the French side of the border, however, the cable cars seated only four and consisted of trios of tinny little cabins that swayed ominously in the wind. For the traverse of the Mer de Glace, a huge glacier whose name means "sea of ice," there was no exposed rock on which to build support towers. Instead cabins were suspended from a thin cable that ran between a pair of ridges on either side of the glacier. When the wind blew, the whole system shook and swayed. My wife, who is even more subject to vertigo than I, turned greener with each wind gust and could barely keep her breakfast down. When we reached the Aiguille du Midi, the first way-stop on the way down on the French side of the mountain, she had had as much as she could take. We rested there for a couple of hours while she regained her balance and calmed her digestion. At that point we decided that the saner course was to scrap the rest of the trip to Chamonix and return to Courmayeur.

Our next trip to the Valle d'Aosta came several years later. It was to Cogne in the Gran Paradiso National Park. The park's origin had been as a royal hunting preserve. After the abolition of the monarchy in 1946, it was opened to the public as one of the Italy's most beautiful national parks. Cogne is a delightful village, strung out linearly along a brook. On the opposite bank of the brook is a lush green valley leading towards the highest peaks of the Gran Paradiso group. On our first day there we took a short hike through the spruce forest just above the village and were rewarded with sightings of a small group of *camosci* with their short, hooked horns. On our second day we took a much longer hike into the heart of the park and ran into several herds of both *camosci* and their larger cousins, the *stambecchi* with their enormous curved horns. The *stambecchi* had been hunted to extinction throughout the Alps, except in this park; recent efforts to reintroduce these magnificent animals elsewhere in the Alps have borne fruit, and there are now several tens of thousands of them scattered across the Italian, Swiss and Austrian Alps.

Towards the end of our trip to Cogne, I organized a hike up the ridge north of Cogne that separates its valley from the main Valle d'Aosta. Well above the tree line, we came to an ancient *baita*, inhabited by a seemingly more ancient old woman. I struck up a conversation with her. It seems that she was the last of her line. She still migrated to the high pasture each summer with her cows to make cheese, but her sons refused to do such hard work. They had finished high school and had found easier and more remunerative work in a government office in the town of Aosta, to which they could commute on their motor scooters. She welcomed us into her aging cave, which was carved into the mountain side, and offered us samples of her cheeses. Some were fairly new and had the fresh smell of mountain wildflowers and a creamy taste, while others had been aging for several months and had a sharper smell and taste. Of course we had to buy several wedges of her products, and these became the core of our picnics over the next week.

Our most recent trips to the Valle D'Aosta were to Cervinia (Figures 21-4 and 21-5), with our younger son Michael when he was an undergraduate, and to Gressoney (Figures 21-6, 21-7 and 21-8). By then the old way of life in Cervinia had almost completely disappeared. When we hiked up into the mountain meadows, the remaining *baite* were all abandoned, and there were virtually no cows to be seen. In the village of Cervinia itself there remained only a handful of old farmers' cottages, and most of those were tumbled-down ruins. All the rest had been replaced with condos, restaurants, and trendy shops. Even the rustic climbers' hostels had gone upscale. I suppose the old farming families still live there, but now they milk tourists instead of cows. In contrast, Gressoney has been much better preserved, perhaps because it is a less fashionable resort even though it was already a touring center in the mid-1800s, as evidenced by a rusty plaque we encountered in a high pass commemorating Tolstoy's visit on a hiking vacation in 1857. Here I was delighted to find farmers still using scythes to cut hay by hand on steeply pitched fields. This sight reminded me of my earliest youth in Val Salice. Cows continued to populate these Alpine meadows, too, and we found several summertime cheese-making operations in high mountain *baite*.

Even now I enjoy mountain vacations above all others. The vigorous exercise and high mountain grandeur clear my brain and drive all my normal daily concerns out of my consciousness. They are the "play hard" aspect of my life that helps to balance the "work hard" side. The Alps, in particular, must be coded into my DNA. Over the years, my wife and I have taken holidays in the American Rockies, Cascades, and Sierras, as well as in the Italian Dolomites, the Scottish Highlands and Snowdonia in northern Wales. But no mountains appear to me to be as beautiful as the Alps, especially those in the Valle d'Aosta north and west of Torino.

Figure 21-1. Carol, David and Michael, Val Veny, Courmayeur, 1985

Figure 21-2. George, Carol, David and Michael,
Col de Checrouit, Courmayeur, 1985

Figure 21-3. David and Michael before a cheese cave under restoration, Courmayeur, 1985

Figure 21-4. Carol, Plateau Rosa, Cervinia, 1972

Figure 21-5. Il Cervino (the Matterhorn), from Plateau Rosa, 1998

Figure 21-6. Abandoned Baita, Gressoney, 2012

Figure 21-7. Baita sale of butter and cheese, Gressoney, 2012

Figure 21-8. Monte Rosa from Plan Santa Anna, Gressoney, 2012

Chapter 22

Into the Wilds

I was first introduced to mountain beauty and outdoor life on summer trips to our ancestral home in Torino when I was a small child. My parents had also brought to America their love of alpine sports, skiing and hiking—among other European pass-times that set us apart from typical American families. But in one way my much older brothers and I became all American. Both of my brothers were very active in the Boy Scouts. They would go off on backpacking trips with a couple of their friends, trips that would take them through the mountainous state parks in New Jersey and New York that straddled the Appalachian Trail. These parks had been developed by the Civilian Conservation Corps (CCC) during the 1930s and contained a network of well-marked trails. They also had numerous rustic lean-tos which the CCC had built of heavy logs, and each lean-to came with a stone fire pit for cooking and heating. My brothers would come home from these several-day excursions smelling heavily of wood smoke and sweat, but clearly having had a great time on their trips. Growing up, I too was bitten by the camping and backpacking bug and wanted nothing more than to follow their lead on these camping and backpacking adventures.

* * * * *

Like my brothers, I joined the Boy Scouts. And like my brothers, I went to summer camp—Camp Greenbrier—in West Virginia, where we would take group canoe trips to camp on an island in the middle of the Greenbrier River, or be bused up to a camping area higher up in the Blue Ridge Mountains. This was camping at its simplest, but it taught me the basics of living in the wild. Indeed, camping with the Boy Scouts was almost as tame as at Camp Greenbrier, and these trips always felt like an adventure. When I was in the Scouts' eleven to fourteen age group, we would car pool to some location, pitch our tents and cook over open fires. In one case, we went in the dead of winter to a Scout camp with permanent cabins and wood stoves, but it was still pretty primitive. We had to harvest and chop the wood for the stoves, use them for cooking, and deal with outdoor plumbing in zero-degree weather.

In my teens, the trips became more adventuresome. In one we canoed the length of the Delaware and Raritan Canal, approximately forty miles, traveling from Princeton to Raritan Bay past New Brunswick. The Canal had originally been dug to ease the movement of coal from the Pennsylvania coal fields to New York City. When the canal fell into disuse for commercial transport, the old locks had been replaced by small dams that required us to portage several times during the course of our three-day journey. Another time we canoed down the Wading River in the New Jersey Pine Barrens. In this case the hard part was not canoeing but rather fending off the incessant mosquitoes in that swampy area. Shortly after high school, two close friends and I bicycled across New Jersey, first to the northern Poconos in Pennsylvania, then further north to upstate New York, and back to Teaneck. None of us had modern bikes, so our three-speed bikes had to support an arduous week's trek up and down steep hills and small mountains. Along the way, we camped in state parks, swam under waterfalls, and in general had a jolly time.

* * * * *

These early camping experiences gave me an appetite for camping, so when Carol and I were graduate students—and had little money to spend—I suggested we go car-camping at a nearby state park for a weekend getaway. Carol had never camped before but was game to give it a try. So, we headed an hour or so east of Champaign-Urbana to Indiana's Portland Arch to see its natural stone bridge and hike through its sandstone gorge.

On the first evening, I decided to introduce Carol to camping by demonstrating my camp cooking skills. Though I had never attempted biscuits in a Dutch oven over a campfire, I imagined it would not be difficult and mixed the batter, dropped spoonfuls of it onto the bottom of the oven, then put the cover on and waited for the biscuits to bake. At the appropriate time, I open the pot and discovered that I had produced two-toned black and white hockey pucks, stone hard and charred on the bottom and gooey and raw on the top. Since these were clearly inedible, I scooped them out of the pot with a spatula and flung them as far into the woods as I could so that we would not need to smell the odor of charred biscuits for the rest of the weekend. This was not the introduction I had hoped for, but the rest of the planned steak dinner proved more amenable to my campfire cookery talents and we did not starve.

That night we were startled awake by unearthly screeching sounds coming out of the woods behind our campsite. At first neither of us had any idea what might be making those sounds. Then, fearing the worst, I guessed that there was some rabid animal in the woods and that we were in mortal danger. When the sounds seemed to get no louder or closer, I pulled on my hiking boots and, using the flashlight as a guide, walked slowly towards the noises to investigate their source. Suddenly I spied four raccoons fighting over the hockey pucks we had deemed inedible, each making hideous shrieks to drive off competitors from what they clearly relished as choice prizes. I guess it really is true that one person's trash is another's (a raccoon's?) treasure.

Our alarm clock on the trip became the incredibly loud dawn chorus of song birds, each asserting its territorial rights for whatever goodies there might be in or near its home tree. We spent the day hiking in the gorge, admiring the arch and wading in the creek that flowed lazily through both. In the evening we were treated to another bird chorus as the birds all made one last territorial assertion before going to sleep for the night. The Indigo Bunting's song was especially haunting. This bright blue creature perched on the other side of the meadow and serenaded us a most beautiful and complex evening song. As darkness fell, two nocturnal birds, a Bob White quail and a whippoorwill, closed out the evening chorus with their onomatopoetic notes. And my cooking improved. On our second night we had grilled chicken topped off with toasted marshmallows.

Despite fighting raccoons, early mornings, and imperfect camp cuisine, Carol took to camping and the following summer we went on another camping trip to Indiana, this time on the weekend that included the first moon landing. Our destination was Brown County in the rolling forested hills of the southern part of that state. We were joined by a couple of fellow students, Arthur and Marsha Jane (MJ) Solomon. From the map we received at the park entrance, we selected a trail that circled a small lake for an afternoon's hike. As we progressed on this trail, we discovered that it was little used and heavily overgrown with brush and vines, notably poison ivy. We avoided contact with the poison ivy but were concerned we might have picked up some parasites in the brush. When we got back to camp, we soon discovered that both Arthur and MJ had several ticks stuck on their bodies, which they had to remove with hot match heads and tweezers. Ouch!

At the end of the trip we drove back to their house in Champaign-Urbana to watch the astronauts take their first steps on the moon. As we watched I began to itch all over and noticed that the others were scratching too. It turned out that while we had indeed avoided the poison ivy we were instead infested with chiggers, barely visible red mites that burrow into the skin. MJ looked up the remedy for chiggers, which was to paint their burrows with nail polish to suffocate them. I guess it worked, but it took many days before the horrid itching stopped.

* * * * *

These experiences and misadventures, however, did not diminish our love of camping. The following summer Carol and I decided to take up back-packing for real. We were introduced to this activity by two fellow grad students, Brant Miller and his fiancée, Karen Sweikovich. Brant, a Canadian by birth, was highly experienced in backpacking and he led our group in planning a trip to the Bridger Wilderness in Wyoming's Wind River Range. Our plan was to drive up to the northern end of the wilderness area near the Green River Lakes and then hike a several-day loop though the high country above tree line (Figures 22-1 and 22-1). Our first day out took us up a tributary of the Green River. I felt a frisson of excitement as we signed out at the ranger station for our first real wilderness experience.

Initially we walked along the river through a heavy forest. We encountered two or three other parties coming down the river as we gradually climbed, following the river up-stream. Late in the afternoon, we pitched camp in a small clearing near the river and proceeded to set up cooking for our supper. In preparation of the trip, Carol and I had sampled a wide variety of freeze-dried foods, selecting those that seemed to taste best, or more to the point, those that tasted least worst, for our trip. I enthusiastically selected one packet for our dinner, and proceeded to boil it up into a bland glop which we ate with gusto. It was certainly better than the hockey pucks of our earlier camp cooking experience.

The next morning we broke camp and resumed our hike, gradually climbing upwards as the forest gave way first to scrub and then to open alpine meadows with phenomenal views of high snow-covered peaks and rolling meadows dotted with small melt-water lakes and their outflow streams. At this point we were faced with the need to cross a rushing stream with no bridge, crossing logs or stepping stones. We followed Brant's lead in shedding our boots and socks, rolling up our pants and wading through knee-deep ice-cold water. At more than one point I felt as though the pressure of the rushing water was going to sweep me off my feet and immerse all of me in this gelid stream, but somehow we all got across with no untoward accidents. As we sat on the stream's bank drying our feet in the warm sunshine, we enjoyed the profusion of Indian paintbrush, anemones, sweet-scented lupines and other wildflowers that were blooming all around us. In moments like these all seemed right with the world.

After another several hours hiking we reached the second of our planned campsites, Three Forks Park (Figure22-3). This so-called *park* was really an open meadow in a wide shallow bowl between two peaks—and just a gorgeous place to camp with a rivulet for drinking water and a luxurious growth of soft grass to sleep on. We pitched our tents and proceeded to cook up our glop for dinner. After dinner I felt a strong urge for the bathroom. There being no cover above tree line, I walked away from our camp until I came to a pile of talus (rough stones that had been heaped up by the glacier that had originally filled this "park"). This afforded me a bit of privacy. As I answered my call of nature, a bevy of little grey picas emerged from the heap of stones, squealing loudly at me. No doubt they were protesting that I was fouling their home. "Tough luck, little guys." I thought to myself. "I'm bigger than you are." I returned to our camp post-sunset, and as the sky grew darker and darker, a dazzling array of stars came out. The four of us lay in the grass watching the stars twinkle, sleepily sipping cups of tea and enjoying the tranquility of the place.

After a night under the stars, we arose to brilliant sunshine, ate a quick breakfast of instant porridge, powdered milk and raisins (more glop!) and broke camp. As we surveyed our surroundings to orient ourselves for the next day's hike, we discovered that our maps from the US Coast and Geodetic Service had some serious errors; they were based on the work of an exploratory expedition in 1909 and were drawn before the days of aerial surveys let alone satellite imaging; they showed mountains and rivers that were either non-existent or seriously misplaced. Despite this issue, we hiked all day, enjoying the sunshine and mountain flowers. We climbed up to a pass (Figure 22-4) where we stopped for a lunch of dry crackers, hard salami and well-aged cheese. After summiting the pass, we descended slightly into a high valley where we made our third camp in a sloping meadow surrounded by low tree-line scrub. This camp was near a raging torrent that had carved a gully about fifteen to twenty feet deep. From this, we perilously drew water to cook our evening's glop. We slept soundly that night, lulled to sleep by the sound of the rushing water of the nearby creek.

Carol and I were awakened at dawn by a snuffling sound outside our tent. I peeked through the flaps to see a mother raccoon and her two kits trying to undo our knapsacks to get at our store of food. I yelled at them and loudly clapped my hands, but they seemed totally unfazed by this noise and went on about their business. So I climbed out of the tent, grabbed my walking stick and began to gently prod the mother, all the while making as much noise as I could. She merely backed off a few feet, just out of range of my stick. I then took a couple of steps forward and threatened her with my stick, but she simply backed off an equal distance, again staying just out of range. It was clear she was no more frightened of me than of the man in the moon. I began to harass her by tossing small pebbles at her, and at last she gave up on the idea of a free meal at our expense and retreated with her kits into the high mountain scrub.

As the four of us were eating our breakfast glops, Brant quietly motioned to us to look downhill. Carol and I turned to see a horse-sized mother moose and her calf ambling up the hill, nibbling on the grass all around our camp. The two of them came within maybe twenty or thirty feet of us, but paid us no heed. They just continued to eat their breakfast as we ate ours, and then disappeared over a hillock between our camp and the small marshy lake that was the source of the torrent by our camp. We were having a real wilderness experience with animals so unused to humans that they did not see us as creatures to fear. Indeed, we probably feared them much more than they feared us because mothers will attack anyone who might threaten their young, raccoons can carry rabies, and moose are notoriously temperamental.

From that camp we proceeded back down from the high mountain meadows towards our cars parked near the Green River Lakes. On the way down I noticed a patch of *porcini* mushrooms in the pine forest, the first time I had ever found these in the wild (Figure 22-5). We collected them and feasted when we got back late that afternoon. This was a major improvement over the freeze-dried glop we had been eating for the preceding several days.

As our trek in the Wind Rivers ended, our group split up. Carol and I headed northwest to the Tetons for another round of backpacking while Brant and Karen headed northeast to Canada to visit his family in Saskatchewan.

* * * * *

Wyoming's Tetons are a range of high peaks without foothills to their east, strung out north to south with a beautiful chain of jewel-like lakes sprinkled at their feet. Our plan was to climb up Granite Canyon at the southern end of the chain, hike the Teton Crest Trail, camp for a several nights in the high passes and then return to our base camp near Jenny Lake on the eastern side of the mountains (Figure 22-6). To reach the trailhead we hitchhiked to the southern end of the national park with a family who had just come from a week's stay at the Triangle X dude ranch about twenty miles to the east in the foothills of the Gros Ventre Range. They spoke so excitedly about their stay at the dude ranch that we both made mental notes to visit it sometime in the future. We ultimately returned to Triangle X many years later with our children.

We parted company with the family from Triangle X at our trail head and set off on our new adventure. The upward climb turned out to be a hard slog uphill with an elevation change of about five thousand feet. Because the Tetons have no foothills on their eastern flank, all hikes into them are terribly steep. As we broke out of the forest at tree-line, we found ourselves on a trail with steeply angled slopes to either side of us. On the right was a sharp upward pitch of the mountain side and on our left an equally sharp downward pitch that fell several thousand feet into a canyon bottom. Suddenly a loud boom threw both of us to the ground. The source of the boom was a hotshot Air Force pilot who had decided at that moment to break the sound barrier while flying just above the mountain tops. It was his jet's shock wave that had knocked us to the ground.

Our upward climb continued as soon as we had recovered, eventually passing Marion Lake, a very pretty tarn (from the Old Norse *tjörn*, or "pond," for a pot shaped mountain lake created by glacial erosion). At the top we crossed onto the western slope of the Tetons and proceeded along the Teton Crest Trail to the gently sloping alpine meadows of the Alaska Basin (Figure 22-7). The western side of the Tetons contrasted dramatically with the steep eastern face of that mountain range. We pitched camp near a glacial tarn, ate our glop, and settled in for the night in this idyllic setting. At about two AM we awoke to more terrible booms. At first I thought it was the Air Force boys out getting their kicks again, but I soon realized that we were about to be hit with an epic thunderstorm. Just as a torrential rain began to beat on our tent, a fierce wind whipped up, collapsing our tent on top of us. I tried to re-erect it in the wind and rain, only to have the wind collapse it again. Fortunately, the storm only lasted about half an hour, and we were able to put our tent up and get back to sleep.

We had to wait for our tent and other gear to dry out in the morning sun before we could pack it all up, so we had a leisurely breakfast before continuing on our second day's hike along the Teton Crest Trail. Climbing up an easy slope to another pass, we crossed back to the eastern side of the mountains, down the southern arm of Cascade Canyon, and then up its northern branch, where we arrived at Lake Solitude (Figure 22-8). This lake clearly should have been named Lake *Multitude* as there were quite a few other campers there, unlike the quiet isolation and beauty of the Alaska Basin. They were attracted to this spot for its spectacular view of the highest peaks in the Tetons just to its south. We spent the night at "Lake Multitude" and then hiked up further to a pass that led to Paintbrush Canyon and its brilliant array of wildflowers, including thousands of Indian paintbrush in colors ranging from a creamy white to a deep crimson (Figure 22-9). Curiously, as soon as we left Lake Multitude we found ourselves alone again in the wilderness as if to say that the hikers who had reached the lake were too exhausted to go on. We then spent our afternoon in a relaxed descent through Paintbrush Canyon and arrived at the end of the day back at our base camp at Jenny Lake (Figure 22-10).

Tired of our glops, Carol and I decided to go out to dinner. The park ranger at the campground suggested an all-you-can-eat chuck wagon joint just outside the park boundary. We did so, and took the owners at their word for *all-you-can-eat*. I'm sure they lost money on us and were glad to see us leave.

Shortly after we got back to our campsite at Jenny Lake, a thirty-ish woman wandered into our campsite. She told us she had just come back from a backpacking trip and had gotten to Jenny Lake too late to get a campsite of her own and asked if we would be willing to let her share our site. We reluctantly agreed and were surprised when she did not pitch a tent. Instead she just unrolled her sleeping bag and slept under the stars. That night we had another violent thunderstorm, and Carol and I wondered how she was managing, sleeping under the now invisible stars. In the morning, we found her and her soggy sleeping bag under our car. At breakfast our still damp companion told us that she had just come back from a very isolated campsite near Leigh Lake where she had gotten a "beautiful sun tan." Then she packed up her gear and left.

The quietness of Leigh Lake appealed to us, especially after the raucous noisiness of the Jenny Lake campground, so we signed up for campsite at the ranger station and were rejuvenated after our strenuous trek along the Teton Crest Trail by a couple of days of rest and relaxation there. While talking with the ranger, he told us the following tale. Two days previously a middle-aged couple had stormed into his station all in a huff. It seems that they had been hiking along the eastern shore of Leigh Lake and had seen a young woman, presumably our camp-mate of the night before, skinny dipping on the opposite shore. They were SHOCKED! SHOCKED! SHOCKED! And what was worse, they then saw two little old ladies hiking along their side of the lake who also had been exposed to this indecency. And, worst of all, the little old ladies then doffed their clothes and jumped in as well. "What" they asked the ranger, "are you going to do to put a stop to such goings on?" He never did tell us what he did about it, but I suspect he just laughed it all off.

* * * * *

The storms we had experienced in the Tetons was the leading edge of the fall rains that had evidently just begun, so the hiking season in Wyoming was pretty much over. For the last part of our backpacking vacation, we headed south to Colorado's Rocky Mountain National Park—several hundred miles south and east of the Tetons—where we assumed the summer weather would still hold for another week or two.

In the Colorado park we planned a loop trek going westbound from Bear Lake to the resort town of Grand Lake along the Great Divide Trail and returning along the North Inlet trail (Figure 22-10). We set off on a gray day climbing out of the forest into the high-mountain tundra. At one point we stopped to rest and I noticed that a lichen covered rock had seemed to move. Then I looked again and realized that it was a ptarmigan hen whose coloration blended almost completely into the background of speckled stones, lichens, and dry grasses. As Carol and I watched her for a few minutes, it became apparent she had half a dozen chicks scattered among the rocks. Their camouflage markings so completely blended into the background that we could not see them except when they moved to peck at a seed or bug. Perhaps it was just the effect of the heavily overcast sky or perhaps it was a result of our being quite tired after a couple of weeks of trekking, but we found the scenery in this part of the Rockies much less interesting than that in either the Wind Rivers or the Tetons. In any case, we plodded on, made camp in the mountain meadows, ate our glop and crawled into our tent for the night (Figures 22-12 and 22-13).

At about this time, the leaden skies yielded to steady pouring rain. We slept as best we could on that cold and damp night. Our tent held up reasonably well and we kept more or less dry as we slept, but the next morning all of our clothes were damp and clammy. The rain let up around dawn, so we got up, ate our breakfast, packed up our damp gear and continued on our way towards Grand Lake on the western edge of the park. The overnight downpour had made the trail very muddy and rendered all the vegetation sopping wet. Soon we were both very muddy and very wet as well. The sun came out briefly, turning our damp surroundings into a steam bath which only added to our misery. The only saving grace was spotting a herd of majestic elk near Grand Lake at the western end of the trail.

Our four-thousand-foot descent from the mountain heights to Grand Lake brought us to its eponymous resort town, where we decided we were not up to completing our planned trip and would hitchhike from Grand Lake back to the east side of the park where we had left our car. Looking filthy and bedraggled, we put out our thumbs, and almost at once a police car pulled up. We had only just come out of the woods and had barely reached the highway that ran back through the park but we were still in the city limits. The cop rolled down the window of his cruiser and snarled at us to get out of town if we did not want to be jailed as vagrants. To add emphasis to his words, he suggested that we perform rectal indecencies with our thumbs.

Trudging north along the highway until we passed the city limits sign (to avoid jail time), we then put our thumbs out again. The first couple of cars flew right by us, but then a white van pulled over to offer us a ride, which we gladly accepted. The driver was a woman in her forties with two elementary-school-aged children in the back seat. They were on their way back to the eastern side of the mountains. After thanking her profusely for picking us up, and to excuse our muddy clothes and bedraggled looks, we explained that we had been rained out while we were on a backpacking trek. In the course of our discussion, we learned that she was a professor of anthropology at Colorado State University and had been on a drive with her kids looking for Indian burial mounds.

Despite our discouraging experience on this particular trek, we talked with her and her kids about our exciting expeditions of the previous several weeks and of some of the things we had seen and found along the way. When Carol told her about our finding *porcini* mushrooms in Wyoming, her eyes widened up. She asked her son to show us the mushrooms they had found earlier that day and she asked us if we knew how to identify them. With one look we identified them as *porcini* and told her they were not only edible but highly prized. She seemed somewhat skeptical and was clearly nervous about the prospect of eating them.

When we got to our car at the western edge of Estes Park she invited us to spend the night at her house in Fort Collins, a town that straddles the dividing line between the Great Plains and the foothills of the Rocky Mountains that was just an hour's drive further on. Hot showers and a change out of our mud-caked hiking clothes—this was an offer we could not refuse. We followed her van to her house, showered and changed into clean dry clothes, and then brought out our mushroom book to show her what she and her children had picked. To repay her hospitality, Carol and I cooked up a supper for her family, all based around their *porcini*.

As we ate breakfast with our hostess and her family the following morning, we noticed the prairie dog colony behind their house. The colony covered an oval area roughly sixty feet by forty, with several dozen entrances scattered over its surface. A dog wandered by one end of the colony and began to sniff at one of the entrances. As the dog examined the hole in the ground, a prairie dog popped out of an entrance at the opposite end of the colony and whistled at the dog. The dog immediately bounded to that end in pursuit of the rodent who had just taunted him. The prairie dog ducked down his hole, and reappeared [or was it another prairie dog?] at the opposite end of the colony, looked at the dog and whistled again. The dog reversed direction and raced back to where it had first arrived, hoping to catch the whistler. But as soon as the dog approached the prairie dog, the latter ducked into his hole, and another one popped up in another part of the colony. Another whistle; another chase; another duck down the hole; and another prairie dog popping up elsewhere and whistling. The dog and the prairie dogs kept this game up for at least half an hour before the dog tired of it and left. After breakfast, we thanked our hostess and began the long drive back to Champaign-Urbana.

* * * * *

From my earliest days I had loved being immersed in nature. While the Italian model of Alpine adventure was to take day hikes through dramatic scenery and then return to an inn in the evening for a well-cooked dinner and a good night's sleep in a proper bed, the American model was much rougher. Perhaps this reflects the country's rougher culture and pioneering past. After the relatively tame camping experiences of my youth and early forays with Carol, our treks in Wyoming's Wind Rivers and the Tetons evoked the feeling of seeing nature in its primeval state, and a sense of what it must have been like for the early explorers who traversed this region in the nineteenth and early twentieth centuries. Undertaking adventures of this sort reinforced the lesson that we could master almost any challenge. And we learned to rely on each other and see extraordinary beauty of a true wilderness however unforgiving that environment might seem.

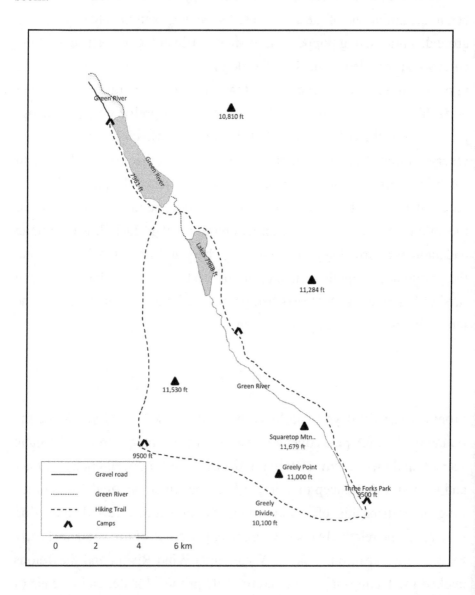

Figure 22-1. Route of the Bridger Wilderness trek Wyoming, 1969

Figure 22-2. Squaretop Mountain and the Upper Green River Lake

Figure 22-3. Pitching Camp, Three Forks Park

Figure 22-4. George and Carol, Greely Divide

Figure 22-5. George and Carol with Porcini

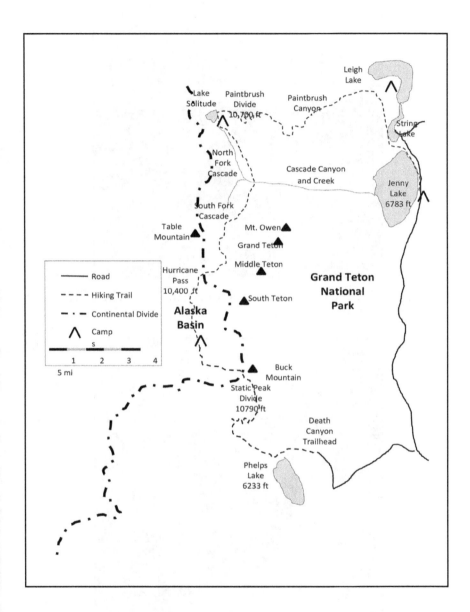

Figure 22-6. Route of the Teton Crest trek Grand Teton National Park WY

Figure 22-7. George in the Alaska Basin, Teton Crest Trail

Figure 22-8. Lake Solitude, Teton Crest Trail

Figure 22-9. Paintbrush Canyon, Teton Crest Trail

Figure 22-10. Cow elk near trail's end, Jenny Lake

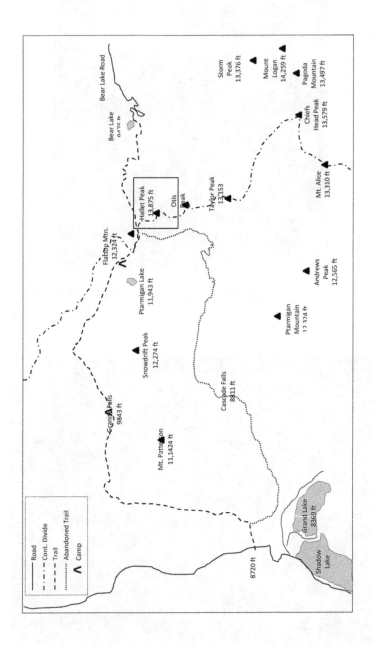

Figure 22-11. Rocky Mountain Crest trek, Rocky Mt. National Park, CO

Figure 22-12. George and Carol at Odessa Lake,
Rocky Mountain National Park, on a return visit in 2009

Figure 22-13. George and Carol atop Chiquita Mountain, 4000m,
Rocky Mountain National Park, 2009

Chapter 23

The Adirondacks

The Adirondacks in far upstate New York had been a remote wilderness area when it was visited in 1858 by Ralph Waldo Emerson and a group of his Transcendentalist friends. Emerson's group had made an arduous trip by train, boat and wagon from Concord Massachusetts to canoe through the unspoiled lakes and rivers that surrounded its High Peaks Region. In the last quarter of the 1800s, Winslow Homer repeatedly visited this region. During those years the region went from wilderness to an area of "rustic" camps for Gilded Age plutocrats from New York City. Homer sought to capture this wilderness in paint before it was lost to posterity. During my lifetime I also have witnessed a similar loss in the replacement of the old way of life in the Italian Alps with tourism.

At fifty-three hundred feet, Mount Marcy, the highest peak in the Adirondacks, is at the southern end of a U-shaped ridge of 4000-5000 foot peaks. Guidebooks still term this a "Wilderness Area" but it is quite civilized compared to the really rugged wilderness of the American West. This ridge surrounds a large mountain bowl on three sides and is crisscrossed with well-marked and well-maintained trails. There are also lodges and lean-tos that probably were built by the Civilian Conservation Corps (CCC) of the 1930s and are now maintained by the Adirondack Mountain Club (AMC). The main access to this bowl is from the village of Keene Valley about fifteen miles from the principal town of the Adirondacks, Lake Placid, the site of two Winter Olympics. Lake Placid claims that "There is always snow in Lake Placid", and to prove the claim, a town employee stores winter snow in a freezer then shovels some of it into the main square every day of the Adirondacks' short non-winter season.

During the summer between my two years at the Institute for Advanced Study in Princeton, Carol and I decided to hike into this central bowl about one day's march from Keene Valley, set up a base camp for ourselves in one of the lean-tos, and summit most of the surrounding 4000 foot peaks. This plan had the further advantage that our base camp would be at around 2600 feet, which would give us a solid head start on the intense vertical climbs (Figure 23-1).

The uneventful five-mile, 1500-foot climb from the village to a lean-to followed the Johns Brook Trail through heavy forest that allowed only occasional glimpses of the high peaks that nearly surrounded us. By mid-afternoon, we reached our chosen lean-to, which had a convenient shelf along one of its side walls where we could store our camp stove, fuel bottles, flashlights, batteries and extra photographic film. After I had extracted our sleeping bags from their stuff sacks and fluffed them up, I filled the now empty sacks with our foodstuffs and hung them well out of reach of the Adirondacks' notorious bears. While I was hanging the bags of food, Carol went down to the brook to refill our water bottles. Suddenly she called out to me, "George! There are lobsters in the brook!" I rolled my eyes and answered, "That's impossible; lobsters live only in salt water and this is fresh." I then ambled down to the brook to see these famous

349

"lobsters". Carol had just seen her first crayfish, which to her credit did look like a two-inch-long lobster.

That evening, Carol and I had a fine dinner cooked over an open fire made up of the fresh foods we had carried up to our base camp for the first day. We were delighted that we did not have to share our lean-to with another party, if you didn't count the one-eyed red squirrel perched on one of the rafters and staring at us rather menacingly. These feisty, reddish-brown animals, smaller than the much more common grey squirrels, are ubiquitous in the Adirondacks, and spotting them scrambling up and down ancient trees is a visual treat and a reminder that this region still preserves species that have become rare elsewhere. We savored that first meal knowing that for the rest of the trip we would be eating freeze-dried glops with indistinguishable flavors. As we were eating, I noticed the one-eyed red squirrel had moved to a branch in a nearby tree, though he continued staring at us with what seemed to be a very angry facial expression. I guess he thought of the lean-to as his home turf and did not take kindly to sharing it with us as his uninvited guests.

We had selected the two highest peaks on the northwestern end of the mountainous ridge—Yard (4100 feet) and Big Slide (4300 feet)— for our first day's summits. At six miles they were a relatively short distance from camp and would be a good warm-up for Marcy. The forested climb punctuated by rocky outcroppings revealed a number of scenic views, the most spectacular of which were views of shark-fin peaks and their sheer rock-face sides. While the way up wasn't difficult, the way down was very steep and ladder-like rock stairs, probably built by the CCC and currently maintained by the AMC, helped us make a safe descent back to our base camp lean-to. This day's hike was an excellent foretaste of what was to come in the follow in the coming days.

But when we got back to camp, we discovered our flashlights, batteries, and cans of spare photographic film—which we had carefully placed out of reach of bears—had all been heavily chewed. Also we found a newly chewed hole in the bottom of one of our hanging stuff sacks containing our food supply; when I took inventory of the sack's contents I found that a small bag of gorp was missing and that one of our bags of freeze-fried glop had been torn open and was no longer fit to be eaten. And then I spied the one-eyed squirrel on the roof of the lean-to, seemingly mocking us with an evil grin. There, for sure, was the guilty party. I was furious. The thievery from our food stash posed a threat to our whole trip. His other chewing and its pointless collateral damage threatened our basic camp comfort. Clearly we would not be able to leave our food behind when we went out on our day hikes.

After we made an inventory of all the damage that the one-eyed squirrel had caused, Carol went down to the brook to refill our water bottles. Suddenly she called out me, "George there are fish in the brook! Come look!" Again I made my way down to join her. After the previous day's "lobsters" I rolled my eyes again, expecting to find minnows, but this time her find was a great one. Carol had spotted a small brook trout. She and I then wandered up and down the brook, hopping from rock to rock, hoping to find more such fish. At one point I peered into a deeper pool and spotted a trout just big enough to be legal to catch. I immediately ran back to our lean-to to retrieve the bit of fishing tackle I had packed and raced back to the brook to try my luck.

I tried each of the handful of flies in my fishing kit, but none of them seemed to appeal to the fish. I guess my reputation as a totally inept fisherman had spread as far as the fish in John's Brook. At one point I almost thought I could hear the fish laughing at me. After watching my rapidly increasing frustration for half an hour, Carol dug up a grub and suggested that we try it as real bait. Skeptically, I took her worm and put it on a hook and dropped it into a quiet pool. Immediately I felt a bite…the bugger had stolen the bait…but this was progress. I urged Carol to find me more bait, and within ten minutes I landed our first fish; it was small but certainly an edible keeper. Then Carol and I swapped roles, with my job being to find more bait and hers to catch more fish. Soon we had three eating-sized fish, enough to replace the bag of glop that the squirrel had ripped open with a much finer dinner. Luckily, no game warden came along to inquire after our non-existent fishing licenses.

We had had the foresight to bring along a bit of flour and cooking oil on this trip, which gave us the wherewithal to fry up our catch after I cleaned the fish, carefully burying the waste a couple of hundred yards from our campsite to avoid the smell of rotting fish guts that could spoil our trip and attract the unwelcome visits of predators. For the second night, we had real food for dinner. For dessert we gathered wild blueberries—smaller and sweeter than commercial blueberries—from the bushes that thrive in cold northern climates and that plentifully lined the path between our lean-to and the brook.

As Carol and I were sipping our after-dinner tea, a park ranger came up the trail carrying a shotgun. At first we were disturbed at the sight of the gun, but the ranger quickly put us at ease when he asked, "Have you guys seen a one-eyed red squirrel hereabouts?" We then recounted our several encounters with such a creature, to which the ranger replied, "Yup! That's the one." It seemed that our one-eyed nemesis had quite a reputation in those parts. But of course, when the ranger came along with his gun, that very crafty squirrel had high-tailed it out of the area.

We were now ready for Mount Marcy. There were several adjacent peaks around the 5300-foot Mount Marcy: Little Marcy at 4800 feet; Little Haystack at 4600; and Haystack at 5000. The climb took us up along John's Brook, past Bushnell Falls, and eventually above tree line. As we broke above tree line, we were beset by some black flies that had apparently not died off along with their brothers and sisters at the end of black fly season in the preceding month. We quickly broke out our supply of Old Woodsman, a stinky, black pine-tar-based bug repellent that is the only product I know that defends against the black fly. From the summit of Marcy we spotted Lake Tear of the Clouds, a puddle-sized mountain tarn that is considered to be the source of New York's mighty Hudson River. Sitting on the summit and eating our cheese, crackers, and dried fruits, we felt the glow of accomplishment. It was hard work, and the views—a loop of rocky summits with forested lower slopes rimmed by a string of shimmering lakes and rivers at their bases—highlighted why even now the Adirondacks is a "forever wild" landscape protected by the New York State constitution.

That evening as we ate our glop supper, we exulted in the day's climb and decided to hike the entire ridge on the east side of the U-shaped mountain bowl. This aggressive trip would be about nine miles and require us to summit six 4000-footers starting with Lower and Upper Wolf Jaws (each 4200 feet), followed by Mount Armstrong (also 4200), Gothic Mountain (4700), Saddleback (4500) and Basin Mountain (4800). It would be a grueling trip, but the views of the fabled Ausable lakes and gorge on the east side of the ridge would be well worth it. Also, we knew that if the plan was too aggressive, we could take a trail down from the ridge that forked off between Gothic and Saddleback.

The climb up Lower Wolf Jaw turned out to be very steep, and we stopped to take a longer than normal break on the summit. At that point it looked as though we would need to take the Gothic/Saddleback bail-out. But as we continued along the crest of the ridge, summiting mountain after mountain, we became more and more exhilarated with our successes. By the time we got to the bail-out trail, any thought of going down it had evaporated, and we pushed on. When we finally got back down to our camp, the sun was setting, we were exhausted but terribly proud of ourselves. We felt so happy that we even found our evening glop a tasty concoction fit for royalty. On our last morning in the Adirondacks, we awoke late, still feeling happy from our mountain rambles and lazily packed up for our final walk out of the woods and back to civilization.

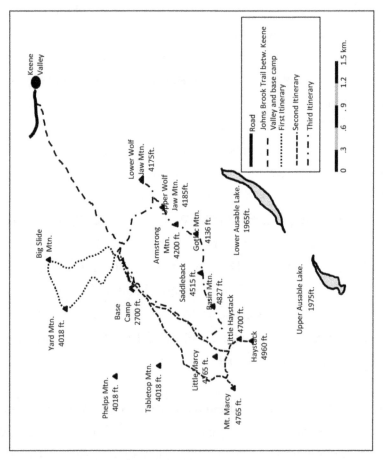

Figure 23-1. The Adirondacks Treks

Chapter 24

The Canadian Rockies, Part 1

The summer President Nixon was fighting Congress to avoid impeachment over the Watergate scandal (in which he was accused of subverting
the electoral process in his 1972 reelection campaign by having his op-
eratives break into the Washington DC headquarters of the Democratic
Party to steal information), an academic conference at the University of
Calgary brought us within proximity of the Canadian Rockies. Having
cut our trekking teeth in the Wind Rivers, Tetons, Colorado Rockies, and
Adirondacks, Carol and I set our mountain sights higher and decided to
take advantage of the conference and a break from American politics by
organizing an expedition to the Canadian Rockies.

I found a great hiking guide to the region, the *Canadian Rockies Trail
Guide*, in the Princeton University library. I also found a wonderful book,
Camping in the Canadian Rockies by Walter Wilcox, an Andover and Yale
graduate (1893) who was one of the early explorers of the back country of
that fabulous region. Wilcox is credited with several first ascents. These
volumes whetted our appetite for our proposed Canadian adventure.

In the back of the *Trail Guide* was a short chapter on the Great Divide Trail, a route which tracks the crest of the Canadian Rockies from the Waterton Lakes National Park on US border to Mt. Robson in the northern part of Jasper National Park. This trail meanders back and forth across the divide which separates British Columbia from Alberta. The guide and maps helped us decide to do a trek from Spray Lake (near Canmore, Alberta, roughly forty-seven miles southeast of Banff) to Kicking Horse Pass (on the TransCanada Highway, about thirty miles northwest of Lake Louise). The trek itself was about 100 miles for which we allowed two weeks, including rest days.

Our plan entailed complex logistics because we were not going to be able to carry two weeks' worth of food and clothes with us. We would need to leave a cache of food, fuel and clean clothes somewhere along the way. Fortunately, the one road that crossed our proposed route, the highway from Banff west to Radium Hot Springs in British Columbia, was pretty much at the half-way point and would be a great place for us to leave a cache. It would be a challenge to find appropriate containers for our cache of food, fuel and clothing, however. We knew that the Canadian Rockies were home to both grizzly and black bears as well as many smaller creatures that would delight in finding a cache of food to eat and soft textiles with which to line their dens; we remembered all too well the one-eyed squirrel who had plagued us during our trip to the Adirondacks. Furthermore, the containers would have to be waterproof to protect our goods from being ruined by rain and/or floods caused by sudden downpours. After several weeks of fruitless efforts to come up with appropriate containers, I happened into a store selling military surplus goods. In one corner were several steel cans, each of which had once contained four shells for heavy artillery. These rectangular cans, roughly twelve inches square and two feet long, were made of heavy gauge steel. Their tight-fitting lids were secured with a screw-type locking mechanism. *Voilà.* These looked about as water-, bear-, and squirrel-proof as anything we could hope to find. So I bought out their entire inventory of four artillery cans.

We then began to acquire supplies for our trip. From our experience of the preceding years, we knew that the freeze-dried soups and glops that would constitute our dinners varied in flavor from the bland and tolerable to dreadful, so we spent several weeks preparing various versions of these "foods" to find which were acceptable and which were so disgusting that we could not force ourselves to eat them. In addition to these freeze-dried provisions, we laid in a stock of powdered whole milk, oatmeal, chocolate powder, nuts, raisins, crackers, hard dry cheeses and other non-perishable foods. We then stuffed our artillery cans tightly with our supplies, packed our knapsacks and set off for Canada.

At the time Carol and I were living in Princeton, New Jersey, where I was completing a post-doctoral research fellowship at the Institute for Advanced Study. To get to the Canadian Rockies, we opted to drive to Montreal and then take the train from there to Lake Louise. In order to save money (post docs in those days were paid only a few thousand dollars a year), Carol and I shared a single berth in the Pullman car for the several days' journey. The railroad trip was spectacular, especially once we got past the densely populated parts of Quebec and Ontario. The train had several observation cars with elevated viewing domes. The wild and rocky north shore of Lake Superior reminded me of coastal Maine. The endless fields of wheat and rapeseed in the Canadian prairies had their own charm; in those parts, the human population was so sparse that we routinely saw deer, antelope and other big game along the way. When the train approached Calgary, the Rockies came into view, though they were still forty or fifty miles away. Just after the train left the main station in that city, it was run though a railroad carwash so that the windows and observation domes would be crystal clear for the ride through the mountains.

The train continued westward in the late afternoon and began to climb through the foothills of the Rockies following closely the valley of the Bow River. The first stop after Calgary was the mountain resort of Banff with its hot springs and Scottish baronial style Banff Springs Hotel.

At the stop for the village of Lake Louise we got off at a curious station made of logs and collected our belongings from the baggage car, including our artillery shell cans. Notwithstanding the logs, the station was anything but primitive; in fact, it was quite elegant. Parked on a side track next to the station was a massive red and black snowplow with a fifteen foot high plow blade for keeping the railroad route through the mountains clear during the fearsome Canadian winters.

Once in Lake Louise, Carol and I dragged all our gear across the tracks to the car rental office. We needed the car to reach various trailheads, shop for the last of our supplies, and also to deposit our cache. We also planned to spend a couple of days taking day hikes in and around Lake Louise to acclimatize ourselves to the altitude while staying in a motel just down the hill from the lake. The lake itself is surrounded on three sides by massive glaciated peaks; on the fourth side is the majestic Chateau Lake Louise Hotel. The lake has a remarkable turquoise color from all the glacial flour (pulverized rock) suspended in the water that flows into it from the many glaciers on Mount Victoria at its western end. Our first day's hike was along the lake and up the flanks of Mount Victoria. For our second day's hike, we drove to Moraine Lake, a deep blue lake with a wall of ten closely packed peaks along its southern edge, and then hiked over Sentinel Pass into Paradise Valley and back to Lake Louise. In our descent from Sentinel Pass, we encountered a large, steeply sloped snow field, which we glissaded down while sitting on our rain ponchos.

That evening we watched the television news which even in Canada seemed to be dominated by Nixon's success at stonewalling the House impeachment proceedings. It looked like Tricky Dick Nixon was going to beat the rap, as he had on several other occasions in his up and down political career. This was our last exposure to the outside world before heading off into the back-country for a couple of weeks.

Before we began our two-week trek, we left our luggage (other than our artillery shell cans and backpacks) with the motel keeper and drove down to Banff and then west toward Radium Hot Springs to find the place where our route made its one road crossing to stash our cache of food, fuel and clean clothes. Without much trouble we found the trail crossing and then hunted around for a well-hidden spot for our cache. It had to be a spot that we could easily find again but that would not draw the attention of vandals who might steal our goods. After poking about for a few minutes we selected a spot under a clump of scrubby pines adjacent to a decrepit outhouse whose state of collapse was sure to discourage entry by any but the truly desperate. There we stashed our artillery shell cans as well as several aluminum (or *aluminium* as they say in Canada) bottles of stove fuel.

When we returned to Banff to register our planned itinerary at the ranger station and turn in our rental car, the ranger asked us to walk him though our proposed route. So we began by explaining that we planned to hike or hitch a ride up a park service road leading to Spray Lake to begin our trek. From there we were going to hike up to Mount Assiniboine in the Assiniboine Provincial Park on the British Columbia side of the Great Divide, and then to hike north to Kicking Horse Pass, some thirty miles northwest of Lake Louise (Figure 24-1). Just as I was about to launch into a more detailed listing of our itinerary, the ranger stopped me. He told us point blank that we could not do this trip because Spray River was in flood: the service road had been washed out and the trail along the shore of Spray

Lake was under water. When we asked him what our alternatives might be, he shrugged his shoulders and said he had no ideas. We were defeated even before we started.

Just at that moment, another man, Jim Davies, came into the ranger station to complete some paperwork. It turned out Davies ran a helicopter service that brought supplies and guests up to various back-country lodges. He had just come in to register a run planned for later that morning to bring supplies to Assiniboine Lodge near Mount Assiniboine, which was a just a few miles from where we had planned to pick up the Great Divide Trail. When he heard about our problem, he indicated he had two empty seats in his copter, and if our backpacks did not weigh too much, he could ferry us up to the lodge. We agreed on a price, hurried off to drop our bags at Davies' helipad, and drove into town to turn in our rental car. Not only had Jim saved our trip, he also saved us what had promised to be a brutal two day climb from Spray Lake to Mount Assiniboine.

An hour later we were back at the helipad to load our backpacks into a big net under the chopper along with hundreds of pounds of food and half a dozen large cylinders of propane for the lodge. Carol and I felt leery about riding with large cylinders of compressed cooking gas under us, but we figured he had been transporting the stuff for years and was still alive, so it had to be safe enough. We climbed into the empty seats in the helicopter and Jim passed us each a pair of giant padded headphones. I wondered why he had given us the headphones until he revved up the engine to prepare for takeoff. The engine was so unbelievably loud that we had to speak with him through the microphones that hung down from the headphones. The intense vibration made me glad that my teeth, bones and hindquarters were firmly attached to the rest of my body.

As the helicopter rose into the air, Jim nudged the stick forward and it began to head toward the mountains. He flew up the valley of the Brewster River, which paralleled the Spray River valley where we had planned to hike before we learned that our planned route was washed out. Gradually the helicopter climbed, flying just a few hundred feet above the trees that lined the tops of the ridges to either side of the river, and we began chatting with Jim. We learned that Assiniboine Lodge was owned by his ex-wife; their business relationship (in which he ferried guests and supplies to her lodge) had outlasted their marriage. Fifteen minutes or so into the ride, Jim began to point out the various high peaks of the Great Divide. About twenty-five minutes in, we were just above the tree line, flying south on the British Columbia side of the Great Divide towards Assiniboine Lodge with the great pyramid of Mount Assiniboine looming in the distance (Figure 24-2). Soon we spotted the lodge several miles ahead, and Jim began to ease the helicopter down, landing on a flat clearing in the alpine scrub, a couple of hundred yards from the lodge.

After Jim shut down the engine, we climbed out of the helicopter and helped him unload our bags and the provisions he was delivering (Figure 24-3). In a couple of minutes, several employees came out from the lodge to collect their supplies. As Jim turned to get back into his helicopter for the return trip to Banff, we thanked him once more for saving our trip and then backed away from his landing area so that he could take off again. As soon as his noisy machine was gone, we sat down to enjoy the unbelievable view. The day was absolutely clear, with not a single cloud in the sky. The pyramid of Mount Assiniboine with its pointy top dominated the view to our west, and all about us were other snowy peaks and alpine meadows that stretched as far as the eye could see.

Before setting off on our trek north to Lake Louise, we decided to head south sans backpacks about two miles to Lake Gog and Wonder Pass to see what we had missed by not coming up on foot from Spray Lake. The view from the pass back onto the high peaks of Alberta's Banff National Park was breathtaking, and we were a tad sorry that we had missed the initial part of our adventure. We then returned to Assiniboine Lodge, making a stop at Lake Magog for a brief lunch of cheese and the fresh bread and fruit we had brought along for our first day. We relished this last taste of real food. For the rest of the trip it was going to be glop and other dried stuff. It was hard to tear ourselves away from the awe-inspiring view of Mount Assiniboine reflected in the absolutely still water of the lake, but we had to push on. So we shouldered our heavy knapsacks [groan!] and set off to the north-northwest from Assiniboine Lodge. After about five hours of walking in the high alpine meadows in full spring bloom, we stopped for the day on the shore of Magog's smaller companion, Lake Og. We sat by the lake enjoying the late northerly sunset and the evening light on the now distant Mount Assiniboine. Supper was soup, glop and dried fruits. On Day 1 of our trek, we had covered approximately eight miles including our backtrack to Lake Gog and Wonder Pass.

The next morning, we arose early, shortly after dawn, prepared our breakfast porridge, packed up our camp—taking in our final view of Mount Assiniboine—and set off on a two-hour walk through the rather desolate Valley of the Rocks. This dry stony valley was remarkably different from the moist and florid alpine meadows we traversed the preceding day. At the end of the Valley of the Rocks, we began the long slow climb up to Citadel Pass to cross back into Alberta and Banff National Park. Due east of us was the aptly named Fatigue Mountain and just to its south, Fatigue Pass, whose name alone was enough to make me glad we were not planning to go through it. Climbing towards Citadel Pass, I spied two tiny white shapes in the distance on a crag well above our trail. This was our first sighting of Rocky Mountain goats with their long white and incredibly clean hair fluttering in the breeze.

We crossed through Citadel Pass at 8000 feet, then climbed a bit more, almost exactly following the Great Divide for about one and a half miles, and then made a short uphill detour to visit Citadel Lake, where we camped for the night. Citadel Lake was a shallow high-mountain tarn surrounded by open alpine meadows and backed by the lone sentinel of Citadel Mountain. The beauty of the spot more than made up for our usual evening meal of reconstituted soup and freeze-dried glop. We had covered another eight miles on Day 2.

At dawn the next day we gave ourselves sponge baths with the frigid water of Citadel Lake, wolfed down some porridge for breakfast and set off. From the lake we made a gradual one-mile descent to Lake Howard Douglas (Figure 24-4), which along with Citadel Lake empties into Brewster Creek. We had ascended this valley in Jim Davies' helicopter two days before. From Lake Howard Douglas we made a steep climb to the top of Quartz Ridge, where we crossed back into British Columbia's Kootenay National Park and began a slow descent towards a pass that took us back into Alberta and ultimately to Sunshine Village.

Sunshine Village is the top of a ski area. There we saw other humans for the first time since we had left Assiniboine Lodge. These people had taken the ski lifts up to the top and seemed awed that we had hiked there from about twenty miles to the south. Like most ski areas in the summer, Sunshine Village was not a particularly attractive spot; it was full of full ski lift equipment and raw scars in the alpine tundra and mountain scrub that marked the ski trails down towards the Banff-Lake Louise highway. After chatting briefly with the ski lift tourists, we shouldered our backpacks and headed north again. We hoped to get to Simpson Pass before nightfall. On our way up to Simpson Pass we encountered several ptarmigan hens and their broods of chicks, which we watched for fifteen minutes or so. They paid us no heed while we sat down and snacked on gorp and dry crackers;

they just kept on pecking at the bugs and seeds on the ground. But as soon as we got up to leave, they rushed in to consume our crumbs.

Just over Simpson Pass and back into British Columbia we entered into the Healy Meadows, a broad alpine meadow which was at the peak of its summer bloom (Figure 24-5). There we pitched our camp for the night. For some reason the lakes in that area all had Egyptian names (Egypt, Pharaoh, Sphinx and Scarab Lakes). Day 3 had been long and hard with a lot of climbs and descents. We had covered about nine miles.

Day 4 started with our usual breakfasting on porridge and raisins and packing up our gear. Our trail began by crossing through the beautiful Healy Meadows with its amazing array of wildflowers and rushing brooks. Our goal was to travel across the meadows, hike through Healy Pass and descend to Egypt Lake, a relatively short five-mile day so we could take a bit of a break. Our morning's walk included many stops in the meadows to enjoy the views. In our climb up to Healy Pass we encountered our first snowfield crossing, which we did carefully so as to stay on the packed trail and not sink into snow up to our hips off the trail's edge.

We got to Egypt Lake in mid-afternoon and were delighted to see that it was teeming with trout (Figure 24-6). Remembering our trout dinner in the Adirondacks, we thought, "Aha! Let's catch one of these fish and get a break from our usual soup and glop dinners." In moments camp was set up and a small fishing kit in use—I had brought along the kit for just this purpose. The fish were congregating in the shallows where the water was slightly warmer than further out. I sequentially tried all of the several different flies in the kit to discover what type of bug would appeal most strongly to these large fat trout, but the fish seemed to have no interest in any of them. I did not get a single nibble. Carol suggested that we try to dig up some worms or grubs on the theory that we would have better luck with live bait. Again I had no luck. Then Carol, whose father had taken her fishing many times during her girlhood, said that she would show me how to catch fish. Her luck was no better than mine. It seemed that the water was so cold that the fish were too sluggish to bite. Finally, I had the bright idea that maybe they were so sluggish that I could catch one with my bare hands. So I took off my boots and socks, rolled up my pants, and waded into the freezing water to try to grab a fish. They were sluggish, but not THAT sluggish. As soon as I got close to one, it would give a quick flick of its tail and swim just out of reach. After fifteen minutes of this game, my feet were totally numb and we gave up on our dream of a fish dinner. Supper that evening was another round of reconstituted soup and freeze-dried glop.

Day 5 entailed climbing up through Whistling Pass. This pass had a large slope of talus on one side and another snowfield for us to cross on the other. Upon reaching the talus, we understood where the pass got its name. Hidden among the rocks were at least a dozen marmots. Whenever we would approach one of them, it would give a loud whistle to warn its mates of our passage, and then duck into a hole among the rocks. Many years later, I learned that these whistling marmots are also known as whistle pigs.

Near the top of the pass we saw where some wag had spelled out "BC" with an arrangement of stones, even though the pass is fully in Alberta and merely separates two different river valleys both of which drain to the east, and whose waters ultimately flow to the Atlantic. After we hiked over the pass and slid down the snow field on its northerly face, we descended towards Haiduk Lake, where we were tempted by more fat trout, but by this time we were convinced that we could not catch them, so we continued on our way. Haiduk Lake was just below tree line, and the meadows around it were well watered by several brooks (Figure 24-7). After we passed the meadows we reached the foot of Ball Pass, a pass into British Columbia from Alberta that we would not be crossing. Instead we camped at the foot of the pass, near a rushing stream and with a magnificent view of Mount Ball with its impressive glacier and beautiful ice fall. This day, we had covered about seven miles.

For Day 6 we planned to hike from the foot of Ball Pass to Twin Lakes, a distance of some seven or eight miles with a steep climb up and over Gibbon Pass. The day was filled with eye-popping views, but individual events weren't remarkable until we reached Twin Lakes. There we were immediately beset by swarms of flies, the only insect pests that we had encountered up to that time. These flies did not bite, thank goodness, but they swarmed around us, flying into our eyes, ears, noses and mouths. We quickly set up our tent and retreated into it to gain the protection of its mosquito netting. After a rest in the tent we debated about the best way to prepare our dinner. Fire risk ruled out cooking in the tent, so I ventured out, set up our backpacking stove and began boiling up water for our soup and glop. Immediately the flies descended on me and it was all I could do to keep them out of our food. They seemed most enthusiastic about our glop. The minute that the soup was hot, I got the glop pot on the stove and retreated into the tent, where we sipped our soup. When we had consumed our soup, I dashed outside to grab the glop pot and set the soup pot on to boil for dishwashing water. I retreated to the tent again, and Carol and I ate our glop; mercifully, we had to pick out only one or two well-cooked flies from it. Then we both ran back outside, washed our dishes and pots, and retreated yet again to our tent, this time for the entire night, even though it was still several hours to sunset.

On Day 7 of our trip, we awoke at dawn, but we stayed in the tent for fear of being attacked again by flies. When we could wait no longer for our breakfast, we ventured out to prepare it. Amazingly, there were no flies.

It was so cold that morning that the flies had all gone to hide in some protected place until the sun would warm the air enough for them the swarm again. We hurried through our breakfast porridge and packed up. We skipped our usual morning ice water sponge bath, for fear of the flies. Instead, we set off on our hike before the flies came out.

Day 7 was going to be a big day for us. Upper Twin Lake was only four miles above the Route 93 crossing and our cache. We hiked at top speed that morning, reaching the road crossing by eleven AM. Without any difficulty we found our cache, which had not been disturbed by man or beast during the preceding week. In a flash, we undid the screw-mechanisms that sealed our artillery shell cases, pulled out all the new food and clean clothes, and stripped. Our hiking clothes were really grubby by this time and I have never before or since enjoyed putting on clean clothes as much as I did that morning. The dirty clothes and food wrappers and other detritus that had been in our backpacks were transferred into the artillery shell cans and hidden in the same place as before.

Our backpacks now overflowed with our new goodies, including full bottles of stove fuel. We mounted these newly heavy bags on our backs and set off for Floe Lake, a six and half mile climb up from our cache on Route 93. The hike started off in a heavily forested slope of spruce trees. We had to climb over 2000 vertical feet back up to tree line before evening. We plodded on through the forest until it began to thin out, when we stopped for lunch. We continued on a more gradual slope until we reached Floe Lake. The lake was well named. On the opposite shore was a small glacier whose tongue floated out onto the lake, periodically calving off small icebergs (Figure 24-8). We pitched camp a short distance down the outflow stream from the lake, and prepared our supper. Although our cache had contained some different varieties of freeze-dried glop from what we had been eating before, the flavor did not seem much changed. After dinner,

Carol and I decided that we needed to bathe since we had skipped our morning bath earlier that day. Carol insisted that we had to go into the lake and submerge ourselves so we would be as clean as our new clothes. That immersion lasted about ten seconds as the water with floating cakes of ice in it was absolutely intolerable for any longer than that.

The Floe Lake campground had one other amenity that we had not seen in a week…an outhouse…and one that was not particularly smelly either. When Carol went to use the outhouse, she immediately called me to come check it out. Mystified as to what could be so interesting about a back-country outhouse, I walked over to where she was. She asked me to look inside where I noticed that the seat was all chewed up. We speculated that the chewer had been a porcupine who was so starved for salt that he chewed the seat for whatever residues might have been on it from the bodies of previous sitters. Porcupines were reputed to exhibit such behaviors with axe handles, work gloves and boots, and I guess also toilet seats. Thus ended our seventh day, one in which we had trekked over ten miles with several thousand feet of ascents and descents.

The following morning, Day 8, we awoke at dawn as usual, but I was feeling under the weather. I had a headache and a bit of a fever. We decided that we would take a rest day and see whether I would recover, figuring that if I were seriously ill, we could simply hike back down to the highway and hitchhike back to Banff, where there was a small hospital. The stopover did not worry us since we had expected to take one or two during the course of our trip. I did not eat much that day, and mostly slept, while Carol enjoyed wandering among the flowers in the meadows along the brook and around the lake. Periodically, she would come back to the tent to give me some ice water to drink and otherwise comfort me. By evening, my fever had broken, and I was able to take a bit of soup and crackers for supper, but no glop.

Day 9 of our trek, I awoke with no fever and was eager to get moving again. So we ate our breakfast, packed up, and set off towards Numa Pass skirting the base of the Rockwall, a long ridge immediately to our west. Our target was to reach the Numa Creek Forks about seven miles further north. Climbing up to the pass, I felt much more tired than I had felt in previous climbs of similar elevation change. Evidently my brief illness of the preceding day had taken more out of me than I had realized.

We then descended to Numa Creek, which we had to cross to get to the designated campsite at the Forks. This crossing presented us with a difficult choice. The creek was much too deep and fast to wade through. One place where we could cross it was on a snow bridge, which had the risk that we could fall through and land in the creek (Figure 24-9). The alternative was to cross on a dead tree that had fallen across the creek. One misstep on the trunk of that tree would have landed us in the frigid drink where we would have been swept downstream by the rushing water (Figure 24-10). Once we had considered our options, we decided on the snow bridge, though with serious concern about whether we were making the right choice.

Having finally crossed the creek and reached the Numa Creek Forks, we set up camp and prepared our supper soup and glop. A park ranger happened by on foot and struck up a conversation with us. I asked him, "By the way, what do porcupines eat besides toilet seats?" "Oh!" he replied, "You must have been up to up to Floe Lake!" Apparently the Floe Lake outhouse with its well chewed seat had quite a reputation.

That evening we considered whether we should continue our trip in light of my exhaustion and consulted our guide book and maps to see what our alternatives might be. To continue would require us to climb through four more passes and cover about twenty-two more miles until we reached the

369

TransCanada Highway in Kicking Horse Pass. I expected that it would take us three or four more days of walking. We had plenty of supplies, so that was not an issue. The question was whether I had been so tired out by my brief illness that I could not complete the planned trek.

The map showed an alternative, which was to descend along Numa Creek and take us back down to Highway 93 near its summit at Vermillion Pass on the border between British Columbia and Alberta. This second option entailed a hike of about six miles, almost all downhill. We decided to sleep on it and see how I felt in the morning before making a decision. When I awoke in the morning I was still feeling very tired. That decided the issue for us. We would take the second alternative, even if it meant cutting short our expedition.

So on the morning of our Day 10 we glumly packed up our gear and set off down Numa Creek to the highway. When we got to Route 93, we put out our thumbs, but this road went pretty much from nowhere to nowhere else so there was not much traffic. Finally, after about half an hour, a fellow in a pick-up truck came by and offered us a lift back down to Banff. Once we got to town, I rented a car and we retraced out steps down Route 93 to retrieve our artillery shell cans with our trash and dirty clothes. We then reversed course, and drove back to our motel near Lake Louise for hot showers, a decent meal with both taste and texture, and a laundry to wash all of our camping gear. While waiting for our clothes to dry, we turned on the TV and learned that the House investigators had gotten hold of a "smoking gun" White House tape which recorded Nixon ordering the cover-up of his involvement in the Watergate break-in. The House was preparing to vote on a bill of impeachment. When we had left on our trek, it had looked as though he was going to get away with his misdeeds. A lot had happened since then.

One of the real pleasures of wilderness backpacking is that the beauty of the scenery and the physical effort required force you to focus on the moment and totally tune out the outside world. We had just had a ten-day vacation from the carryings-on in Washington. That night we slept in a real bed for the first night in a week and a half, a comfort marred only by the thought that we were again forced to pay attention to the foul deeds of Tricky Dick Nixon.

On Day 11 we drove up to Kicking Horse Pass and the trailhead where we had originally planned to come out. The trail head was actually a five-mile private road leading to the Lake O'Hara campground and lodge. By good luck, the gate on the road was open so we drove down to Lake O'Hara, parked our car, and began walking south along the Great Divide Trail towards Lake McArthur and McArthur Pass. Unencumbered by heavy backpacks, we made rapid progress, and after covering about half the seventeen-mile distance from Lake O'Hara to the Numa Creek Forks, we turned around to collect our car at the campground and returned to our motel at Lake Louise. Thus we very nearly completed our originally planned itinerary.

It was now time to go to my academic conference and begin doing mathematics again. We drove down to Calgary and checked into our room in the university dorm. When we checked in we found a note from a local friend, Professor Verena Dyson on the University of Calgary mathematics faculty. She had invited us to dinner along with several other conference attendees. A change of clothes helped us look more presentable and we drove to her house not far from the campus. When we got there, she informed us that the House of Representatives had just voted to impeach Nixon and that he was about to resign. As we sat down to dinner, Verena turned on her television, which was broadcasting Nixon's resignation speech. Just after Nixon ended his speech, Verena's telephone rang. The caller was one of her adult children whose television had blown up just as Nixon was about to pronounce the word *resign*, which prompted a lot of paranoid jokes about Nixon having the FBI plant bombs in the television sets of his long lists of political enemies.

This was not the end of our Canadian Rockies exploits. About two weeks into the conference, Carol and I talked Verena into joining us for a week-end backpacking trip in the Rockies east of Lake Louise. The highlight of that trip occurred on that Saturday night. In the middle of the night I woke up screaming from a nightmare. Carol asked me, "What's the matter? Are you OK?" to which I replied, "I just dreamt that I had reached for my glasses and felt a bear's foot on them." "Oh ridiculous!" she replied. "Just roll over and go back to sleep," which I did. Hiking out to our car that morning, we passed another party who had been camping a couple of miles downstream from us. The asked, "Did you guys see the grizzly bear that wandered down along the river and through our camp last night?" I have long suspected that the cause of my peculiar nightmare the preceding night was that I sensed the bear in my sleep. And with that final note on the Canadian Rockies, we returned to our daily lives of mathematics and the political upheavals of 1974.

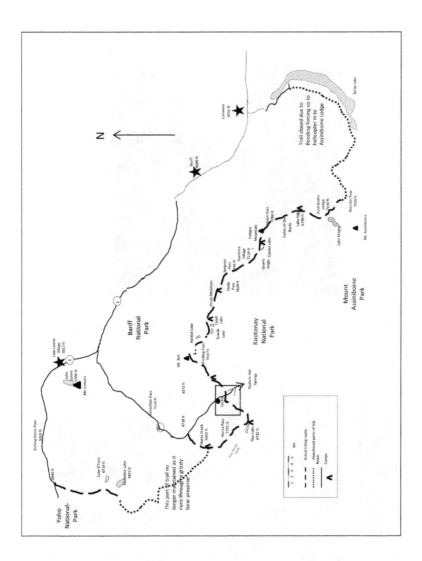

Figure 24-1. The Canadian Rockies Trek

Figure 24-2. Mt. Assiniboine from Assiniboine Lodge

Figure 24-3. Unloading the helicopter

24-4. Carol near Lake Howard Douglas

Figure 24-5. Carol among the wildflowers of Healy Meadows

Figure 24-6. Carol Fishing Egypt Lake.

24-7. Carol in Haiduk Lake meadows

24-8. Our camp at Floe Lake

Figures 24-9 and 24-10. A choice between Scylla and Charybdis in crossing Numa Creek

Chapter 25

The Canadian Rockies, Part 2, Our Return

When our sons David and Michael were in their tweens, Carol and I decided to introduce them to the beautiful region of the Canadian Rockies. We flew from Boston to Calgary, Alberta, for the start of our trip. Before heading west into the mountains, we drove in the opposite direction to Drumheller, a town about forty miles east of Calgary in the ranch and oil country of the Alberta plains. Drumheller is on the edge of a large area of badlands, whose canyon walls have yielded many dinosaur fossils and we hoped to find some of our own. We spent several hours wandering in one hot dusty canyon and out another, thinking we had seen fossils protruding from the mudstone walls but never making a great discovery of a new T. Rex or brachiosaurus skeleton. Thoroughly tired and more than a little disappointed, we went into Drumheller's paleontology museum, where we finally made our dinosaur "discoveries". The museum exhibits included thousands of absolutely amazing dinosaur fossils from nearby canyons.

Late that afternoon, we left Drumheller and headed west about 100 miles to Lake Louise in the heart of the Rockies. The next morning we decided to take a short two- or three-mile hike above the northern side of the lake to acclimatize ourselves to the altitude in preparation for the more vigorous trips that we planned to take in the coming days. Even this short hike afforded us spectacular views of the turquoise Lake Louise and the heavily glaciated massif of Mount Victoria at its westerly end. This view gave us all of a wonderful foretaste of how beautiful the hikes would be in the coming ten days.

Our second day in the Lake Louise area, Carol and I decided to repeat a hike we had taken more than a decade ago from Moraine Lake to Lake Louise, passing over Sentinel Pass and down Paradise Valley. We drove with our kids about ten miles south to the trail head at the western end of Moraine Lake, admiring the spectacular view of the ten snow-covered peaks that line the southern shore of the lake and taking a few family pictures. Slogging up the mountains on the northerly side of the lake in the blazing sun for about three hours, we reached the summit of Sentinel Pass. There we were greeted by a blast of northern air that immediately cooled our sweat-soaked bodies. We found a picnic spot sheltered from the wind and sat down for lunch before beginning the long downward journey towards Lake Louise.

The first part of the descent was down the very steep headwall of the northern side of the pass. The headwall and the high mountains to either side of it kept it perpetually in the shade, which was a welcome relief from the sun that had fried us during our ascent. About half-way down the headwall we encountered a large snow field that had survived this late into the summer because of this shade. We crossed the snow field with a combination of walking and sliding, reaching a field of large stones at its bottom. I took the lead crossing these stones by hopping from one to the next. The stones were quite steady as each was firmly wedged into the spaces between the stones under it. After about ten

380

hops, I landed on a large stone that, unbeknownst to me, was only balancing on the stones below it. This stone rolled forward, pitching me in the same direction and crushing the toe of my left boot between it and the stone immediately adjacent to it.

I knew at once that I had broken one or more toes. I spied a small patch of snow just beyond the adjacent stone, tore off my boot and sock and thrust my entire foot into the snow to cut down on the swelling. As the family caught up with me, I resolved to minimize the incident so as not to alarm them and told them that my foot was merely bruised.

In point of fact I was very concerned. I asked the kids to go into the spruce scrub to find me a suitable walking stick, which they did in a matter of minutes, and we set off. My pace was a slow hobble. At this point we should have been three and a half hours' walk from the nearest road, but with my battered foot it would surely take us more than an hour longer. After half an hour or so, we began to reenter the forest and I stopped to rest my throbbing foot. Transferring part of my weight to the stick on each alternate step enabled me to pick up the pace somewhat, and soon we were traveling at nearly a full walking speed. Nonetheless I continued to require frequent respites due to the pain, the net effect of which was an average speed of only about one and a half miles per hour.

It took us five hours before Lake Louise and the eponymous Chateau came into view, but with that view came the promise of a longer rest stop. We entered into the main lounge on the ground floor with its magnificent view of the lake and Mount Victoria. I plopped down into the first easy chair I saw to take my weight off my much-abused foot and confessed that I thought I had broken one or more bones in my foot. We decided that Carol would seek a ranger to drive her back to Moraine Lake to fetch our rental car, while I would wait in the lounge with our sons. After a half hour's rest, I hobbled over to the concierge desk to inquire where I could find a doctor to look after my foot. The concierge indicated that there was a clinic in the hotel, but that the doctor had already left for the day. I was advised to return the next morning.

Another hour passed when I suddenly heard a cheery "hello" from Carol who had completed a very quick round trip to Moraine Lake to retrieve our car. We decided to have dinner at the Chateau Lake Louise while we considered how to reorganize our vacation around my new disability. As were seated in the formal dining room, all looking rather grubby since we were still dressed in our sweaty hiking clothes, I asked the somewhat startled waiter for an extra chair, a kitchen towel, and a plastic bag filled with ice. When he returned with these items, I proceeded to shock him further, by removing the boot and socks from my left foot, elevating the naked, smelly foot by resting it on the chair and then topping it off with the towel-wrapped bag of ice.

As we ate our dinners, the four of us decided I should visit the doctor as soon as he got in the next morning. If he said that I could continue to hike, Plan A was that we would return to Moraine Lake and hike along its eastern end and southern shore. If he told me that I needed to keep off it, Plan B would be for me to sit in the café overlooking the lake and the mountains on either side of it while the others hiked. The next morning we returned to the hotel and went straight to the clinic. The doctor took one look at my very black, blue and swollen foot and announced that I had broken a bone in my great toe. A quick x-ray showed that only one bone was broken, and that it had not been displaced. The good doctor then told me very matter-of-factly that there was nothing to be done about this broken toe. If I merely kept off it for six weeks, and kept it elevated and iced for the first week it would heal on its own. This sounded like the absolute end of our vacation.

We then had a quick lunch in the hotel coffee shop and drove to Moraine Lake to put Plan B into motion. I set myself up at a table on the café's terrace, nursing a cup of coffee and reading a book, all the while keeping my left foot elevated and iced. In the meantime Carol, David and Michael set off on their planned hike. After about an hour, a brief passing shower drove me inside the café, where I had to endure a non-stop three hours of repeated playing of Berlioz' *Symphonie Fantastique*. While I was inside, I noticed a rack of brochures for various organized excursions in the Rockies. Two in particular caught my eye. The first offered guided horse trips into the mountains and the second white water rafting trips on the Athabasca River, a fast-moving outflow stream from the Columbia Ice Fields that drained northward towards the Great Slave Lake and the Arctic Ocean. These struck me as the obvious solutions for Rocky Mountain adventures for a man who could not walk. When Carol and the boys got back late that afternoon, I shared my ideas. They immediately agreed and we booked a horse trip up to the shoulders of Mount Victoria for the next day.

The packer who would be taking us on this trip met us at a livery stable near the Chateau Lake Louise, along with another eight people who had booked the trip. The packer matched each rider with a suitable horse, double checked the saddles and tack, and took the lead. The horses had made this particular trip so many times there was no need for us to direct them. We just sat on their backs as they queued up and followed the guide up the mountain. At one point we encountered a downward sloping snowfield, which the horses crossed by assuming a half-sitting posture and sliding down the snow until they reach the mud at the bottom of the short slope. If horses could be trained to ski, I am sure this is how they would go about it.

The idea that a horse excursion would be better for a man who should stay off his foot did not prove accurate, however. After about an hour in the saddle, my hindquarters began to hurt from all the pounding I received

383

from my horse's irregular gait as it picked its way up the trail and after two hours my buttocks hurt more than my foot with its broken toe. In addition, it was a hot day, and horse sweat created a foul odor (distinctly fouler than human body-odor) that mixed with the scent of the digestive gas that the horses emitted in great quantity. Toward the end of our pack trip I wanted to distance myself from the horses and concluded I could walk more comfortably than I could ride. Henceforth we would walk in preference to riding horses.

The following morning we drove north from Lake Louise to the Crowfoot Glacier, a large glacier that used to come close to the Icefield highway but has now receded well back from the highway. We hiked up its outflow creek and then along its foot for a picnic lunch on a ridge overlooking the glacier's flank. My concerns about my broken toe had suggested that we keep this initial hike on it reasonably short. While we ate, I soaked my broken toe in the icy melt water dribbling from a nearby snowfield. As the boys played among the rocks, I noticed a shiny bit on one of the slabs of shale that they displaced. On closer examination, I discovered that it was a tiny flake of natural gold that had been squeezed flat by the geological forces that had formed the shale from what had once been riverside silt. I then began to separate the layers of the shale slab and found additional bits of gold as well as thin flakes of natural copper. I kept a small fragment of this shale with a few barely visible dots of gold in it as a souvenir. Had this not been a national park, I might also have filed a mining claim.

That evening we stayed at Num-Ti-Jah Lodge on the shores of Bow Lake, the lake that captures the meltwater of the Bow Glacier and feeds the Bow River that flows south and east towards Calgary and beyond to Hudson's Bay. Num-Ti-Jah had been built in the 1930s and 40s by Jimmy Simpson, a legendary mountain guide and pack-trip leader from the earliest days of tourist visits to the Canadian Rockies. When it was built, Num-Ti-Jah had been the northern terminus of the Icefields Highway, though this highway now extends all the way to Jasper. As we were eating supper in the lodge's dining room and enjoying its spectacular view, we saw a number of men running out of the woods and gathering in the hotel parking lot. In an instant all the guests left the dining room to join the men in the parking lot to learn the cause of their commotion. Just as we got outside we saw a final man emerge from the woods carrying a picnic cooler which he dropped at the edge of the parking lot as he ran to join the crowd that had gathered in the middle. This last man was soon followed by a mid-sized grizzly bear that stopped to inspect his picnic cooler. The bear deftly opened the cooler and began to sniff at its contents. The first thing he pulled out was a wedge of cheese, which he downed in an instant. Next he pulled out a brownie which he also ate with gusto. Then the bear bit into a large grapefruit, which he immediately spat out as being much too sour for his taste. After the bear finished eating the remaining items in the cooler, it turned and ambled back into the woods.

At this point I struck up a conversation with the man whose picnic cooler had just been raided. It seems that he and the other men we had seen emerging from the woods were working in a road improvement detail along the Icefields Highway. They had been camping along Bow Lake in order to save money that they otherwise would have had to spend to rent cabins for the summer. They were all in the habit of fishing in the evenings after work to relax and to enjoy the bounty of free meals. About a week earlier, this bear had begun to raid their camps to steal their evenings' catch. After a day or two, the bear had begun to systematically attack every successive campsite as it made its rounds of the lake each evening between seven and eight PM.

The following morning as we were getting ready to take our first substantive hike together since I had broken my toe, a truck pulled into the hotel parking lot bearing the logo of Parks Canada and carrying a large cage. Three park rangers climbed out of the truck and began to confer among themselves on how best to deploy this trap so that they could catch the offending bear and haul it off to the back country. When one of them asked me where we planned to hike, I responded that we planned to go along the north shore of the lake and up to Bow Falls above it. The ranger suggested that we reconsider our itinerary, particularly since we had children with us. I guess he thought the bear would view our boys as tasty snacks and, what would have been worse from the rangers' point of view, we might have distracted the bear from the trap that they planned to place at the edge the parking lot near the remains of the picnic cooler from the previous evening. So we were forced to change our hiking plans yet again.

Carol and I consulted our hiking guide and decided we should drive further north to the Columbia Icefields, where there was a nice hike up a moraine that ran between two of the largest glaciers and was reputed to offer panoramic views of the vast Columbia Icefield. So we all piled into our rental car and set off for Bow Summit, the pass that divided the waters between those that flowed south and east (towards Hudson's Bay and the Atlantic) and those that flowed north (to the Arctic). When we got to Bow Summit, my heart sank at the sight of an enormous parking lot with hundreds of cars. To one side was the largest gew-gaw shop I had ever seen, with endless displays if kitschy Canadiana such as ersatz "Eskimo" carvings (made in China). On the other side was the toe of the Athabasca Glacier with dozens of bright red, smoke-belching snow-coaches on it, transporting the passengers from all the cars up onto the glaciers. We quickly found the entrance to the Parker Ridge trail and beat a hasty retreat from the parking lot mob. Mercifully, by the time we had walked ten minutes, we had completely left the crowd behind, and we were alone to enjoy the magnificent scenery. The trail climbed up a steep lateral moraine that separates the Saskatchewan Glacier from the Athabasca. As we continued to climb, the snow coaches shrank to insignificance and appeared more as oversized red ants than as noisy tourist buses emitting clouds of noxious black smoke from their diesel engines. As we approached the top of the trail the views got better and better. When we stopped for lunch, we were transfixed as we stared endlessly at the vast sea of ice below and the snow-covered summit that marks the triple continental divide, separating the flow of waters among the Atlantic, Pacific and Arctic Oceans. We then hiked back down to the parking lot and continued our journey north to Jasper. I felt very proud of myself for having taken on this hike despite my temporary disability.

At the conclusion of the hike, we continued our drive north along the Banff Jasper highway, encountering numerous species of the big game that inhabits those beautiful national parks: mountain goats with their long white hair, Dall or big-horned sheep with their elaborately spiraled horns, long-eared mule deer, hulking moose, grizzly and black bears, and stately elk with their magnificent racks of antlers. That evening we celebrated my return to hiking with a fine game dinner at the Jasper Park Lodge. Among the four of us we sampled the meats of bison, elk, deer and caribou.

On the subsequent days we alternated walking and non-walking excursions so as to rest my foot and returned each night to the Jasper Park Lodge. The first excursion was white water rafting on the frigid Athabasca River that I had discovered from the rack of brochures. We have a photograph of me on this trip; although my raft had six passengers, only I am visible above the waves as we shot the rapids (Figure 25-1). Our second day in Jasper we hiked up to the Alpine meadows facing Mount Edith Cavell, a mountain named after a British nurse who was executed by the Germans during World War I for helping a number of captured British and French soldiers escape from German-occupied Belgium. On our third day in Jasper we took a steamer cruise on Maligne Lake whose southern end is surrounded by immense glaciers. On our last full day in Jasper we took a leisurely hike through Maligne canyon, an amazingly deep and narrow canyon (in many places only three-five feet wide) that had been carved by the river draining Maligne Lake.

On our last day we drove for many hours through the endless birch forests between Jasper and Edmonton, Alberta, to the airport and our flight home. All in all, it had been a very memorable and satisfying trip despite our having to reorganize it on the fly to deal with a bit of an accident that could have derailed the trip completely. Indeed, it was perhaps made more memorable on account of that accident and how we dealt with its consequences.

From this trip and our earlier visits to the Alps, our sons developed a strong love of the mountains. They each have each gone on a number of wilderness trips in the Rockies and California. The love of the mountains which my parents passed on to me and I to Carol and our children is now entering a new generation, I note with considerable delight that our grandchildren are catching the mountain and camping bugs.

Figure 25-4. George and family (hidden by the waves), whitewater
rafting in the Athabasca River

Chapter 26

Many Shores

Behold the Sea,
The opaline, the plentiful and strong,
Yet beautiful as is the rose in June,
Fresh as the trickling rainbow of July;
Sea full of food, the nourisher of kinds,
Purger of earth, and medicine of men;
Creating a sweet climate by my breath

--Ralph Waldo Emerson

I have often sought rest and relaxation at the beach. It is my second-most favorite vacation, second only to hiking in the mountains. The seaside has been a way to rebalance my life, especially at times when I needed a stretch of play to offset the heavy demands of my professional life. As a result, I have been to the shore in dozens of places. Generally ex-

perienced as a family, the beach has deepened and enriched the genera-
tion-spanning bonds of both my childhood family and my relationships
with my wife and children. In some cases, it has served as a cross-cultural education, while in others it simply represented a way to enjoy the
beauty and variety of nature. And that variety extends to the different
ways in how different cultures approach the sea. I continue to be struck
by the uniqueness of each beach experience and the most remarkable
ways different compounds can be formulated from the ancient chemical
elements of earth, air, water, and fiery sun, as shown by the next several
vignettes.

Portofino

My earliest shore memory, was of a trip to Portofino, near Genoa, on
the Italian Riviera in 1948, when I was not quite three years old. At the
time Portofino was a small fishing port that had become a fashionable
resort sometime in the 1920s. The most vivid mental image I have is
of the look of the place. The town is wrapped around a small almost
rectangular harbor, hemmed in by steep hills that tumble directly into
the Mediterranean. The picture etched onto my mind is of a street with
ambling pedestrians looking at the fishing boats tied up on one side and
the row of houses and shops in three- and four-story buildings on the
other. There were also a moderate number of people seated at outdoor
tables at the restaurants and cafes, engaged in leisurely conversations or
reading newspapers. The stucco exteriors of the buildings were painted
in various shades of ocher and red, or else pale, whitish tints, contrasting
sharply with the intense blue of the water. Interestingly, I do not recall
ever being in the water.

Today the single road into the town is choked with traffic. The main street
around the port is so clogged with pedestrians that it is hard to get about.

The fishing boats have largely been displaced by mega-yachts of the rich and famous. And now all the restaurants overlooking the sea have several-hour waits for tables. The fishing lifestyle there has since been replaced by a tourism economy, much as has happened to the dairying economy in most of the Alpine valleys. Even fifty years after my first visit to Portofino, however, there remains the same remarkable blueness of the sea and the brilliant reds and yellows of the buildings. From my childhood visits I have retained deep memories of past ways of life, some of which are preserved while others, like Portofino, are now mere folklore of earlier times.

Truro

My second memory of the beach was of going to Truro on Cape Cod with my parents and brothers in 1949. I was nearly four years old. My parents had rented a cottage right on the beach on the Cape Cod Bay side of town. On the bay side, between our cottage and the main highway through town, were high sand dunes, giving the feeling of quiet and isolation. Once a day, that quiet was interrupted by the passage of a single train that was hauling pure Cape Cod sand to a glass works near the town of Sandwich.

The beach outside our front door sloped gradually into the bay. On the dunes by the bay were clumps of beach plum bushes, loaded with ripening fruit. My mother, who had learned the art of making home-made preserves during the war, led us in gathering a large basket of the plums, which she turned into a dark-red, slightly tart jam.

Unlike the ocean side beaches, the bay side beach had no surf. It made up for this lack with an incredible array of sea creatures. Even in my shallow water domain, where I encountered almost daily horseshoe, fiddler and hermit crabs, innumerable varieties of mollusks lived among other crustaceans along the beach. I would gather these in a small bucket filled with sea water and then later return them to the sea. Once dozens of starfish moved into the shallows, perhaps to prey on the plentiful clams. Another time, the shallow water played host to hundreds of tiny seahorses--all of whom were gone by the next day. The beauty of this bay shore was made even more otherworldly during a sunset swim with my mother and older brothers where the brilliant red-orange ball appeared to settle into the water, causing the water itself to take on the same brilliant color, as if it were on fire. The light from the setting sun reflected in the bay was so intense that I could barely see my family as they swam out into the deeper water.

Nearly sixty years later I attended an exhibition of Edward Hopper's paintings at Boston's Museum of Fine Arts, which included several oils of the same area in Truro. I still recognized many of the cottages, the Cape Cod Lighthouse, and the Coast Guard Station that I had first glimpsed during that delightful August of 1949, and more poignant for me, Hopper had preternaturally captured the brilliant, clear colors of the wild outer parts of Cape Cod. Much of the raw beauty of the dunes and shoreline that Hopper preserved is now protected as part of the Cape Cod National Seashore where there are sharp limitations on construction and development.

Falmouth

My next beach remembrance was of Falmouth on the southern coast of Cape Cod where my parents had rented a cottage when I was nearly six years old. The cottage was on a shallow tidal inlet that had only a small opening to Nantucket Sound but came with a small dock and a row boat. My older brothers, Albert and Peter, and I spent countless hours rowing about the inlet, relishing the freedom from our parents' supervision that this craft gave us. On one of our rowing expeditions, Peter noticed that there were hundreds of Atlantic blue crabs scuttling along the bottom of our inlet. Once we returned to the cottage for lunch, Peter and Albert asked my father if he would buy us a net to catch these crabs. Our father readily assented, though little did he know what the consequences would be.

During low tide early the following morning, Albert, Peter and I set out in the rowboat with our newly acquired crab net and a large bucket to hold our hoped-for catch. My father was quite sure that the bucket was entirely superfluous because he expected the crabs to easily outrun us, but he consented to letting us take it in any case. And so we set off. Being small and light, I sat in the bow of the boat as the spotter. Albert as the oldest and strongest of us sat in the middle, rowing, while Peter sat in the stern with the net, ready to scoop up the crabs as the boat passed over them. Peter missed the first several crabs he tried to net but he soon got his technique down pat, and with lighting speed he began netting crabs as fast as Albert could row the boat around the inlet

Soon our bucket was full with about two dozen large crabs; we returned triumphantly to our dock. Our parents examined the fruits of our morning's labors, nodded approvingly and suggested it was now time to return the crabs to the sea. Albert did not see the point of letting these creatures go after all the work he had done rowing us about to catch them. He asked if we could boil them up and eat them instead. Well aware of my mother's thriftiness, Albert pointed out that we had just brought home a free lunch and it would be a pity to waste it. Reluctantly, she agreed to serve them.

My mother, who had never set foot in a kitchen before she came to America, consulted her cookbooks to determine how best to prepare the crabs and discovered they had to be plunged alive into boiling water, whereupon she decided she was not up to the task and refused to have anything more to do with the project. Seeing the disappointed looks on the faces of us boys, my father announced he would boil the crabs. This was an act of sheer bravado, as I do not recall my father ever having cooked anything more complicated than boiled eggs before or since.

My father read the recipe in the cookbook for boiled crab and decided this was going to be an easy task. The first instruction was to bring a large pot of salted water to boil on the kitchen stove, which my father completed successfully. The second instruction was to quickly drop the crabs into the boiling water and let them cook for ten minutes. No sooner did my father pour the crabs from our bucket into the water then they all jumped back out of the boiling water and onto the floor—my father had missed the cookbook's third instruction, to slam a heavy lid on the pot after adding the crabs to the boiling water. Soon we had two dozen slightly-boiled crabs scrambling across the floor of our cottage in an effort to escape. My mother screamed and ran outdoors. My father and brothers then spent the next hour recapturing all the crabs, many of which had sought shelter in dark, hard to access corners under the furniture. I was too afraid of the crabs' pinchers to join in the effort. Instead I went out to try to calm my mother. Resolutely, my father made a second effort to boil them, this time covering the pot, and we had a deluxe crab-meat luncheon. Even my mother was willing to join in this meal despite her earlier crab trauma.

Santa Margherita

My father announced at *Val Salice* one year (I was nearly nine at the time) that my parents, my brother, Peter, and I would go to the seashore at Santa Margherita in a few days. This announcement of a seashore Santa Margherita puzzled me as the only Santa Margherita I knew was

395

a church about one kilometer from our country villa where our servants and farm tenants went to mass every Sunday. The church, and the surrounding hamlet of the same name, sat a couple of hundred kilometers from the sea. To relieve my confusion, my father described how the towns with saint's names typically had grown up around a (Catholic) church named for that saint. There were not enough saints for every church to be named for a different one, he explained, which resulted in many churches named for any given saint, and therefore, many towns in Italy had the same name. The seashore Santa Margherita was known as Santa Margherita Ligure because it was the town of that name in the region of Liguria. In fact, this particular Santa Margherita was not all that far from Portofino, where I had been some years previously.

On the appointed day we all piled into my father's Fiat Millecento and set off for the coast to our south. Our car climbed the steep mountains that separate Piemonte from Liguria on the highway which began to alternate between tunnels and long viaducts over precipitous gorges. At the crest of the mountain range, we turned southeastward, away from Genoa and toward the resorts south and east of that city. The highway then wound its way down the foothills towards the shore, veering in a more southerly direction. The nearer we came to the Mediterranean the more the vegetation became nearly tropical, dominated by palm trees, citrus, and century plants, even though we were at the same latitude as Halifax, Nova Scotia. The highway now twisted in and out, following that heavily indented coast line that is defined by steep hills dropping straight into the sea.

The large white stone building that was our hotel in the seashore Santa Margherita faced the sea and was surrounded by a magnificent garden. It sat on the landward side of the main roadway along the seafront and I remember there was a dark, musty pedestrian tunnel passing under the road to the water and a long stone pier extending out into the water, perhaps a couple of hundred feet or more, where many guests chose to sunbathe. The hotel's "beach" was mostly rocks with little patches of sand between them.

The incredible clarity of the water, with the bottom clearly visible even though the steep hillside of the shore extended below the surface, impressed Peter and me, and we immediately asked our parents to buy us masks and snorkels so that we could explore the underwater world. We only received masks, however. My parents had heard too many stories of scuba accidents, and I think they confused the simple snorkels we asked for with the much more complicated scuba systems. In any case, equipped with just our masks Peter and I began our explorations.

By far the most common creatures on that shore were large sea urchins. These particular urchins had blackish-purplish spines and central bodies that were perhaps a hand-breadth wide. Overall, when measured from spine tip to spine tip, they were as much as a foot in diameter. We wanted to bring a few specimens to the surface to show our parents but were afraid to pick them up because of their sharp spines. Then Peter had the idea to devise a special tool for collecting sea urchins. He made large pair of "tweezers" by loosely tying two sticks together at one end with some heavy twine and wrapping more twine around the free ends of the sticks. With this tool we could safely pick up substantial specimens without risk to our hands.

We brought up half a dozen of these creatures from the sea floor and showed them proudly to our parents. They nodded approvingly and then told us quite firmly that we had to return them to the water. I suspect they still remembered the crab debacle from Falmouth several years before and did not want to risk our asking to eat them—although the idea of eating them had not crossed our minds. Just as Peter and I brought them to the end of the pier to toss them back into the water, we were approached by a balding thirty-ish man who asked if he could have one. He then broke off the spines, cracked open the shell around the central body, and proceeded to eat the raw, orange-colored interior. Sushi not yet having become fashionable in the West, I found the whole idea absolutely revolting but at the same time also fascinating. Peter and I then gave the man the rest of our sea urchin collection and he proceeded to down them all in short order. When our parents later asked whether we had successfully disposed of the urchins, we indicated we had done so but without specifying *how*.

My other recollection of our visit to Santa Margherita was of the Italian institution of *la passeggiata*. Each evening, after supper in the hotel's formal dining room, we would join hundreds of other families from our and other nearby hotels to walk up and down the road along the shoreline. This parading continued until almost exactly 9:30, when seemingly instantaneously everyone returned to his lodgings and the roadway was once again given over to cars. These communal evening walks were so different from our experience in America, where we would be the only family out for a walk after supper.

Scheveningen

In 1956, my parents decided that we should make a vacation stop in Holland. My mother and I had never been there, and my father had not been there since the 1920s. We spent several days seeing the sights in Amsterdam, including an inadvertent walk through Amsterdam's red-light district when we got lost one day, a sight I am sure my parents would have preferred that I had not seen. We then rented a car to visit such picturesque provincial towns as Delft, Haarlem, and the royal capital of The Hague. We wandered around The Hague for several hours and unexpectedly my father got it in his head that we should have a picnic on the beach at Scheveningen, a town on the nearby shore of the North Sea. Scheveningen had been a fashionable beach resort in the late 1800s patronized by the Dutch royal family and the royal court. The idea sounded exotic to us.

My father had a long career of devising clever but totally impractical schemes, however, and this beach trip turned out to be a prime example. We stopped along the way at a grocer's to pick up the makings for our picnic, and then drove down to the beach. The day was a perfect Dutch summer's day: that is, the sky was leaden, the temperature was in the low 60s, and a light drizzle blew in from the sea and fell on the damp sand. Along the beach, I noticed small groups of hardy Dutch beach-go-ers coming down to the beach in their bikinis, spreading out their blankets on the damp sand, and then crawling *under* their beach blankets in an effort to keep warm. On the beach, we munched on our bread and cheese in damp misery until my mother suggested that we give up on the picnic. Thus ended our visit to Scheveningen, and instead we went in search of a tea house where we could try to extract the chill and damp from our bones. Our association of the beach with warm summer days was clearly at odds with what the Dutch consider to be the perfect time for a visit to the sea shore.

Maine and Nova Scotia

A happier example of my father's sense of seashore adventure was a summer trip to Maine and Nova Scotia. Our first stop was at Bar Harbor in Maine, where we spent several days exploring the mountains, islands, and harbors that make up Acadia National Park. On one of the few sandy beaches on that rocky coast, my parents encouraged Peter and me

399

to go in for a swim. We got into that frigid water only up to our knees, and by that time our feet were completely numb and blue from the cold. Although my parents had by then lived in America for fifteen years and should have known better, they had expected the water to be warm, as it is on the sub-tropical Italian Riviera.

From there, we took the ferry, aptly named MV Bluenose, to Yarmouth at the southern end of Nova Scotia—I was both bitterly cold and seasick on the overnight crossing of the Gulf of Maine—and commenced our drive along the southern and eastern coasts of Nova Scotia. Our aim was to find a seaside village where we could stop for a few days to have a sojourn by the sea. The coastal towns along the rocky shore were indeed picturesque, but the water in Nova Scotia turned out to be (predictably) even colder than in Maine. This was not the place for a beach vacation.

At one of the winsome fishing villages where we stopped for the night, my father decided we should make the best of the situation. During the preceding day or two he had learned that the most important sport in the area was fishing for Atlantic blue-fin tuna and thought we should give it a try. At the time, Nova Scotians fished for these huge creatures from dories that they rowed out from their home ports into the open Atlantic, and the sport could be quite a challenge. My father, brother and I rallied to the idea of the blue-fin tuna challenge and found a tourist information kiosk on the village green where we hoped to learn more about tuna fishing and get a recommendation for a fishing guide. An elderly gentleman in a white safari jacket and pith helmet staffed the tourist office. In response to our inquiries, the old man looked at us earnestly and began telling us the following story, saying the words very slowly and deliberately:

"There ... was ... a ... nice ... young ... fellah ... heah ... in ... town ... who ... took ... people ... out ... fishin' ... .

He ... was ... very ... good ... at ... it ... , ah yuh! ... .

They ... say ... that ... a ... couple ... of ... months ... back ... he ... went ... out ... in ... his ... skiff ... and ... hooked ... a ... big ... tunah, ... and ... that ... he's ... not ... been ... seen ... since.

And ... the ... pity ... is, ... they ... never ... found ... his ... boat ... neithah ... . Ah ... yuh!"

Maybe tuna fishing was not such a wise idea after all. My parents caucused, looked at their maps of Nova Scotia, and decided we should go inland to one of the many lakes. There the water would surely be warm enough for a beach vacation. We found the perfect place, and checked into a small inn on the shore of one of the many beautiful lakes that dot the interior of Nova Scotia. The inn had a grassy lawn leading down to a dock, where there were several canoes tied up. The lake itself was a couple of miles across, and had many small inlets; it was, surrounded by dark green pines. My brother and I enjoyed fishing there from a pair of canoes, though I had my usual non-luck and caught nothing. Paddling around I began to hear a haunting bird call but could not see what was making that call. A few minutes later, a large water bird, swimming with most of its body below the surface, ducked under the water, stayed out of sight for a minute or two and then popped up again farther away, voicing the eerie cry I had hear earlier. I had met my first loon.

Having spent several days at the lake, my father decided that he wanted to see Nova Scotia's Bay of Fundy on that province's west coast. Fundy is famous for its seventy-foot tides and surprisingly warm water for such a northerly arm of the sea. We left our lake paradise and drove to a hotel right on a sandy beach on the bay. It didn't take me long to change into my bathing suit and run down to the beach for a swim. The water was so pleasantly warm, that I could stay in for hours at a time, and only my mother's call to come and dress for dinner got me out.

But I was ready to get right back in the water the next day. However, I unhappily discovered the water had retreated about a mile and half away. It was now low tide. Where I had been swimming eighteen hours earlier there was now an endless expanse of mud flats, beached boats, and a small army of clam diggers with their rakes and buckets. The water would not return for about five hours. I tried to make the best of the situation by digging in the sand, but this certainly did not feel like I was at the beach. As I think back on this vacation, I realize we experienced within a relatively short distance of each other stark images of remarkable contrast, from the frigid and frightening Atlantic shore and calm beauty of the lakeside canoes, to what I would describe as the intermittent beaches of the Bay of Fundy. From the bay, we packed up and headed back for Yarmouth, the Bluenose, Maine, and home.

Montauk

Late in the summer of 1960, my father announced at dinner that he wanted to take the family for a short vacation to the Hamptons, on Long Island. The next day he informed my mother and me that he had booked rooms for us at a beach-side inn in Montauk at the extreme tip of Long Island and that we would be heading there the following weekend. This particular inn had been recommended by Eddie Treves, our cousin and the son of my father's business partner.

My parents had quite a row that first night. When they were especially angry with each other they argued in Piemontese, and that evening it was all
Piemontese. It seems that my thrifty mother thought the place too extrav-
agant whereas my father thought the place was just dandy and appropriate
to the lifestyle in which my parents had both grown up in pre-war Italy.

A night's sleep did nothing to quell the considerable ill will between my
parents, so I thought it best that I leave them to themselves. I grabbed a
towel, ran out to the beach, and was awed by the towering breakers that
were rolling in off the open ocean. Within minutes, my towel lay on the
sand while I ran headlong down to the water to swim out to the point
where the waves were breaking. I had a grand time diving though the
waves just as they began to curl over.

This sport continued until I mistimed a wave and it broke over me, drag-
ging me through the rough sand and pebbles on the bottom, and holding
me underwater for what seemed to be an eternity. The wave pushed me a
considerable distance towards the shore before it gave up its grip on me,
and I could stand on the ocean bottom, get my head out of the water and
take a deep breath. Never did a whiff of ocean air smell as sweet! But I
was in big trouble. The wave had swept away my bathing suit. I stood in
waist-deep water wearing not a stitch. Given the crowd of hotel guests on
the beach, it seemed out of the question to run up unto the sand to cover
myself with my towel. I quickly spied my suit floating on the crest of
another wave about twenty yards away and began swimming as hard as
I could towards it, fearing that my suit would float off to Portugal before
I could get to it. A certain amount of rather desperate swimming ensued
as I caught up to my suit and slipped it back on with the result that I was
spared the embarrassment of having to run up onto the beach stark naked
in front of dozens of hotel guests. My parents, who had seen the whole
spectacle, drew great amusement from my discomfiture and forgot their

dispute. We immersed ourselves in the guiltless pleasures of sun and surf for the rest of the week, relaxed and able now to enjoy each other's company anew.

Monterey

Towards the end of my graduate-student days, I gave a talk on my doctoral thesis at a symposium at the University of California, Berkeley. The symposium was in honor of the 70th birthday of the great Polish mathematician, Alfred Tarski, and included several days of back-to-back presentations on mathematical logic. The entire body of conference attendees was then bused down to the Asilomar Conference Center at Point Lobos, near Monterrey, California, where the conference continued at a decidedly lower key.

At Asilomar, I awoke early the first morning and ran down to the beach for a before-breakfast swim. The beach was absolutely empty, save for a few dozen sea gulls, which I ascribed to the earliness of the hour. I quickly waded into the surf and dove through the breaking waves. While the water was brisk, I thought nothing of it, until I became aware that I had company in the waves. About half a dozen seals had joined me to cavort in the surf. They were clearly enjoying themselves, barking to each other as they glided down the fronts of the waves. My northerly companions made me aware of the intense coldness of the water and I hastened out to the beach to warm up in the California sun.

Once I had dried off, I wandered back to the conference center for breakfast. A middle-aged professor and his wife sat down to eat with me, and I began to relate my morning's adventure. They looked at me in disbelief, and said, "Are you crazy? Nobody swims in the ocean around here without a wet suit. If you want to swim, there is a nice heated pool beyond the terrace." No wonder the beach was empty! Although I did enjoy the company of my pinniped swimming friends, I suspect it is not something I am likely to try again.

North Wales

Towards the end of the year that Carol and I spent in England, while on a NATO research fellowship at Oxford, we went on holiday to the Snowdonia region of North Wales. That area combines some of my most favorite landscapes with rugged, heather-covered mountains rising directly from the sea, separated by lush green valleys dotted with large flocks of long-tailed Welsh sheep. We took a day off from about ten days of climbing various peaks to walk along the Conway River to the beach at Aberconwy. There, ominous signs warned people not to play on the dunes and reminded them of the disastrous accident at the nearby town of Aberfan many years earlier where a very steep dune had collapsed, suffocating dozens of schoolchildren.

On the way back to our B&B we found a massive fruiting of one of our favorite mushrooms, *chanterelles*, and gathered a couple of pounds of these delicious yellow gems to bring back to our B&B. Our landlady very reluctantly agreed to prepare them for supper. Like the vast majority of Brits, she was deathly afraid of any mushrooms other than the little white ones they sell at the greengrocers, and she was no doubt convinced that by dawn she would have two dead guests. At that point, her husband came into the house from the garden. He saw our collection, and immediately recognized what prizes we had found; it turned out he had been stationed in Germany after World War II as part of the British occupation and had learned to appreciate many varieties of wild mushrooms. We immediately offered to share our prospective feast with him, and he eagerly accepted. Now our landlady was really concerned: not only would she awake to two dead guests she would be a widow to boot. Nonetheless she consented to cook up our mushrooms.

That night I came down with a bout of the flu, accompanied by fever and nausea. Knowing the mushroom paranoia in those parts, I knew I could not visit a doctor—he would immediately conclude that I had mushroom poisoning and order some unpleasant treatment. To avoid this, I had to tough it out. We abandoned our hiking plans and instead drove past Caernarvon Castle to the beach on the nearby the Lleynn Peninsula. I hoped there to recover from the fever, congestion and nausea that were plaguing me and spend a few restful days on the shores of the Irish Sea.

Since our B&B was near the beach, we decided to take advantage of the idyllic August weather and walk along the beach to get a sense of the place. Temperatures were in the 60s, the sun was shining, and there was a gentle breeze making this much more pleasant than my childhood memory of the cold North Sea beach at Scheveningen. Here and there on the beach were small family groups consisting of parents sitting in low chairs with their children building elaborate and very realistic castles of sand. Of course the children had great models for their structures, as Wales is dotted with dozens of well-preserved castles dating back to the English conquest of Wales in the 1200s.

While we were taking in the sand castles, we were confronted by an incredibly odd sight. Walking briskly towards us, a barefoot Englishman, with his long trousers rolled up half-way to his knees, sported the stereotypical English beach uniform. He wore a long-sleeved white shirt, and may or may not have had on a necktie. His face was scarlet as this had been his only day in the sun in the preceding twelvemonth, and wrapped around his balding head was a white handkerchief fastened with tight knots at the four corners. He was clearly the most peculiar compound of earth, air, water, and fire that we had ever seen, on a beach or off. The sight of this strange fellow made me forget my ailments and by the next day I was fully recovered.

Nantucket

I immediately fell in love with the idea of living on an island thirty miles out to sea when I made the childhood discovery of a map of the US East Coast that included the island of Nantucket. Of course, I had never been there and had no idea what the place might be like, but that only added to the romantic attraction. My older brother Peter must have felt the same, because he and his wife Bonnie began to spend a month or more each summer on that island after they married. Through them, I realized a bit of those childhood Nantucket dreams and delighted in the island's quaint charms.

The island had been settled by Europeans during the 1600s, and over time, it developed into the center of the American trade in whale oil, the pre-ferred lighting fuel of the time. Initially Nantucketers hunted whales in the immediate vicinity of their island, but they gradually expanded their whale hunting territory to cover the oceans of the entire world. By the ear-ly 1800s Nantucket whalers routinely sailed as far as the South Pacific in pursuit of their lucrative trade in whale oil, baleen, spermaceti and other whale-derived products. A Nantucket whale ship was the first to locate the descendants of the mutineers from the HMS Bounty on Pitcairn's Island. The voyage and ultimate destruction of a Nantucket whaler, the Essex, by an infuriated whale became the core historical event around which Mel-ville's classic novel, *Moby Dick*, was written.

The island's residents grew rich on the trade in whale products, and some of the simple shingle-clad cottages of the earliest settlers gave way to grand houses, especially in the center of the main town. Then in 1859, with the discovery in western Pennsylvania that petroleum could be cheaply extracted with shallow wells, the market for whale oil collapsed. A thriving Nantucket went into a 100-year sleep. It did not reawaken until the 1960s when it became a fashionable seaside resort. While much of Nantucket's shoreline is dotted with the vacation houses of the mega-rich, the island community did an excellent job of preserving its historic atmosphere, maintaining its cobblestone streets and requiring that all new construction conform to the style of the older buildings. It also preserved a large portion of its moorland interior and the Cotue and Great Point peninsulas, keeping them forever wild even as the town center has become ever busier. By intelligent preservation, Nantucket has maintained a beautiful environment even as the local population and its primary occupations have radically changed.

Monhegan Island

Ever since my boyhood, I had had a fascination with Monhegan Island off the coast of Maine, although I did not get there until my own sons were boys. I think my fixation on that island derived from reading an article about the place in *National Geographic* in a dentist's waiting room in the 1950s.

Monhegan is essentially a large block of granite covering about one square mile, some twenty miles out in the Gulf of Maine, with a year-round population of around seventy-five, most of whom earn their livings lobstering or running guest houses for the summer visitors. Perhaps its attraction was its isolation from the hustle and bustle of coastal Maine. Possibly I pictured images of its spectacular seascapes with great waves crashing onto its granite cliffs. It could be I imagined the intrigue of its tiny working harbor, colorful lobster boats, and innumerable sailing yachts belonging to well-heeled visitors from the mainland. Or perhaps I remembered an exhibit of paintings from the active artist colony that has thrived on that island for many decades, led by the several generations of the painterly Wyeth family. Or just maybe I was drawn by its anachronistic refusal to permit automobiles on the island or to allow the construction of a power plant. At any rate, Carol and I got it in our heads that we should take our school-aged sons out to Monhegan for a few days to experience life from a simpler time, without electricity, television, or automobiles. This way they could gain a deeper respect for the more important things in life.

The ferry to Monhegan leaves from Port Clyde near the mouth of Penobscot Bay. Two dozen or so other people accompanied us on the two-hour trip into the harbor, or rather the narrow strait between Monhegan and the much smaller nearby islet, Smuttynose; to give some shelter in that so-called harbor, one end was partly blocked by a granite jetty. We disembarked, and walked up the hill towards the little town and our guest house, where we dropped our bags. A small shop sold the makings of a picnic and off we went for a circuit of our idyllic little island.

We entered the forest between the town and the cliffs on the opposite side of the island, where we began to find tiny houses generally no more than a few inches high, made of sticks, bark and moss. According to the island residents, making such tiny houses for the fairies and other wee folk thought to inhabit the woods is an island tradition. Our children delighted in hunting for these tiny dwellings, though in retrospect, I suspect that the residents had no such tradition and instead gullible tourists were the real builders of these houses.

We wandered through the woods, emerging on the windward shore, took in the sights of the cliffs and surf and then stopped to eat our picnic. Following the shore line, and stopping occasionally to pick wild raspberries and blueberries, we came to the oft-painted shipwrecked tugboat, high and dry on the rocks, at the low southern end of the island. This was an invitation to while away an afternoon poking about the rusty wreck and the adjacent tidal pools. On our walk back towards the village, I began to look forward to a simple dinner at our guest house followed by a quiet evening of reading and board games by candlelight.

We sat down to dinner a bit before the late mid-summer sunset and I noted the as-yet unlit hurricane lamps on the tables, a sure sign of forthcoming rusticity. No sooner were we seated than I noted a waiter systematically lighting the lamps on all the tables. This lamp lighting was interrupted by a loud roar, and soon a second, even louder roar started up, and then a third, and a fourth—it sounded like a Mack truck had just pulled up to the guest house on this island without terrestrial motor vehicles. I startled our waiter with a question about the commotion, who looked at me strangely, as if I were from Mars, and said "That's just the generators, so we can all watch TV and see what we are doing when it gets dark out." And with that comment, he switched on the electric lights in the dining room. Dinner over, I tried to concentrate on reading the book I had brought with me but was too distracted by the blaring of the television in the guest house lounge. This wasn't the lesson I had hoped to teach our children about life before the advent of electricity!

As an antidote, we decided to explore the northern end of the island on the following day. We bought the makings for a bread-and-cheese picnic at the town's general store and then set out through the woods. The northerly coast was not quite as dramatic as that which we had traversed the previous day, but the trail to it also had many fewer people on it. The path was not nearly as well-worn and in places was almost overgrown with brambles bearing succulent blackberries. The quiet was more what I had expected from Monhegan and a welcome respite from the roaring generators.

We returned to town, eager to see how the resident painters and sculptors would capture the essence of the island's fishermen, cottages, harbor and wild seascapes. Surely their muses would be working overtime with Monhegan's raw beauty. A half a dozen visits to various galleries and artist's studios made it clear, however, that some of the local artists were long on inspiration but short on talent, while others produced technically excellent but uninspired work. The works ranged from the pedestrian to the mildly original, and none evoked the drama and originality of the Wyeths' oils. Clearly it takes a true master artist to capture on canvas this island's rugged beauty. In short, Monhegan was a delight visually with its wild seascapes and gastronomically with its wild berries, but I regret that my romantic plan to introduce my children to an island without electricity or television was dashed so completely.

Ansedonia

Carol and I took our sons back to Italy when they were in their early teens. Our custom on such trips was to break up what could be an overwhelming sensory deluge of art museums, grand cathedrals and antiquities with trips to the mountains or seashore for a change of scene and pace. This particular trip started off with several days in Rome with its vast quantities of classical and Renaissance treasures to explore. On our first day we visited the Coliseum, the Circus Maximus and the old Roman forum. Our children were particularly impressed by the Arch of Titus with its frieze of the Hebrew captives being paraded through Rome following their disastrous revolt of 67-70 CE, carrying the Menorah from the just-destroyed temple of Jerusalem.

Our day at the Vatican began with our being inspected by the guards at St. Peter's who were making sure all who entered were decently attired. The guards seemed particularly concerned with women whose shirts were

411

too low-cut, whose skirts were too short, or whose trousers fit too snugly. A bit later, as we stood in a very long and slowly moving line to view the then newly restored Michelangelo frescoes in the Sistine Chapel, one of our sons noticed a continuing stream of men who would disappear behind the enormous pillars of the cathedral. The men seemed to pair off briefly, exchange small packages, and then disappear quickly out a side door. St. Peter's was evidently the New York Stock Exchange of Roman drug dealing. The guards seemed to totally ignore this activity—they were too busy shooing out women whose clothing they deemed too revealing.

A week in the heat and dust of a Roman summer left us longing for a few days at the seashore. Luckily, my cousins Emanuele and Annalisa had invited us to visit them at their seaside house in Ansedonia in southern Tuscany. We hired a car and drove north from the city on the ancient Roman coastal highway, the Via Aurelia. Emanuele met us at Cerveteri, a very well-preserved Etruscan necropolis half-way between Rome and Ansedonia. Emanuele, an architect by profession, gave us a detailed tour of this city of the dead built by a people who seem to have lavished much more of their design and construction skills on the dead than on the living.

From this city of the dead, we drove together to Ansedonia. Emanuele and Annalisa's house was on a hillside overlooking the Mediterranean, perhaps a mile back from the shore. Standing on the terrace, I saw a number of houses on the lower slopes of the hill, interspersed with groves of ancient olive trees and their incredibly twisted trunks and gnarled branches. In the distance was the small port of Orbetello. After we greeted Annalisa, who had not joined Emanuele at Cerveteri, and their daughter Marta and her soon-to-be-husband, Emanuele suggested that we all drive down to the beach for a swim. We eagerly agreed to their suggestion, changed into our suits, and drove down to the beach with them.

The beach was separated from the highway by a forest of maritime pines, trees that supply the *pignoli* [pine nuts] that are such an important staple of Italian cuisine. This forest had been planted in the 1920s by Mussolini's government to provide an added source of income for the local farmers and was one of the few good acts committed by that otherwise criminal regime. We crossed through the dark coolness of the forest and emerged onto a wide, sandy and sparsely populated beach. Each of the few families seemed to have staked out a substantial territory for itself quite distant from its neighbors.

We selected a spot for ourselves well away from all the others and marked our territory with our towels, shoes and other paraphernalia. One of our sons offered to guard our things while the rest of us went swimming. In reality he was very tired and promptly dozed off in the warm sun. He was awakened quite forcefully by a female voice asking, *"Scusi, che ore sono?"* [Excuse me, what time is it?]. Having been asleep, he only half heard her. He then rubbed his eyes open as she repeated, *"Scusi, che ore sono?"* Now that he was awake and his eyes were fully open, he found himself looking straight at a large pair of naked female breasts. Quite surprised by this sight he completely lost his tongue and could not utter a single word in either English or Italian. The woman asked again, this time a bit impatiently, *"Scusi, che ore sono?"* Again, our son could not give a single word in reply. In the end, the woman picked up his arm, glanced at his watch, and stormed off muttering, *"Che ragazzo cretino!"* ["What an idiotic child"]. We teased him mildly, to which he tried to save face by complaining about her plain features and "thunder thighs" as if to say, "Who me? Look at her chest? Never!" but no amount of face saving could ease his embarrassment.

A final word on this experience: the following year Carol and I took the boys to the south of France where we spent the first several days of our vacation on the French Riviera. This same son, who had never been able to get himself out of bed before noon except on school days, was up by 7:00 every morning and on the topless beaches as soon as they opened, taking in the sights. This was a somewhat different educational experience for him from what my wife and I had intended when we planned our family trip to Provence.

* * * * *

Thinking back on the wide-ranging assortment of seas and shores that I experienced as a child and later brought my family to experience, I am aware that some of my earliest and most lasting memories are of the shore. These memories remind me of how I have lived in two worlds—connecting continents, old worlds and new—and have witnessed the passage of time as old ways of life fade away and are often replaced by something artificial that can turn the beauty of the natural world into a Disney-like sanitized parody of itself. I am also keenly aware of how the shore has always provided a renewing escape from my hard-driving work-focused life. In closing, all I can say is that for these reasons I adore beach vacations. And, quite frankly, I cannot decide which type of beach suits me best. They all leave me with thoughts of magical times by the sea, times that allow me to reflect on my relationships with family and friends, and to delight in sharing with them a love for the beauty of the world around me.

Afterword: *Memories of Memories, Revisited*

About five years after I published *Remembrance and Renewal*, I began to think about writing a book about my own life. I knew I did not want to write a conventional memoir: "When I was 22 I did THIS, and then the next year I did THAT, and in the third year I did SOMETHING ELSE." Such a book smacked of egotism and would have been a colossal bore.

Instead I decided to write a series of essays on a variety of topics based on experiences in my life. The topics might vary quite widely, from memories of *Val Salice* and its importance in my life, to issues of family and relationships, my several educations, and the nature of various types of work – as well as the wonders, to me, of the mountains and the sea. The theory was that through these essays I might be able to convey some of the beauty in life that I had enjoyed and some of the values that I developed and hold dear.

This theory sounded good, but I soon learned that while some topics leant themselves well to this structure, others proved very challenging.

The result was that this project moved in fits and starts. There would be high-energy bursts that might run for a few weeks in which I could draft a substantial essay every few days. Then there would be long periods, often lasting the better part of a year, in which I could make no headway whatsoever. At times I despaired of ever finishing the book.

Some of the essays, especially those about my ancestors' past exiles (including those occasioned by the Spanish Inquisition and the Italian Fascists) never seemed "done." I kept uncovering new avenues of research into my family's history. For example, in 2015 I learned that in 1939, a street in the Piemontese town of Santena (formerly a part of Chieri) had been named for my great grandfather, Cav. Emanuele Sacerdote. He had been an important figure in local politics and a significant benefactor to the town's citizenry. Fascists "aryanized" this street name; they replaced his name with that of Guglielmo Marconi in order to erase the memory of a local Hebrew notable. After a fair amount of pressure from our family and a local journalist from Santena, this insult was undone in 2017. Plaques were put up acknowledging the street's former name (Figures A-1, A-2, and A-3).

More recently I learned that one of my maternal ancestors was a Spanish nobleman and crypto-Jew named Luis de Carvajal. He and his family moved to Mexico in the mid-1500s to escape the Inquisition, where he became a huge landowner and governor of a much of northern Mexico and Texas. When the Inquisition was introduced into Mexico, this man and much of his family fell into its dreaded hands with deadly consequences, with much of the family dying in the Inquisitions dungeons and autos-da-fe. However three of his nephews one of his grand-nephews escaped. The grandnephew reached Italy, assumed the name Montefiore and married Rachele Olivetti in Pesaro in 1620. My great-great grandmother Rachele Montefiore is presumably a descendant of this family. These are all stories that need further research, perhaps a useful project for one of my children or grandchildren.

For other essays, current life experiences caused me to call up experiences for earlier times. For example, the summer before my older grandson, Nathan, entered kindergarten, I spent an afternoon chatting with my daughter-in-law Dorothy about what it might be like for him. That discussion brought back a great many memories about my elementary school years, and I then wrote the "Kindergarten Babies" chapter in just a few days. In similar fashion, when I had to prepare some remarks for the memorial service for my late cousin Marc Sacerdote, I focused on some of our childhood experiences together at my grandmother's Italian country villa, *Val Salice*, and the influence that they had on his life and my own. From there it was a short step to expand on the topic and write about what that place meant to me and how my view of it changed over the years as I grew up.

The hardest topics to tackle proved to be the ones closest to me. While I could write as an observer about a trek in the wilderness or a walk on the beach, I found it very difficult to find the right balance between my role as a participant and my role as a reporter when I talked about family, friends, and colleagues. In short, I found that it took many drafts before I could hit the right tone in writing about the people who had the greatest influence on shaping my life such as my older brother Peter, my wife or my children.

What finally pushed me to complete this book was an odd experience that I had one spring afternoon. My wife and I had gone to the college graduation of our nephew Jonathan Schoeller. The afternoon before the official ceremonies, as Jonathan took us on a campus tour, we wandered into the Engineering Quadrangle. On one side of the quad was a statue of a man with upraised arms, which my sister-in-law, Carol's sister Lisa Schoeller, explained commemorated a wealthy Wall Street banker who had given a large donation to the engineering school. The statue looked vaguely familiar, and when I read the plaque at its base, I turned to my wife and exclaimed, "Carol, we know this man! His name is Ed Hajim; he was a very close friend of my late brother's and we dined with him on the evening before Peter's memorial service." When we returned home two days later, I sent Ed a brief note, which started an email correspondence. In one of his notes to me, he said that he had been trying for several years to write his memoirs and was now on his third ghost writer, with still not a lot to show for his effort.

Ed's note brought to mind this book which seemed totally stuck and not likely to see the light of day. I had not worked on it for the preceding ten months. I printed off a copy of the draft such as it was at the time, and discovered two important facts: First of all, I already had about 150 pages written, and only needed another thirty to forty to wrap up a first draft. Secondly, I really liked the material I had written and was eager to see it in print. In fact, the existing text appeared to need only a round of light editing before it would be done.

In the following several months I worked almost every day to complete my first draft. I then took another couple of months to crisp up the language. Finally, I selected a small assortment of pictures with which to illustrate it, and sent the completed manuscript out to be printed. In retrospect, writing this book was a bit like the birth of our older son—a long labor followed by an intensely emotional moment when the product finally came out.

I began this book with some of my earliest recollections of yet earlier times. Now that I am a man in his seventies, one who has retired from work, and whose children are fully grown and well launched into careers of their own, I find myself reminiscing once again. I have enjoyed my life.

Yes, there have been a few disappointments and on occasion I have had to deviate from the path I intended to follow, but these negative moments are far outweighed by other experiences and by those closest to me whom I have loved with all my heart. In writing this book, I have had the privilege of reliving those experiences, and reflecting on those relationships.

In recalling the events and people that have shaped my life, I have also thought about some of the lessons I have learned over its course. In the next few pages I will sketch some of the more important observations in the hope that a few of them might help those who get this far in my book to live a better and happier life.

I have always endeavored to do the right thing on behalf of family, friends, colleagues and clients. When ADL lost sight of this principle and its leadership replaced an ethic of doing the right thing for clients and colleagues with an inwardly focused demand of obeisance to those higher up on the organization chart, the company went into a decade-long downward spiral that ended in bankruptcy. In constantly focusing on doing the right thing, I have been able to build others' trust in me, the essential glue that binds people together and enables them to achieve great things together. Conversely, if I had sought merely to further my own aims at the expense of the trust of my family, friends, colleagues, or clients, my relationships with them would have lost their vigor. Likewise, I am always ready to help others if and when they need help; they have usually returned the favor at a time when I have most needed it. But I have also learned to be wary of those who are only takers and never give back. They have almost always turned out to be traitors.

I have come to highly value personal resilience. My ancestors often faced difficult times such as being forced into exile by the Spanish Inquisition and, later on, the Fascist Racial Laws, or to having been locked into ghettoes for nearly a century and a half. In each case, they learned how to deal with the problem and prosper anew after a wrenching change in their circumstances. Every once in a while life has thrown me a hard knock or two. I have learned from my own experience and observation of others that those who have suffered a setback and then have found a new way forward will experience renewed joys and successes in life. Conversely, I have seen time and again that those who allow themselves to become mired in self-pity after a hard knock tend to fall by the wayside.

I have striven to be diligent in all that I have done. I have always sought to do important work to the best of my abilities, for clients, for the various non-profit organizations I have supported, and especially for those dearest to me.

I have developed a love for the beauty of the world around me. My best memories are of beautiful places and wonderful times I have enjoyed with family and friends. If I blinked at the wrong times I would have missed the best parts of life.

Our family has always put a heavy emphasis on gaining an education that is both broad and deep. Intellectual capital is something no one can take away from you. My parents invested heavily in my education and I did my part by taking on extra-challenging programs at every step in the process. In turn, my wife and I devoted a great deal of time, money and effort towards our children's educations and they stepped up to their part in the process.

My work often had a large component of developing new ideas and approaches and then teaching them to clients and colleagues. I have viewed ignorance as a generally remediable condition, but have also learned to be on my guard against those who are proud of their ignorance. I have observed repeatedly that trying to educate the latter is akin to Robert

Heinlein's famous line: "Never try to teach a pig to sing. It wastes your time and annoys the pig."

Growing up as a kid who was always a bit different from my peers, I have had to find the right balance. I do not call too much attention to my differentness, but I also do not hide in the bushes when I have something substantive and unique to offer others. I have repeatedly seen that people will shun a loudmouthed self-promoter or someone they perceive as too unlike themselves, but that they give no heed to others who are shrinking violets and lose the benefit of those "others'" experience and talents.

I have come to believe that it is very important to understand where I and those about me have come from. I have observed that people's histories have a nasty habit of trying to repeat themselves when you least expect them to. By understanding my background and theirs, I have been able to profit from life's positive lessons while generally avoiding repetitions of its negative ones.

Finally, I have learned the importance of having a long-range, multi-generational view of the future. It is this capability that has enabled me to have successful relationships with top-level executives at some of America's most successful companies. While it is necessary to deal with daily life, it is even more imperative to be aware of the bigger picture of where things are going and to adjust to the world accordingly. My parents had the foresight to see the threats posed by the Fascist Racial Laws and the looming entry of Italy into the war. They took radical action that saved their lives and those of my brothers, and made it possible for me to enter this world. Our family has prospered over many generations precisely because we have repeatedly thought in terms of generations and not just in terms of the here and now.

As I close this small volume, I am led to wonder about my children and grandchildren, and my nieces and nephews. What memories will they have of their parents and grandparents? What lessons will they learn in the course of their lives? And, finally, how will they pass their lessons and their values on to their children and grandchildren?

Figures A-1 and A-2. Emanuele Sacerdote, Micky Treves, and the mayor of Santena unveil a plaque acknowledging the original name of the street which honored our common ancestor Cav. Emanuele Sacerdote of Chieri, February, 2018

Figure A-3. The main piazza of Santena with its fountain
celebrating the region's famous asparagus